SUGAR RAY

THE SUGAR RAY ROBINSON STORY

SUGAR RAY
THE SUGAR RAY ROBINSON STORY

SUGAR RAY ROBINSON
with
DAVE ANDERSON

Robson Books

This Robson paperback edition first published in 1996 by
Robson Books Ltd, Bolsover House, 5-6 Clipstone Street,
London W1P 8LE
Originally published 1970. Revised hardback edition 1992.

British Library Cataloguing in Publication Data
A catalogue record for this book is available from the
British Library

Acknowledgments
The Hearst Corporation: for excerpts from Leonard
Lewin's column from the *Daily Mirror*, June 24, 1952,
Copyright 1952, The Hearst Corporation; and excerpts
from Jimmy Cannon's column from the *Journal-American*,
January 20, 1955, Copyright © 1955, The Hearst Cor-
poration. Reprinted by permission.
    The New York Times: for excerpts from Arthur Daley's
column of January 20, 1955, © 1955 by the New York
Times Company. Reprinted by permission.
    Chapter 26, "Cassius Clay", originally appeared in
Playboy.

Printed in Great Britain by WBC Book Manufacturers Ltd,
Bridgend, Mid-Glamorgan

TO MILLIE

for giving my career a happy ending

Contents

Foreword
by Dave Anderson

Don't be fooled by the title. This is not Sugar Ray Leonard's autobiography. This is the real Sugar Ray's book.

Sugar Ray Robinson.

The real Sugar Ray should have copyrighted his nickname. For those who think Sugar Ray Leonard was a good fighter, think again. The real Sugar Ray, the original Sugar Ray, the *only* Sugar Ray, would have flattened Leonard with either hand. No later than the sixth round. But the real Sugar Ray never seemed to resent Leonard's usurping his nickname.

"He asked me," the real Sugar Ray once said, "if I minded him using my name and I said, 'No, go ahead.'"

Maybe the real Sugar Ray didn't mind, but others did. In boxing, it seems that anybody named Ray is automatically Sugar Ray — not only Sugar Ray Leonard, but another American boxer named Sugar Ray Seales and surely the next good prospect whose first name happens to be Ray.

To all those who remember Sugar Ray Robinson as "pound for pound the best boxer in history," there has been only one Sugar Ray.

One morning in the late Summer of 1950 my father noticed in the New York newspapers that Sugar Ray was fighting that holiday afternoon in the Coney Island Velodrome, a little outdoor wooden arena not far from our Brooklyn apartment.

"Let's go," he said. "You've got to see this guy fight."

Sugar Ray was between titles. He had been the world

welterweight champion from 1946 to 1949 and now he was campaigning as a middleweight. His opponent that Labor Day was Billy Brown, durable but not overly talented. Sugar Ray earned a 10-round decision without breaking much of a sweat. Five months later he would stop Jake LaMotta in Chicago to win the middleweight title for the first of five times.

Over a quarter of a century, from 1940 to 1965, he had 175 victories against 19 losses, but five of those losses occurred in the last six months of his career after he turned 44.

He registered 110 knockouts, but he was never knocked out and he was stopped only once. In a 1952 light heavyweight title bout with Joey Maxim, he was far ahead on the cards of the referee and the two judges. He needed only to finish the 15th round to reign as the light heavyweight champion. But in the 100-degree heat at Yankee Stadium that steamy Summer night in New York he collapsed after the 13th round. Maxim was awarded a 14th-round knockout.

To appreciate Sugar Ray's reign, consider that he was undefeated in his first 40 bouts with 29 knockouts, lost a 10-round decision to Jake LaMotta in 1943, then extended his record to 128-1-2 with 84 knockouts while holding the welterweight and middleweight titles.

In the last year of Sugar Ray's career I was writing boxing for the New York *Journal-American*. But by then he was boxing's version of a sideshow freak, a name who would fight a nobody. One day I accompanied him to Pittsfield, Massachusetts, a leafy town of about 60,000 in the Berkshire mountains, where he would go against another nobody. He didn't have to do much to win, just throw a few left hooks that fooled the judges into thinking he still had something left. When it was over, he got paid.

"About $700," promoter Sam Silverman told me.

In his big years, that wouldn't have covered the drinks at the victory party in "Sugar Ray's" cafe on Seventh Avenue in Harlem. But by now he had gone through about $3 million and he was all but broke. After he put together a few victories against some other stiffs, he had one more decent payday for that era: $10,000 to fight middleweight contender Joey Archer in Pittsburgh.

This was Sugar Ray's last stand until Archer, a gentle puncher, knocked him down in the eighth round.

About a year later I began collaborating with Sugar Ray on this book. He was living with his third wife, Millie, in a Riverside Drive apartment, less than half an hour's drive from my New Jersey home. Once or twice a week I drove over there and he reminisced into a tape-recorder. But in less than an hour he would sigh.

"You're my man," he would say to me, "but I'm tired. I can't talk anymore. That tape-recorder wears me out."

"Tired?" I would tease him. "You went 15 rounds with Jake LaMotta, but you can't go an hour with a tape-recorder?"

Looking back now, I've often wondered if that weariness represented the first signs of Alzheimer's disease. Along with diabetes, Alzheimer's contributed to his eventual death on April 12, 1989, less than a month short of what would have been the 68th birthday for the real Sugar Ray, the original Sugar Ray.

The only Sugar Ray.

DAVE ANDERSON

SUGAR RAY
THE SUGAR RAY ROBINSON STORY

1

The Ego and I

In my big years, a five-dollar bill was tip money. I mean if I was in my Harlem café when a kid came in hawking the *News* and the *Mirror,* I'd give him a five and tell him to keep the change. Or if I got a manicure, the girl had an automatic five. Or if I was in a hotel, the chambermaid always had a five waiting for her every morning under the pillow. I never thought I'd find a five under my pillow, as I did one night near the end of 1965.

"Where'd this come from?" I wondered, holding it up.

"Priscilla must've put it there," my wife Millie said.

I had stopped boxing and I was in money trouble. I had to borrow to keep up appearances. Not many people cared, but a few remembered, like Priscilla Williams. She's a sweet little lady who used to work in my dry-cleaning shop in Harlem when I was a big man there. She always took personal care of my clothes, especially the blue-and-white satin robe I wore into the ring. Her husband, Bob, used to drive me around in my big, flamingo-pink convertible.

I wasn't famous any more, but Priscilla liked to visit Millie in our Riverside Drive apartment and fuss over my clothes.

To her, a five-dollar bill was important money. And at that time it was important to me, too. I had earned about four million dollars in and out of the ring, but it was gone. I also had earned a reputation, as sports columnist Red Smith once wrote, as "the only man in the world who can unbutton a promoter's shirt from behind while wearing boxing gloves and remove the victim's pants and bankroll without attracting attention."

I also was the only man in the world who could blow that bankroll without attracting *my* attention.

But damn it, I didn't need money as bad as Priscilla did. The next day, I had Millie sneak the five-dollar bill into Priscilla's purse when she wasn't looking. That way, both of us were happy. She thought she had helped me, and my ego hadn't let her.

My ego makes me tick. In the ring it would sometimes tick like a time bomb.

I was in Philadelphia once for a fight with George Costner, a tough puncher who also liked to call himself Sugar. In the days before the fight, he kept telling the sportswriters how there was going to be only one Sugar, meaning him. But after the referee gave us the instructions in the middle of the ring, I held out my gloves.

"Better touch gloves now," I told Costner, "because this is the only round. Your name ain't Sugar, *mine* is."

Two minutes and forty-nine seconds later, Costner didn't look so sweet. Another time I was in Wilkes-Barre for a non-title fight but my opponent, Gene Buffalo, came in under 147 pounds. That meant that technically my welterweight title was at stake.

"We can call it off," the promoter said.

"Forget it," I said. "I'll handle him."

He went in the first round, too. When I was at my peak, some of the people around me used to plead with me to demand a certain referee or certain judges to be sure I got a fair shake, but I refused.

"Here's the referee," I'd say, holding up my fists.

In those years I was described as "pound for pound, the greatest fighter of all time." That phrase has been like part of my name whenever I'm introduced anywhere. My ego enjoys it, but it wasn't my accomplishment. God gave me the gift. I'm a blessed man, a chosen man. As a boy, I wanted to be a doctor, but that dream ended when I quit school in the ninth grade. Another dream began: to be a gladiator.

And like a true gladiator, I never lost. Something just happened to keep me from winning.

Not that I enjoyed being a gladiator. I didn't, but I did enjoy performing for people, being on stage in the ring. I enjoyed the money I earned, and I enjoyed the fame. With my fame I didn't have to struggle for acceptance, but I knew what acceptance meant to my people. I was instrumental in New York Mayor Vincent Impellitteri's appointing the first Negro deputy police commissioner, Billy Rowe, and I was instrumental in averting a Harlem riot when policemen allegedly roughed up a woman in arresting her.

But mostly, I prefer to march on my own, to the beat of God's drum.

As a blessed man, a chosen man, I believe there's a task somewhere ahead for me. I thought that task was about to be assigned to me when I agreed to work for Senator Robert F. Kennedy if he received the Democratic nomination for President in 1968. But one night that June, my phone woke me.

"Ray," a voice said, "this is Stephen Smith out in Los Angeles. Bobby's been shot."

Several days earlier, Bobby had promised to come to my apartment soon to discuss campaign plans. When he died, I cried, just as I had cried when the Reverend Martin Luther King, Jr., had been assassinated. Not because one was white, or because one was black, but because both were Americans, two wonderful people.

My beliefs have sprung from my belief in God. I believe that of himself man can do nothing, that he needs God to guide him and bless him. I don't go to any special church, I believe that it's more important to have a church inside a man than a man inside a church. From childhood, I was taught to obey the Ten Commandments and I have—except for the one about adultery, and I'm not proud of having broken it.

But as you'll see, I'm neither saint nor sinner. I'm a gladiator.

2

Junior

It was known as Black Bottom. And it was.
Black because we lived there, Bottom because
that's where we were at.

It was only a few blocks from downtown Detroit. And a
few miles farther was Grosse Pointe, out where the Fords
live. But the only time anybody in Black Bottom got close
to a Ford was if he bought one. My father, Walker Smith,
had a black model-T and that made him a big man in Black
Bottom. He had grown up on a farm outside Dublin, Georgia. So had my mother, whose maiden name was Leila
Hurst. When they got married, they had their own little
farm near Dublin. My oldest sister, Marie, was born there
in 1917. Evelyn came along in 1919. About that time one
of my mother's sisters, Lillie, and her husband, Herman
Hayes, had moved to Detroit. They wrote back about how
easy it was to get a job and how good the salaries were. Pop
didn't have to be coaxed. He was making maybe ten dollars
a week raising cotton, corn, and peanuts—mostly cotton.

"And if you got a boll weevil in that cotton," he told me
years later, "you worked the whole year for nothin'."

Pop decided to go to Detroit and see what it was like. He
got a job with the construction company where Herman

Hayes worked. On Pop's first payday, his boss peeled off sixty dollars.

"The man made a mistake," Pop told Herman.

"No, he didn't," Herman said. "That's your right salary."

"Well, now," Pop said, "and no boll weevils."

Pop was a wiry little guy, five foot seven and a hundred and fifty pounds, with a dazzling smile that lit up his dark-brown face. And he was strong. His job was digging out cellar shells for buildings. Bulldozers do that now, but in those days there were no bulldozers. He dug those shells with a shovel. The paydays made it worth while. After he saved money, he sent Mom a train ticket to Detroit. Mom traveled with Marie and Evelyn and me, although I was still a few weeks away. Black Bottom was made up of wooden houses, mostly two-story, on flat, dusty streets. Pop had rented the first floor of a wooden frame house on McComb Street. That's where I was born on May 3, 1921. No hospital for me. No doctor, either. I arrived in Mom's bed with a midwife officiating at my first weigh-in. Seven pounds, twelve ounces. When Pop got home that night, he had my name picked out.

"Junior," he told Mom. "My first boy baby has got to be a junior."

Walker Smith, Junior. No middle name. Pop always called me Junior. When I was a kid nobody ever called me Walker. After we moved to Canfield Street, I can remember my sister Marie yelling, "Junior, Juuuuuuunnnniooor," when she wanted me home. That was a nice little two-story yellow-brick house. We lived downstairs, and during the day Marie was the boss. Mom was working downtown as a chambermaid at the Statler Hotel. Mom was a husky woman, with a round face and complexion the color of coffee with cream. But by now Pop had two jobs. He mixed cement in the daytime. At night he worked on a sewer project. He had to get up at six in the morning and he'd get home close to midnight. Six days a week.

The only day I really saw him was Sunday. After wearing work clothes all week, he liked to get dressed up on Sunday. He was a good dresser. Conservative, but stylish. He liked dark suits—blues, grays, and browns. And I can remember that in the summer he wore two-tone shoes and a white Panama hat.

I always wanted to be with him more. One time I hid in the rumble seat of his Ford. When I hopped out, he had to drive me home. He didn't like that because he had to use more gas. And that meant he was wasting money. He worked hard for his money and he didn't like me wasting it. Another time I remember I came home with my shirt ripped.

"How'd that happen, Junior?" he said.

"Some boys and me were wrestlin', Pop," I said, "and in all the scramblin', the shirt got tore."

"Then defend yourself, Junior," he said. "I got to pay for the clothes you wear."

Money was always a problem around the house. We had moved twice more, trying to find a lower rent, and we were in a narrow white wooden house alongside an alley on Willis Street. Pop used to have a few drinks now and then, and when he'd come home, Mom would argue with him about it. Sometimes their yelling would wake me up and I'd hear Mom saying, "Don't you talk to me about money when you drink up more money than I spend."

That would set Pop off, and he'd have his say because Mom liked to drink, too. That was her relaxation.

When she was a country girl in Georgia, her family made their own moonshine. I can remember Mom coming home on a Saturday night from her job at the hotel—she had been promoted to seamstress—and she'd have a bottle with her. Gin, I think it was. I never really cared what it was. I knew

I didn't want any part of it. All that arguing about drinking and listening to how they acted . . . I used to pull the covers up around me in my little bed and tell myself I'd never touch that hard liquor.

And I never have.

The arguments between Mom and Pop kept getting worse. One night Mom came home from work and started to pack up some clothes for my sisters and me. For weeks before that, she had been making us clothes. The strange part was, she'd make me a shirt that fit me, then she'd sew another one a size larger. She did the same thing for my sisters with dresses. And shoes, she must have bought us each two or three pairs, one larger than the other. The night she started packing, we all stood around staring at her.

"Where we goin', Mom?" Marie said.

"To Georgia," she said. "But don't tell your Pop. He don't know about it."

"Why don't he know?" Evelyn said.

"Because he ain't comin' with us," Mom said. "When he gets home tonight, you give him a big kiss good-by. But don't tell him nothin'. Promise now."

That night, Pop was sitting at the kitchen table when my sisters and I went to kiss him. He didn't know what to make of it. Usually we were asleep when he came home.

"How come everybody got up to kiss me?" he said.

" 'Cause we love you, Pop," I said. "That's why."

The next morning Pop was up early to go to work. As soon as he was out of the house, Mom woke us up. We got dressed and piled our little satchels on the trolley and rode to the railroad station to take the train to Georgia. Some years later Mom told me that Pop "never settled down," that's why she left him. Pop never understood.

"I wasn't loafin' around," he once told me. "I was out working for my family. And one day my family was gone."

Mom brought us down to our grandma's farm, her mother's, outside Glenwood, Georgia. Then Mom returned to Detroit. It was in March 1927, shortly before I turned six, and it was a whole new life for me. One of my first days in Georgia I can remember walking barefoot in that red clay with one of my uncles, Herschel Hurst. We called him Uncle JB. We were out hunting. We had a big black dog, Bob, that chased a raccoon up a tree and Uncle JB shot it dead. Other times Uncle JB would hunt with a slingshot. He assigned me to find rocks for him.

"Junior," he'd say to me, "you are my ammunition man. Look for little *round* rocks."

Uncle JB once told me, "We're going bird hunting." I had heard people talk about quail and I thought that's what he meant, big birds. We were tramping through the woods when Uncle JB stopped in his tracks.

"There's one," he whispered.

Up on a branch, a blue jay was perched pretty. Uncle JB let fly one of my little round rocks from his slingshot. That blue jay squawked a little and dropped onto the dirt.

"What a pretty bird," I said, feeling sad.

"It tastes prettier," Uncle JB said.

It wasn't bad tasting at that, but I never got to like it. On the farm we had hogs and chickens. Uncle JB killed them, too, for eating, but Grandma didn't want me to watch.

"Junior," she always said, "you go stand behind the smokehouse and don't peek."

But one day I did peek. I saw Uncle JB smash one of the hogs over the head with an ax. Then Uncle JB stabbed him in the throat to bleed him. At dinnertime that night Grandma was fixing my plate when she told me, "Junior, wait'll you taste this hog meat."

"No, no, Grandma," I said, "don't you put none of that dead hog on my plate. I'm not eatin' none of that dead hog."

Grandma and Uncle JB thought that was funny. But I didn't think it was. I wanted no part of that dead hog. Most of the time I gobbled up everything on the table. I took my meals standing up then. The table was high and the bench was low. If I sat down, my eyes would be just about level with the table. So I had to stand up. And that way, I was able to reach around. When I finished my plate, I'd use my fork to stab some meat off Marie's plate—"pretty meat" I used to call the white meat of the chicken. Then I'd stab some meat off Evelyn's plate. When I couldn't reach anybody's plate, I'd climb onto the table and stab some meat off the platter. Not that I didn't get whacked for it, but a few pieces of meat were worth a few whacks.

We ate well. We had fresh milk from a big cow named Duck. I used to say, "Go out in the woods, Duck, and bring back some more milk for tomorrow."

I remember something else, too. Our school was a box-shaped house, unpainted, with a dirt playground. It was about a mile away. We were walking home one day along the railroad tracks, maybe a dozen of us kids, when some white teen-agers started throwing rocks at us. All I could do was run around picking up rocks for the older kinds to throw. Nobody got hurt, as I remember, but when it was over I asked my Aunt Maude why anybody would throw rocks at people for no reason.

" 'Cause we're black and they're white," Aunt Maude said. "And they think they're better. But they ain't."

I had never heard of prejudice at that time, and I wouldn't have known how to pronounce or spell it. At that age, though, I really didn't think about it too much. I was more interested in other things. Like on Saturday morning Uncle JB would pile us kids into his truck and drive to the market in Dublin. He'd sell cotton and beans at the market. On the way home JB would stop and buy each of us kids a box of

Cracker Jack. We thought we were really living. But one Saturday when we got back to the farm, Mom was there. She was going to take us back to Detroit.

During the train ride Mom explained how she was trying to get a divorce from Pop but that in order to obtain custody of us she had to have us with her. When we arrived, Mom took us to a little flat she had rented on Palmer Street.

It had been a year almost to the day when we left, but Black Bottom looked the same. The gray of winter was in the sky. The paint was peeling on most of the houses. The yards and alleys were muddy with melting snow. When we had left Georgia, the grass was green, the leaves were on the trees, the azaleas were blooming. But in Black Bottom everything looked bleak.

The people looked bleak, too. Most of the men had jobs. But none of them had butlers.

The first few days, I wandered around the neighborhood to reacquaint myself with things. I strolled over to Dequindre Street and peered down the Grand Trunk railroad tracks. One day a few years earlier I had jumped onto the handrail of a freight car in my Sunday best. But before the car moved, Mom hauled me down and gave me a whack right there in the street. Several blocks on the other side of Dequindre Street was the Brewster Center. I had been around it a few times before we went to Georgia, but now, when we returned, I was almost seven and it appealed to me more. It appealed to Mom, too. She had a new job at the General Linen Supply, sewing uniforms and butchers' coats, and she didn't want me hanging around the streets when she was working.

"Take this quarter," she said to me one day, "and give it to the man at Brewster Center. It's your dues for a month."

Brewster Center looked immense to me then. It was a sprawling, two-story red-brick building, a recreation center operated by the Department of Parks. Inside there were a swimming pool and a basketball court and a boxing ring. In some of the other rooms there were Ping-Pong tables, all kinds of games, anything to keep kids busy. One of my first days there I was watching the activity in the boxing ring when I heard somebody say, "See that big kid, that's Joe Barrow."

Joseph Louis Barrow, his full name was. In another few years, he would be Joe Louis, the world heavyweight champion.

Joe Barrow was the big hero of the neighborhood. He was an amateur boxer, and us little kids used to tag along behind him. He lived a couple of blocks away from me. When it was time for him to go to Brewster Center to train, I'd go over and stand in front of his house waiting for him. When he'd come out, I'd grab the little bag he carried, with his shoes and stuff, and carry it for him. He got to know me and called me Junior, but I don't think that he ever knew my last name then. My sister Marie was in school with him at Garfield High. I remember Pop visited us one day and he asked Marie, "What's Joe Barrow do in school?"

"Pop," she said, "he just looks out the window."

Pop came to see us every so often. And he always had some money for us, sometimes a dollar for each of us.

"What are you doin' that for?" Mom snapped at him one day. "They'll just throw that money away on candy."

"Leila," he said, "they're my kids, too, and if they want to throw that money away, let 'em throw it away."

I always saved a little of that money for my dues at Brewster Center, just in case Mom was having trouble. By that time the stock market had crashed, and things were going from bad to worse for Mom. Not that I knew much about it. She kept her problems to herself and at my age I wasn't concerned with Wall Street. My life centered around Brewster Street. I was too small to put on gloves at the Center, but I watched the older kids in the ring. And on the way home, I'd shadowbox. One day Mom noticed me coming up the block, bobbing and weaving and dancing and throwing punches, and she told me later, "I thought my boy had something wrong with his head, I really did."

She soon discovered what I was doing, because I'd go in the house and take the pillows off my bed and prop them up on a chair and punch them, just as I'd seen the bigger boys punch the big bag.

Other times I'd shadowbox with the other kids. Some of them didn't like it. I had a cousin, Curtis Hurst—we called him Doc. He was a few years older than me and bigger. But when we shadowboxed I danced circles around him and I had fast hands. One day he got mad at me for making him look bad, and when Mom got home he was waiting for her.

"Aunt Leila," he said, "make Junior quit hittin' me."

"Doc," she said, "don't tell me your troubles. You hit him back. Even if Junior is smaller than you. Hit him back and he won't bother you none. You got my permission."

"But Aunt Leila," he said, "I *can't* hit him. Every time I hit at him, he ducks."

Another time a grown-up man, about six feet tall, visited us. After dinner, I was dancing around the living room, and he started to shadowbox with me. But Mom didn't want him to do it.

"You be careful now," she told him, "or Junior will slap your face."

"That little kid?" he said. "He couldn't slap my face on a ladder."

Just as he said it, I leaped off the floor and cuffed him across the jaw with my left hand, just as Mom had warned him. He couldn't believe it. But out on the streets of Black Bottom I never did any real fighting. I was too young to be part of a gang, but I got into trouble every once in a while. Usually from teasing a girl. One time I remember a big girl turned on me and chased me home.

"Marie, Marie!" I was yelling, coming down the block. "Marie, help!"

Marie came roaring out of the house, shaking her fist at that girl, and they started rolling all over the sidewalk. She was my defender and I became devoted to her. With Mom working all day, she used to give Marie the keys to the house and Marie wore them on a string around her neck. She sounded like a bell cow, those keys clanking wherever she went. But she was like a big brother to me, always defending me. I had a nickname for her—Lard, as in a tub of lard. She was a little chubby. But she never got mad at me for calling her that. She was a wonderful sister. Whenever I got into some kind of trouble at Balch School, the teacher would tell me to bring my mother to the classroom after school. But Mom was working, so Marie had to go instead.

Not that it was ever anything really serious. But if scholarships were awarded for mischief, I'd have gone to Harvard.

To me, school was a little dull. In order to liven it up a little, I did things—when the teacher wasn't looking. Like pulling the ribbon on a girl's pigtails, any girl who got close enough. Or snatching her books and spilling them. After a few girls whined about that, the teacher would get angry at me. But Marie always calmed her down. Once in a while I played hooky. With Mom leaving early for her job, the temptation was there every day. One morning I was outside our new flat on Hendrie Street, where the Chrysler Expressway is now, when the truant officer marched up to me.

"Does Walker Smith live here?" he said.

"Yes, sir, he does," I said, trying to think of something.

"Are you Walker Smith?"

"Oh no, sir," I said, pointing down the street, "Walker Smith just went around the corner."

"Thank you," he said, hurrying away.

As soon as he disappeared around that corner, I ran around the other corner. By the time he got back to school, I was in my classroom, a little late but not absent. Marie was in Garfield High by then but Evelyn was still at Balch Grammar School with me. I had a nickname for Evelyn, too. I called her Neck because she had a small, skinny neck. She was a couple of grades ahead of me, but I could persuade her to do whatever I wanted to do. At lunchtime we were supposed to buy a sandwich and milk. Mom gave us money every day.

"Now listen, Neck," I used to say to her, "we don't want any silly sandwich and milk."

"But Junior," she'd say, "you know Mom told us to buy a sandwich and milk with this money. You heard her."

"I know, Neck," I'd say, "but let's go over to the day-old bakery instead, you and me."

Not far from school there was a bakery that sold day-old goods at a discount. You could buy little cupcakes, four for a dime.

"And with the other dime," I'd tell her, "we can buy some peanuts and soda pop."

I doubt if any dietitians would prescribe cupcakes, peanuts, and soda pop, but I thrived on it. Of course I supplemented it with fresh fruit, mostly cherries we used to steal from a tree not far away from our house. There was a big fence around the yard where the tree was. I'd station Evelyn as the lookout and hop the fence and fill my pockets with as many cherries as I could.

"Neck," I'd tell her, "I don't know what I'd do without you."

She helped me deliver my paper route, too, the *Detroit News*. One time I had a cut foot. I could hardly walk. But Evelyn carried me on her back to where I picked up my papers, and she carried both me and the papers along my whole route. I don't know how she did it, but that was the kind of love we kids had for each other. With Pop gone and Mom working, we had to produce our own good times. Mom never took us anyplace. She was too busy working. We understood why Mom wasn't around and we didn't resent it. And when we needed her, Mom was always there.

As a kid I often amused myself by walking on my hands. I could do it the length of the schoolyard, sometimes the length of the block. But one day I put my right hand on a chunk of broken glass. I had all my weight on the hand and the glass sliced into my middle finger. The blood was all over the sidewalk and all over my hand, but I wrapped a handkerchief around it and the bleeding stopped. I threw the bloodstained handkerchief away, so Mom wouldn't find out, but I forgot about the cut. The next morning, the finger was swollen twice its size. Mom had gone to work but when I got to school, my teacher realized the finger was infected.

"When your mother gets home tonight," she told me, "make sure she takes you to a doctor."

I didn't want to tell Mom, but I knew I had to. I showed her the swollen finger and told her that my teacher suggested that a doctor look at it.

"Never mind a doctor," she said, "they charge too much. I'm taking you to the emergency room at the hospital."

The smell there almost made me sick. I had never been in a hospital before and I didn't like anything about it. Not the smell. Not the nurses walking around in those white uniforms. Not even the doctor who looked at my finger.

"It's badly infected," the doctor told Mom. "Your son better stay overnight."

"Overnight!" Mom roared. "No reason for my boy to stay here. Fix it up right now."

"You don't understand," the doctor said. "We'll have to make a decision on this."

"Decision on what?" Mom wanted to know. "Put some stuff on it, wrap it up, and let us go home."

"It's not that simple," the doctor said. "We may have to amputate the finger."

"Not my boy's finger!" she roared. "No need to amputate anything. We're goin' home."

And off we went, me looking at my finger and looking at the scowl on Mom's face and looking at the doctor shrugging his shoulders. The next day Mom took me to another doctor. He agreed with Mom that amputation wasn't necessary, but he had to scrape the bone—it was a bone infection—and drain the pus out of it. My last visit to him, I can remember Mom opening her black purse.

"How much do I owe you for all this?" she asked him.

"That'll be twenty-five dollars," the doctor said, "but you don't have to pay it all at once."

Mom's eyes started to fill.

"I don't make but ten dollars a week to support three children," she said, "but I'll get you the money."

"Take your time," the doctor said.

The next night, Mom showed up at his office with the twenty-five dollars. She had borrowed it. Every so often after that, when I was in my green chair-bed at night, I could hear Mom crying as she sewed. Other times I'd see her crying. Her eyes would be down, trying to hide them from me, but the tears would be on her cheeks.

Seeing her like that, my stomach felt hollow. I'd tell myself that someday I'd buy Mom a big house where she didn't have to worry about money.

I didn't know how I was going to do it. I didn't even

know what I wanted to be when I grew up. But I knew that someday I *would* do it for Mom. And while I was thinking about that, Mom was thinking about something else. Her ten-dollar salary had discouraged her about living in Detroit. One night after dinner she called us kids together.

"Children," she said, "we're taking a bus to New York next week. We're going to live there."

3

Driftwood and Dice

We left Detroit on the Sunday after Election Day in 1932. Franklin Delano Roosevelt had been voted our new President. He had promised everybody a New Deal when he took office in March. But that was too long a wait for Mom. She had written to a friend of hers in New York who arranged for a three-room flat for us. Mom had the address in a letter she had received.

"Four-nineteen West Fifty-third Street," she told us on the trolley to the bus station in Detroit. "That's near Times Square."

The bright lights of Times Square. The crossroads of the world. That sounded great to me and my sisters. Not that we were really dressed for it. I had on an old leather jacket and patched gray knickers. My sisters were wearing faded dresses. But all our clothes were clean. So were the extra clothes we carried in our little cardboard suitcases. Mom had her suitcase and a big bag of bologna sandwiches she had made for us to eat on the bus. We must have looked as if we'd stepped off a poster depicting the Depression. But at the bus station Mom marched up to the ticket window as proud as if she were taking a Mediterranean cruise. The bus pulled out of Detroit in mid-afternoon. It took us down through Cleveland and that night it stopped for half an hour

at Buffalo. My sisters and I had finished most of the sandwiches and we weren't too hungry. But Mom wanted something hot in her stomach in order to keep her strength. She
got off the bus to buy a bowl of soup and a cup of coffee.
While she was gone, I got to talking to the bus driver.

"Where are you going?" he said to me.

"New York," I told him. "My sisters and my Mom are with
me and we're going to live near Times Square."

"You'll like that," he said.

We talked some more and when it was time for the bus
to leave, he handed me a quarter.

"For good luck in New York," he said.

I thanked him and hurried down the aisle and gave the
quarter to Mom. Years later she told me that when she arrived in New York all she had to her name was fifty cents,
including the twenty-five the driver had given me. But at
the time she didn't tell us anything that might dishearten
us. Instead, she kept reminding us that we were starting a
"new chapter" in our lives, a "new adventure." And we
were. Riding into New York that day, I stared out the bus
windows at the skyscrapers. But when we walked up to our
place on West 53rd Street, I was a little disappointed.

"Is this it, Mom?" I said.

"I guess so," she said, checking the address on the glass-
paned wooden door. "This is the right number."

"But where's Times Square?" I said.

Mom opened the door and walked in, but I stayed outside for a few moments and looked around. There were no
bright lights here. It seemed to me that we were in a small
canyon. In Detroit the houses had been lower and most of
them were separated by alleys. When you looked up you
saw the sky. When I looked around that first day in New
York, all I could see were the adjoining brick tenement
houses, all of them five stories high with black iron fire es-

capes jutting out. Above the street was a strip of sky. That's all, just a strip. In Detroit the sky had hung like a big tent over the smaller, separated houses.

As I went upstairs to our three-room flat, the wooden floor creaked. We were in the back of the building, overlooking a dingy courtyard. Behind that was the rear of the house on 54th Street.

All these sights were new. And there were new smells and sounds. The odor of greasy cooking was all through that tenement. It seemed as if you could rub the grease off the doors with your finger. And at night, there was a scratching from inside the wall. Rats, I learned later. I learned a few other things. That Times Square was quite close, a few small canyons away. And that our neighborhood had a nickname: Hell's Kitchen.

I had transferred from Black Bottom to Hell's Kitchen— top that for a couple of fancy prep schools.

Our block on West 53rd Street was just about all Negro people. In fact, it was like that for an area of about six blocks. Outside that, the neighborhood was white, mostly Irish and Italians. I can remember that summer some of us kids used to go down to the Salvation Army place on Eleventh Avenue, around 44th Street, and when we did, we had to go together in order to protect ourselves. To get home, we'd try to hop a ride on the back of a truck. But sometimes we had to walk and that's when we would hear it.

"Hey, nigger," one of the white kids would yell at us, "get back where you belong."

The word *nigger* didn't bother me. Negro people use the word *nigger* more than white folks do. I had heard it all the time when I was growing up in Detroit. But I didn't like the idea of anybody telling me what to do. Mostly, the white kids liked to yell at us and watch us keep moving. Once in a while some of them would stop us and talk tough.

"We're gonna beat your black ass," I remember one of them said to a couple of us one time.

"Now listen, man," I told him, "you do that and the cops will come and we'll all be in trouble. And when you get home, your mom will get after you and you'll be in worse trouble. Don't start nothin', man. It ain't worth it."

It worked. He looked at me and said, "Get movin'," and we did. I was good at sweet-talk even then.

The next day my buddies and I would take our chances and go back to the Salvation Army place. That was an important place to us. They served lunches there, usually hot dogs and beans. It was free and that was a big thing during the Depression. Anytime we got a free meal it was like found money. The day we moved in, Mom had discovered seventy cents under a pile of peeled wallpaper in the kitchen. Add that to the fifty cents she arrived with and she had something to buy groceries. But there were nights in that flat when there wasn't enough food to go around. I realized that in later years. At the time, I didn't understand what Mom and my sisters were doing.

"I'm not hungry, Junior," Mom liked to say, "you take my piece of meat."

"Yeah, Junior," Marie might say, "I've got to watch my weight. You eat mine."

I gobbled up everything I could. I didn't stop to think that they were sacrificing some of their food so I could have my fill. Mom really had a time trying to feed us. She was making twelve dollars a week as a seamstress in a linen-supply firm a couple of blocks away. That was two dollars more a week than she had been getting in Detroit. But our rent was twenty-three dollars a month. That meant she had about twenty-five a month to feed and clothe three kids and herself.

Somehow, she was able to include a few little luxuries.

Her bottle of gin on Saturday night. And dancing school for Evelyn and me.

Mom thought that Evelyn, being a little lighter on her feet than Marie, would make a good dancer. And I was always dancing around, pretending I was Bill Robinson, Bojangles, the best dancer of that era. The Roy Scott Studio was around the corner, on Ninth Avenue. The tuition was fifty cents a week for each of us. They taught ballet there, but Evelyn stuck with me in tap dancing. After a few weeks of it, I got bored. There was no action. Tap, tap, tap. Everything was in slow motion. So one day I conned Evelyn.

"Neck," I said to her, "no use us goin' there any more. We're not learnin' anything. Let's take the money and buy us some goodies instead."

Evelyn screwed up her face, as she always did when she was afraid to do something. She said to me, "Suppose Mom finds out?" But I had an answer for that. Mom was working, she couldn't find out. And after a few minutes, Evelyn agreed. So that afternoon we each spent some of our fifty cents and saved a little of it. When we got home for dinner, Mom was sitting in the kitchen.

"Well, children," she said, "show me the new step you learned in dancing school."

We went through our routine. Tap, tap, tap. In slow motion. Mom had a big smile on her face.

"You certainly are improving on that step," she said. "Someday you might both be professional dancers."

When Evelyn and I were alone later, I told her, "See, Mom can't tell the difference." So for the next few weeks, we both skipped dancing school and pocketed the money. There's no thief like a child thief. But one night after we were supposed to have been in dancing school, Mom asked us to show her our new steps. Again, we did that same old step.

"They're not givin' you much in that school," Mom said.

"All you've learned is one step. I'm goin' to talk to that teacher."

She did. And the teacher, naturally, told her that we hadn't been attending school for several weeks. That night I got a good whipping. For both Evelyn and me. Evelyn, as a sister will, squealed to Mom that I had talked her into it. So Evelyn got off light. I got her share as well as mine. After that, Mom didn't give us any more money for dancing lessons. But that one step I learned soon began to pay off. Where we lived was not only a few blocks from Times Square, it was also only a couple of blocks from many of the famous theaters on Broadway. At night in the summer two or three of us kids would stand outside one of the theaters, and when the customers came out on the street for a smoke at the intermission, we'd dance for them.

And how we would dance. Talk about the current dances being improvised, man, that's all we did.

The one step I learned in dancing school was the basis for it, but after that I just did whatever my hips and feet decided. Those people loved it. We'd keep dancing for about ten minutes, and then the theater doorman, in his gold-braided uniform, would come out and announce that "The second act is about to begin," and some of the men would take change out of their pockets and toss it to us. We'd scramble around, picking it up, and then we'd buy some candy and split up the rest. Sometimes we'd make a couple of dollars apiece on a good night.

One of our favorite spots was the Alvin Theater. We were always good for a few dollars there.

With nothing else to do, we always got there early and hung around outside the lobby. The people got to know us after a while. One night I was the only one there. The other boys had to go somewhere with their folks. But shortly after I got to the Alvin, the manager came through the doors to the lobby and walked toward me. I thought, *Man, I'm through, he's chasin' me.* But then I saw the smile on his face.

"Young man," he said, "this play is closing tomorrow. But the next night there's going to be a men's smoker here. I've seen you dance and you're pretty good. How would you like me to put you on the bill for the smoker?"

I didn't know what to say. I just looked at him and I nodded. He told me to be there at nine o'clock and to come through the stage door. I didn't dare tell Mom or my sisters. I didn't tell any of the other kids who usually danced with me, either. I didn't want anybody that I knew watching me. After dinner that night, I put on some clean clothes and sneaked out of the house. At the theater, I went in through the stage door and the manager was there backstage.

"Here he is," I heard him say to one of the other men. "Wait'll you see this kid go."

I peeked out from behind the curtain and saw all the men whistling at a girl dancer in a pantie costume. All those people.

"Don't be nervous now," the manager told me. "Just do what you do in the street."

I didn't know what he meant. The people didn't scare me. Man, there's nothing scary about people. But for the first time in my life, I had an audience that was expecting to see me dance. The people outside the theater had been different. Some had watched me and some had ignored me. But now, all these men in the theater were waiting to see me and that made me realize that I had to be good.

My hands were sweating, I remember that, but it was because I wanted to please them. The audience itself didn't make me nervous. I was too much of a ham to let an audience bother me.

On the stage, the girl was finishing her dance and as she came off, the men were clapping.

"You're on next," the manager said. "As soon as you hear the music, get out there and dance."

The girl took a bow, the orchestra started to play—but, man, don't ask me what tune it was. All I remember is that I kept dancing until the music stopped. And when it did, I looked out and the men were applauding. Not, I remember, as loud as they did for the dancer. But that was all right with me. I wasn't as pretty as she was.

"You were great," the manager said to me as I ran backstage. "Here's your money."

He handed me two dollars. All for myself. I didn't have to split it with the other guys this time. I had been a *solo*, like Bojangles Robinson. I didn't wait around to watch the rest of the smoker. I hurried home and put the money on the kitchen table. When I told Mom how I got it, she laughed.

"It's about time you paid me back for all that cheatin' you did on dancing school," she said.

Another money-maker was driftwood on the docks along the Hudson River. The river was only a couple of blocks away. From our sidewalk, I could see it between the old green wooden piers. Across the river was New Jersey, but it might as well have been Wyoming. I never got there. I used to roam along the docks, looking at the ocean liners and collecting the driftwood. I'd chop it up and stuff it into bushel baskets. I got twenty-five cents a bushel for it from the junk dealer. I don't know what he did with it because it didn't look good for anything to me. But those quarters always looked good.

I used to roam all over that neighborhood. But I was too young, I guess, to appreciate some of the places.

I understood the theaters. But all the good restaurants

didn't mean anything to me. And there was another place that I never paid any attention to. It was a big gray-brick building on Eighth Avenue between 49th Street and 50th Street. I imagine I walked by it a hundred times and never looked at the marquee that identified it as Madison Square Garden. If I did, I probably thought it had flowers inside.

Not too far away was the Empire State Building, where I had a bad experience.

Riding in one of its elevators I got sick to my stomach. I decided that I wasn't going to ride in an elevator again. Now when I visit people with offices or apartments on a high floor, I walk. I once walked up seventy-six flights, and in my apartment house, I walk up to and from the eighth floor. But at the time I got sick in the Empire State Building, walking up stairs wasn't a problem. We lived one flight up.

Actually, we lived in Hell's Kitchen only about a year before we moved to Harlem.

Mom had found a four-room flat on East 142nd Street for forty-two dollars a month. We stayed a few months, but the rent was a little steep. In the spring of 1934, we settled in a three-room flat on Manhattan Avenue at the corner of 119th Street. We moved a few more times in the following years, but we always lived within a block or two of our original place on Manhattan Avenue. When I speak of my neighborhood as a boy, that's the one I think of because that's where things began to happen. I even had a job there.

Around the corner, on Seventh Avenue, was an old-fashioned market. The groceries were on tall shelves behind the counter. The meat was butchered on a blood-spattered wooden block. Outside, the fresh vegetables and the fresh fruits were on a big wooden stand under a red-and-white striped awning—Dave's Vegetable and Meat Market. Dave was Jewish. His butcher, Nick, was Italian. Nice guys. But their vegetables and fruits were easy pickings for anybody with fast hands. Every time I passed, I grabbed something. An apple one day, a peach the next, sometimes a sweet potato. But one time, as I went to take an apple, I felt a hand clamp around my wrist—Dave's hand.

"Junior," he said, holding my wrist, "you don't have to do that."

"Mister Dave," I said, "I was going to pay you. Look, I got the money right here."

"Junior," he said, "if you paid me, it would've been the first time."

He had me there. He still had me by the hand, too.

"Junior," he said, "I need somebody to make deliveries for me and wait on the people. Are you interested in the job?"

"A job?" I said. "You want to give *me* a job?"

"That's right," he said. "It pays three-fifty a week—after school and all day Saturday."

"You got yourself a worker," I said.

"Good," he said. "Be here tomorrow."

When I arrived the next day, Dave handed me a white apron and led me outside to the fruit-and-vegetable stand.

"You're in charge here," he said. "Watch out for kids stealing stuff."

He turned and walked inside. I had to laugh. He sure knew what he was doing. If it takes a thief to know a thief, he had hired the right man. But the strange thing was, I suddenly had a genuine loyalty to him. Some of my buddies would come strolling down the street toward the market, and just from the way they walked, I could tell they had their eyes on a cantaloupe. But I'd sidle over to where they just couldn't grab anything.

"Hey, Junior, what you doin'?" one of them once said.

"Beat it, man," I said. "I'm workin' here now. If you want somethin', *buy* it."

"Man, you Honest Abe now," he said.

The thing was, I couldn't bring myself to steal anything either. One day I mentioned that to Dave.

"Just *take* what you want," he said.

The free apples never tasted as good as the ones I had stolen, but the three-fifty a week put a little money in my pocket for the first time. Around that neighborhood, a little money was a dangerous thing. Other guys were just looking to take it off you in a dice game. Our pet place was a courtyard behind the tenements on 118th Street. We had to go through the basement to get there and it was a hideaway. One night I was back there shooting craps. I needed to roll a nine.

"Here it is," I was whispering, "here it is."

Just then, whack! I felt an open hand slam me across the back of the head.

"*Here* it is," I heard Mom say.

Mom had seen me coming along the street a few minutes earlier. She had been looking out our window, and she knew I'd had time to get upstairs. When I wasn't there, she came looking for me. She knew where to find me, too. She was always looking to keep me out of trouble. And to tell you the truth, I never went looking for trouble. I never had any trouble with the cops. They might chase us for playing stickball in the streets, something like that, but no cop ever lined me up against the wall about anything. In those years, I went out of my way to avoid trouble. In fact, I never had a street fight until I was pushed into one.

One night after dinner we were having races in the street from sewer to sewer. The sewer covers were in the middle of the street. Usually they were about twenty-five yards apart.

This night we were racing two sewers, about fifty yards. The fastest one on the block was a guy we called Shake— Samuel Royals, his name was. I had to race him two sewers, and I beat him. Not by much, but I beat him. He didn't like the idea of losing, and he started shooting off his mouth.

"Three sewers and I'd beat you, Smith," he said.

"Maybe you would and maybe you wouldn't," I said, satisfied that I had won.

"C'mon," he said, "let's run three sewers."

"Look, man," I said, "we ran two sewers and I beat you. Let's forget it."

"Three sewers, man," he said. "You afraid?"

"I ain't afraid to run," I said. "I'm just too tired to run. Maybe tomorrow."

"Maybe *now*," he said, pushing me.

When he shoved me, I stumbled backwards into our stoop. My sisters were sitting out there and so was Clyde Brewer —Honey we always called him. He was courting Marie and he was around all the time. We got along good. When I stumbled into the stoop, Honey picked me up and shoved me at Shake.

"Go get him, Junior," he said.

Man, I had to do something now. So I started flailing away at Shake. No jabbing or dancing, just swinging. Somehow I popped him on the nose and his blood was all over him and me and the sidewalk. He dropped his hands to look at the blood and I hit him some more and knocked him down. I jumped on top of him and punched him some more until Honey dragged me off. Shake, he just sat there.

"Now who's afraid, Shake?" my sister Evelyn said.

Shake got up slow and walked away. The other guys on the block stared at him. Then they turned and stared at me.

"Junior, you use your hands pretty good," Honey said.

Nobody was any more surprised than me. I was about thirteen then and I was five foot eight, a few inches shorter than I am now, but I weighed only eighty-five pounds. You had to look twice to see me once. My triumph over Shake was big news on the block. Several days later, a little man named Benny Booksinger stopped me on the street. He knew who I was without asking.

"Walker Smith," he said, "I put on boxing shows for the Police Athletic League. I can use you."

I didn't know how to answer him, but I didn't have to. He told me about a show he was having that night. I had seen some of his street shows. He used old orange crates to form a boxing ring.

"Be there at eight o'clock," he said. "Under the street lamp in the middle of your block."

That night Benny matched me with a kid named Harmon, a husky kid. I danced around him and got in a couple of good punches, and I got the decision over three rounds. But after Benny raised my hand, some big guy about seventeen, walked up to me.

"Hey, man," he said, "you just beat my little brother, so that means you got to fight *me* now."

I wanted no part of him, but Benny was pushing me toward the orange crates when Mom came marching across the street. She had seen me fighting Harmon from our apartment window.

"You get back in the house, Junior, and you," she roared at Benny Booksinger, "you get off this block."

He was a little Jewish man, smaller than Mom, and he was backing up, grabbing his equipment, when she swatted him with her open right hand. He didn't come around the block after that, but he knew where to find me. He invited me to go with his PAL teams to boxing shows all over New York City, and I usually went with him. I usually won, too, except for the time at Greenwich House, in the Village. I was in with a tough little Irish kid and he got a three-round decision. Years later, Billy Graham, who once challenged Kid Gavilan for the world welterweight title, reminded me of that fight.

"You know who the kid was?" he said.

"I never saw him again," I answered.

"You're looking at him now," he said. "Before the fight all the kids thought you were Joe Louis's nephew, because you had known him from Detroit. I was scared stiff."

"You didn't fight like it," I said.

Another time I was in with a kid named Buster Pepe at Greenwich House. I worked him over pretty good but after the final bell, the decision was in doubt. In those years a Negro kid didn't always get what he deserved in a bout with a white kid.

"If we don't get it," Benny said to me in the corner, "I'll break their heads."

And he might have, too, but I got the decision. That was the first real victory that did anything for me. It made me realize that I must be pretty good. Pepe was a champ at Greenwich House. Beating a white kid was something special, too. I outgrew that later, but at the time it was important because nobody had to tell me that a Negro kid was as good as a white kid. I had proved it to myself.

Around the neighborhood, some white kids began to challenge me a little, particularly the Irish kids. One day five of them cornered me on a subway platform but I popped each one and got away. After that most of them let me alone. One day Warren Jones, who was in my class at Cooper Junior High School, stopped me on the street.

"Smitty," he said, "I understand that you use your hands pretty good."

Coming from Warren Jones, that meant something. I knew he was a boxer. He had told me that his uncle had trained him in the Salem-Crescent gym in the basement of the Salem

Methodist Church at 129th Street and Seventh Avenue. I had wandered up there a few weeks before that for a big crap game in the alley behind the church. I was on my knees with the dice when all of the other guys started to run. Not me, though. With everybody leaving, I knew it was my chance to scoop up all the money. While I was scooping, somebody grabbed me by the shoulders.

I jumped up, struggling to get away, but out of the corner of my eye, I saw a man with a clerical collar.

I stopped struggling and just stood there. He walked around in front of me and introduced himself.

"I'm Reverend Cullen," he said. "Reverend Frederick Cullen. And this is my church. Son, it's not right to gamble. And especially, it's not right to gamble in the shadow of the Lord's house. When I had a hold on you, it seemed to me that you're a well-muscled young man. Come with me and I'll show you the best way to use those muscles."

He led me to a cellar window of the church. Inside I could see a boxing ring and all the other gear—the punching bags, the rubbing tables, as well as a basketball court and an area for about a thirty-yard dash.

"Young men come here to work out at night," he said. "It not only develops their muscles, it develops their character. I'm not asking you to do me a favor. Do *yourself* a favor and come up here some evening and see for yourself. Try it. You might like it."

"I will, Reverend," I said. "I'll be back here soon."

"Good, you'll enjoy it," he said. "On your way now."

The next day Warren Jones told me about how his uncle took him to upstate New York, over to New Jersey, and sometimes up to Connecticut.

"They're bootleg fights," he said.

"Bootleg?" I said. "What are they?"

"That means that they're supposed to be amateur—you

know, you don't get any money out of it. But you really do. They give you a watch and then they buy it back for ten dollars."

"Who gets the ten?" I said.

"It's all yours," he said.

I started to smile. Maybe there was something to this boxing. I had worked all week in that market for three dollars and fifty cents. And all Warren Jones did was have himself a three-round fight and he made ten dollars.

"But how do you get bootleg fights?" I asked him.

"You've got to do roadwork in the park," he said. "The roadwork builds up your wind."

"What's roadwork?" I said.

"Runnin', man," he said. "Meet me in the park tomorrow after school and we'll run."

Central Park was down at 110th Street, a few blocks away. All the boxers ran there.

"And then tomorrow night," he said, "I'll take you to meet my uncle at the gym."

"What's your uncle's name?"

"George Gainford," he said.

4

Sweet as Sugar

The smell hit me first. In the cellar of the church where George Gainford had his Salem-Crescent Athletic Club, about thirty guys were working out. Sparring in the old ring. Skipping rope. Punching the bags. Doing calisthenics. And sweating, the perspiration dripping like leaky faucets off their bodies. Over the years, the sweat had permeated everything in the gym. The thick stale odor hung in the air and it hung in my nostrils. Later on, it would represent a strange perfume to me, but that first day, I was blowing air up my nose as Warren Jones led me toward a big barrel-chested man.

"Uncle George," he said, "this is my friend Smitty. He wants to be a fighter."

"Him!" Gainford said, sizing me up. "He looks too small to me. Too skinny. Smitty, you better go home and tell your momma to buy you more milk."

"Uncle George, he's worth a look in the ring."

"You want to get Smitty killed? Some of these boys would kill little Smitty," he replied, turning to me. "Be honest with me, Smitty, what do you weigh?"

"Hundred and eleven."

"And how old are you?"

"Fifteen last month."

"You really want to fight?" he said. "If you do, maybe I can try you. I need another flyweight."

"I want to fight," I said, thinking of the ten-dollar bouts that Warren had mentioned. "I really do."

"Come around tomorrow," Gainford said, "and I'll take a look at you, Smitty. I'll let you work."

In those days, George Gainford ruled amateur boxing in Harlem. He developed almost all the Negro boxers in the Golden Gloves program. He had never been much of a fighter himself. There's a gag that he had two fights in his life. The first, when he was knocked out. The second, when they tried to get him to take another fight. But physically, he was impressive. At six foot two and two hundred fifty pounds, he towered over most of the kids in the gym. He had been born in Charleston, South Carolina, but his people had come from British Guiana, and he had their melodious voice. The way he marched around the gym, there was no doubt that he was the man in charge. When I returned there the next day, he handed me wrinkled green satin trunks, scuffed boxing shoes, a jockstrap, and a protective cup.

"Over on that table," he said, "pick out gloves and a headguard that fit you. And then warm up."

I shadowboxed for about ten minutes, then Gainford motioned for me to climb through the ropes. Inside the ring, I noticed that the canvas was dotted with small dark brown spots. Drops of blood that nobody had ever cleaned up. Across from me was an older guy I had never seen before. There was no bell. Gainford would yell "Time!" when he wanted the sparring to start or stop. He had a stop watch for the round, either two minutes or three minutes depending on your experience. Mine was to be two minutes, but it seemed like two hours. In the PAL fights the other kids had slapped or swatted me with big padded gloves. But this

older guy was stinging me in the face with every punch he
threw. I kept waiting for Gainford to yell "Time!" and when
he did, he was shaking his head.

"Smitty," he said, "you come back here tomorrow and
I'll try to teach you a few things."

I had looked awful. And now I felt awful. I had a headache. My nose wasn't bleeding, but I could smell blood
inside it and taste blood inside my mouth. On the way out of
the gym, I was carrying my equipment in a brown paper
bag and Warren Jones was trying to console me.

"You didn't do bad," he said. "You were in with one of
the Golden Glovers."

"Man," I said, glad to be out in the fresh air away from
that sweaty odor, "now I know why they call it 'the bucket
of blood.' All that blood on the canvas. But they ain't ever
going to get any of mine on it."

"Don't be discouraged," he said. "You got good moves. I'll
see you there tomorrow."

"Where you hurrying off to?" I asked. "Ain't you gonna
be on the corner later?"

"I'm going home tonight, man," Warren said. "The fight
is on the radio. Joe Louis."

Not too far away, about forty blocks uptown and across
the Harlem River, my man Joe was going to be in Yankee
Stadium with Max Schmeling, the German with the bushy
eyebrows who had once been the world heavyweight champion. My man Joe had come out of Black Bottom to win
twenty-seven consecutive professional fights, twenty-three
by a knockout. He was on his way to a title bout and in Harlem, man, he was the hero. That night, June 19, 1936, I remember that everybody with a radio had the fight on.
Not only that, they had their windows wide open and the
radio turned up so loud that you could walk along the street
and not miss a punch. I was outside, sitting on our gray ce-

ment stoop, listening to radios all around me, but I couldn't believe what I was hearing. My man Joe couldn't stay away from Schmeling's right hand.

"Louis is down!" I remember the announcer shrieking during the fourth round.

Joe was up almost immediately, but Schmeling continued to dominate the fight. In the twelfth round, the husky German smashed Joe to the canvas again.

". . . nine . . . ten . . . and out!" the announcer yelled.

And out. Nobody on our block could believe it. All over the block, the radios were clicked off one by one until there was a strange silence. On the other stoops and on the fire escapes and in the windows of their drab flats, the men were sitting in their undershirts and the women in their old cotton dresses, as if struck dumb by the outcome. One by one, the people disappeared inside. Soon, as the lights went out, the block was in darkness.

The next day, the newspaper photos made Joe's defeat even more vivid.

His face had been down, turned sideways, as the referee waved his arms ending the bout, and as Schmeling grinned in the background. In another photo, apparently taken seconds after the knockout, Joe had lifted himself to his knees and his head was bowed and he was holding onto the middle rope with his gloves. I've never forgotten that picture because it made me think then that boxing had to be wrong for me. If my man Joe could be knocked out, a skinny kid like me had no chance. Instead of returning to the Salem-Crescent gym, I hocked the boxing equipment that Gainford had given me. I got three dollars for it.

Several days later, Warren Jones came looking for me.

"Uncle George don't care if you don't come back," he said, "but he wants the equipment back tonight."

"I hocked it," I said.

"Give him the money."

"I spent it," I said.

"Then stay out of his way, Smitty, he's really angry. I know him. He'll be coming to get it himself."

That night, I was in the poolroom down the street when Gainford busted through the front door.

"Smitty," he roared, "you owe me money!"

I took off through the side door, and disappeared around the corner. I didn't want any part of that big man catching me. But even though I hadn't returned to the gym, there was one thing about boxing that grabbed me. Other sports never had really interested me too much. Not many kids in our neighborhood had the money for baseball or football equipment. Some played basketball, but not many. About all we ever played was stickball because that didn't cost much. We'd saw off an old broomstick and chip in for a nickel rubber ball, or steal one if we had to. Stickball was our sport. For entertainment, we used to sneak into the subways and ride the trains out to Coney Island with its amusement parks, but they cost money. The big thing about boxing was that it was free.

The trouble was, I didn't dare go back to the Salem-Crescent for several months. I had to send Warren Jones to make peace. Gainford agreed to give me one more chance.

When I showed up, George told me, "One more chance, one *last* chance." And he told me loud. I knew I had to be serious this time. And I was. I worked in that gym every night. I discovered that I wasn't much of a puncher, but I could stay away from punches. I was beginning to enjoy everything about boxing. Punching the bag. The calisthenics. Even the sparring. But not the rope skipping. It was too girlish for me. I preferred to slap time with the rope and dance to the beat. But I made the mistake of telling Mom that I was working out in the gym. One night she stormed in to see George.

"Mister Gainford," she said sternly, "I don't want you making a fighter out of my Junior."

"I ain't making no fighter out of your son, Mrs. Smith. Look, you take your son and get him out of here if you want. I don't need him around."

"No," she said, "I like him here. He's out of trouble here. But I don't want him a fighter."

"He don't have to be a fighter," George said. "He wants to come here, I don't particularly want him here. He's too skinny to be a fighter anyway."

"Good," said Mom, "just let him hang around then."

I did. I was in the gym every night. The trouble was, Warren Jones and the other guys weren't always there. They were traveling to their bootleg fights. Gainford had two or three cars going out almost every night. Up to Poughkeepsie, or somewhere in Connecticut, sometimes all the way to Canada. George had a black '31 Ford coupe, with room for three in the front and a rumble seat for three more in the back. After he got to like me, I tried to talk him into letting me go with him.

"No chance, Smitty," he said, "unless your mother tells me you can go."

I got Mom to agree, on the promise that I wouldn't participate in any of the bouts. And I didn't. But wherever we went, I'd tell George I could've beaten this kid or that kid in my weight class. George had the same answer every time.

"Smitty," he'd say, "you gonna get killed, you can't beat nobody. Now get in the car."

For me, that meant ride in the rumble seat, which was great except when it rained. But instead of discouraging me,

George's words made me all the more determined. One night we were up in Kingston, New York, not far from Albany, when the man running the show, Ben Becker, walked up to George.

"I've got a problem," he said. "I need an opponent for a flyweight."

"Flyweight?" said George. "I don't have a flyweight with me tonight."

I had overheard the conversation and I spoke up. "Sure you do," I said. "I'm a flyweight." George put one of his big arms around me and led me over to the side of the room.

"All right, Smitty," he said and he was smiling, "now I'm going to find out if you can fight."

George went back to talk to Ben Becker, and he motioned toward me. "Here's my flyweight," he told Becker, who had a piece of paper in his hand. They were the Amateur Athletic Union forms, and then Becker asked the question that changed my life.

"What's the kid's name?"

"His name?" George stammered.

"Where's his card?"

In order to fight in amateur shows, you had to have an AAU card to certify that you were an amateur, not a professional. I didn't have a card, but George had a stack of them. He carried all his fighters' cards. He might take half a dozen kids out on a trip but he would have several dozen AAU cards with him.

"Here's his card," George was saying now, shuffling through them. "Here it is. Ray Robinson."

I knew Ray Robinson from around the gym. He had been one of George's bootleg fighters, but he had stopped boxing. George had held onto his card, and now, suddenly, I was using Ray Robinson's AAU card.

"Ray Robinson," George was saying to Ben Becker. "Don't let his skinniness fool you."

He handed the card to Becker, who wrote down my new name on the AAU form sheet.

"Smitty," George said, taking me aside again, "I'm using Ray Robinson's card for you. That's your name tonight. We'll get a card for you later. Now go in the dressing room over there and wait for the doctor to call you."

Half an hour later, I was sitting on a bench in the dressing room. I was thinking about how I'd fight, and my mind wasn't on what was going on around me. I wasn't paying attention when the doctor called out, "Ray Robinson."

Nobody answered, and the doctor asked, "Is there a Ray Robinson here?"

The guy next to me nudged me and said, "That kid Robinson must have been scared off."

"Ray Robinson," I said, realizing who the doctor meant. "I'm Ray Robinson."

After the doctor checked me over, I put on one of the old wrinkled blue-and-white satin robes that George always brought along so that his fighters would look like fighters. He laced my gloves on but he didn't seem to have much faith in me.

"Just do the best you can, Smitty," he said, patting me on the shoulder. "I'll be waiting for you."

He went outside to watch the first fight. He scouted everybody. As soon as he left, I realized that none of the other kids in the room had made a sound. Seven of them were in there with me. I glanced at each one, hoping to start a conversation, anything to take my mind off the fight, but all the kids were staring at the floor or glancing at the ceiling. One was lying on the floor, with his head on a folded towel and another towel draped over his eyes. Anything to avoid a conversation. Nobody knew who he was matched with, and the other kids, who had been through this before, knew that it was bad to get friendly with a kid who might be your opponent a few minutes later. In that ring, man, it didn't pay to be friendly with anybody. In that ring, the kid across from you was your enemy. In the room, the only noise was the bells and the hand-clapping of the people outside. Suddenly, a shout went up.

"Knockout," one of the other kids whispered. "They only shout like that for a knockout."

Moments later, Ben Becker hurried into the room with his big AAU form sheet in his hand. He called two names.

"All right," he said. "Let's get out there. C'mon, everybody's waiting. C'mon, hurry up."

The two kids got to their feet, glanced at each other, and went through the door into the crowd. Moments later, a dark Italian kid in a red bathrobe strutted into the room, his face sweating but smiling.

"What a punch," an older man was saying, pounding him on the back. "What a left hand."

Behind them, another kid in a green bathrobe wobbled into the room. He was trying to focus his eyes. Next to him, a little man in a red cap was shaking his head. He led the kid over to where the kid's clothes were on a hook.

"Tomorrow," the little guy in the red cap snapped, "you be in the gym tomorrow at six."

"No," said the doctor, who had followed them in, "I'm putting your boy on suspension."

The little man in the red cap argued, but the kid didn't say a word. He was blinking slowly, and the doctor made him lie down on the bench. Outside, the crowd wasn't making much noise. They began to stamp their feet, asking for more action. Soon, they were booing and the announcer was saying ". . . on a decision . . ." and Ben Becker was in the room.

"Robinson, Ray Robinson," I heard him say.

I never heard the name of my opponent, but I noticed him stand up and look at me. We walked out of the room and through the aisle leading to the wooden steps behind my corner. Up in the ring, George was waiting for me and when I got there, man, it was like that time I danced at the Alvin Theater. It was like being on that stage.

As scared as I was, I was happy. Happy excited, and I was praying.

"Smitty," said George, "stay away from this kid. I've seen him before."

As he spoke, he soaked a sponge in the water pail and sprayed me with it. Once, twice.

The Father, the Son, I thought, and then I said, "Once more, George."

He sprayed me with the water from the wet sponge again and I thought, *and the Holy Ghost.* In all the years that followed, I had him do that every time I got into the ring. I never told him why I wanted him to spray me three times, as I'd seen a priest do with holy water, but that prayer was my only superstition, if you want to call it that. I never believed in a lucky charm, like a rabbit's foot. Man, a rabbit has four feet, but they're not lucky enough to save him from being killed. I always preferred prayer.

Most of the time it helped, beginning that first night in Kingston.

I was so excited, it's all a blur in my mind now. The other kid's punches, the people yelling, George talking to me between rounds, and the announcer walking into the middle of the ring after the bell ended the third round.

"The winner," he called, pointing to me, "on a unanimous decision, Ray Robinson."

I couldn't believe it. Neither could George. He had stuffed a towel around my neck and then tucked it inside my blue-and-white bathrobe, but now he stared at me. "They ain't all this easy, Smitty," he said. "They ain't all gonna be this easy."

I didn't care. This fight had been easy, that's all I knew. Later on, the money was easy, too. When the card was completed, I went into Ben Becker's office for the ritual I had seen other kids take part in on my earlier trips with George.

"Here's your watch, Robinson, nice fight," Becker said, handing me a round gold watch that train conductors use.

I gave the watch back to him and held out my hand. He put a ten-dollar bill into it. I think it was the first time I'd ever had a ten-dollar bill in my pocket, but it created a problem for me. If Mom ever discovered it, she'd ask how I got it. I wasn't supposed to be fighting.

"What should I do, George?" I asked.

"If you tell your mother you had a fight, you know she won't let you come any more," he said. "And next week, Ben Becker wants you back here, so you better not tell her."

"But where should I hide the money?"

"Put it in your shoe," he suggested.

And I did, but after a few months, I had so much money that I didn't dare leave it in my shoe. I had to tell somebody at home and that meant Marie. She was still my big brother and, as always, she had a solution.

"I'll hide the money in one of my old shoes, Junior," she said. "Mom never looks in my clothes."

I was the boy with three names—Junior at home, Smitty in the gym, and Ray Robinson in the ring. I never did get an AAU card as Walker Smith. I had gone back to Kingston the following week with George and I had boxed as Ray Robinson again. And I had won again. They started to advertise me as Ray Robinson, and the word spread to some of the other places where George took fighters.

"Smitty," George said to me one night, "I think it's too

late to change your name back. You are Ray Robinson."

When Robinson's AAU card expired, I applied for a new one in his name. He had been born on August 26, 1919, in Richmond, Virginia. Now I had his birthday and birthplace. I knew the real Ray Robinson and in the years that followed, he liked to tease me that I'd stolen his name. I couldn't argue with him. The last time I saw him, he was a bartender.

In those months when I was making trips with George, Mom was under the impression I was going along for the ride. To have me out of the house was a break for her. She had enough troubles, trying to pay the rent and feed us, and she trusted George. There were times when we'd get back to Harlem as late as four in the morning and instead of going home, I'd sleep on the couch at George's house. I loved that, because it made it seem that boxing was my whole life. And it was. At night I was either training in the Salem-Crescent gym or on a trip with George. And the rest of the day, I was involved in boxing.

In the morning I'd stroll down to Central Park and do my roadwork. Not the Central Park near the Plaza Hotel, where the men in their top hats stand around horse-drawn carriages, that's 59th Street. The Central Park that I knew was the other end, 110th Street, where the only horses we saw were those pulling junk wagons. In the afternoon I'd hang around Grupp's Gym on 116th Street off Eighth Avenue. At a fancy party years later, a society lady peered over her pince-nez glasses at me and asked, "Mister Robinson, what college did you attend?"

"Grupp's College, ma'am," I said.

"Really," she said, "and what did you major in?"

"Science, ma'am," I replied.

"How interesting," she said.

And in a way, I had. I really had gone to college at

Grupp's. My professors were the old-timers who hung
around there. Famous old fighters like Harry Wills, Kid
Norfolk, Panama Joe Gans. And some not so famous ones
like Soldier Jones. All they did was talk boxing, and all I
did was listen.

"Balance, son," Harry Wills once told me, "balance is a
fighter's most important asset."

Against one of the walls at Grupp's, there was a tall mirror. I never thought much about it, but one day Harry Wills
explained its use.

"The mirror," he said, "shows if you have your guns where
you can use them."

Slowly, my balance improved, and it saved me many
times. In addition to enabling me to put all my power behind a punch, good balance enabled me to keep my
feet when another man might have been knocked down. Balance is so important to an athlete. Joe Louis would have
been an even greater champion if he had developed better
balance. The time Tony Galento flattened him, it wasn't a
great punch. Joe was off balance when Tony nailed him. Balance is hard to describe, but if you've seen Willie Mays
catch a fly ball or Joe Namath throw a pass, you know what
balance is.

I took another course at Grupp's College, a course in anat-
omy.

I learned to aim for my opponent's temple, or for his
heart. It sounds brutal, but boxing is a brutal business. Most
spectators seem to think that the jaw is the primary target,
or maybe the solar plexus. Perhaps it is with some fighters,
but I learned to look for the temple and the heart and the
liver. Hit a man in the liver and his pain is excruciating.

I learned about my own body, too. Soldier Jones used to
wipe some sweat off me with his finger and taste it.

"Salty," he would say. "That's good. The salt is in your system. When it's not salty, it means you're stale."

Soldier Jones had fought in the armories all over New York City, like George Gainford, and over the years, he was with me in the corner. He was the one who taught me about the value of the left jab.

"Always remember," he said, "that if you can catch him with the left hand, you can hit him with the right. The left side is your offensive side, the right your defensive."

Some of my teachers were more my age. Sedgewick Harvey was a famous Golden Gloves champion, maybe ten years older than I was. He was a hero to the kids in the neighborhood, but he was always encouraging little kids like me. He taught me how to cut the ring, how to make my opponent go where I wanted him to go, not where he wanted to.

"If he circles to his right," he explained, "you move to your left, and if he circles to his left, you go right."

As simple as that, but if somebody doesn't take the time to explain it to you, sometimes you never learn it. Kelly hung around Grupp's too. Kelly was a little Irishman in his forties. Kelly was the only name I ever knew him by. He had never had a real fight, but he trained every day as if he was getting ready for a title shot. Kelly had seen all the great fighters, all the way back to Jack Johnson, and he used to tell me about their styles. One day he told me that there was going to be a boxing show at the Golden Gate ballroom in Harlem.

"Have your pop take you," he said.

I didn't say anything, but I guess he could tell from the look on my face that something was wrong.

"What's the matter?" he asked.

"I ain't got a pop," I said. "It's just my mom and my two sisters."

"I'll take you," he said.

He took me quite a few times. It got so that he was like a

father to me. All those old-timers were. But of all the men around me, George Gainford was the most important. Psychologically as well as physically. He was more of a father image than anybody else. As for my boxing, the best thing he did for me was let me alone.

"You know that song, 'It ain't what you do, it's the way that you do it,'" George once told me. "That applies to boxing, too. I like the way you move. Don't copy anybody. Be yourself."

He had begun to show more confidence in me. I had won a few fights, and the spectators always seemed to give me a big hand. Going on those trips upstate with George was the biggest thing in my life. Sometimes, he had more confidence in me than I had in myself. One night I noticed a tough-looking kid about my size on the other team.

"Who's that?" I said to George.

"That's the boy you're fighting," he said.

"Not me," I said.

"What's wrong?"

"Look at him," I said. "His nose is all flat, there's scar tissue around his eyes. He's too tough."

"Smitty," he said, "if he could fight, he wouldn't look like that."

George was correct. The kid couldn't fight. After a few more fights, I started to have more confidence in myself. One time in Poughkeepsie, I was weighing in with my opponent when the man running the show came over and showed us the fancy new wrist watch for the winner.

"Is that the one I'm getting?" my opponent said.

"Oh," I said to the man running the show, "are you giving two watches away?"

"No," the man said, "just one."

"That's what I thought," I said. "Because I know *I'm* going to win this one."

And I did. Another time I was with George in Hartford, Connecticut. The promoter there had George bring me up to fight this kid who was unbeaten. I got the decision, a close one. It broke his winning streak. But he was some fighter, a little Italian kid.

"What's his name again?" I asked somebody after the fight.

"Willie Papaleo," he said, "but around here, Willie Pep."

In later years, Willie Pep would win the world feather-weight championship, and he was the best boxer I ever saw. After that victory, I was getting dressed when a Hartford policeman marched in with one of the local amateur boxing officials.

"Gainford," the cop said, "you and your fighter better come with me."

"What for, officer?" Gainford stammered. "What's going on? What's wrong?"

"Some of the people around here think your fighter has to be a pro if he beat Willie Pep here. I'm going to have to lock you both up for the night until the people here can check with the AAU in New York in the morning."

George exploded, but it didn't do us any good. We went to jail.

The next morning, the Hartford promoter checked with Ben Levine, the AAU boxing man in New York, and he vouched for my amateur standing. Another time we were in Watertown, New York, not far from the Thousand Islands in the St. Lawrence River and not far from the Canadian border. I had put on a little weight, I was up around 118, but there was a Canadian kid about 126 who hadn't lost a fight and was knocking out almost all his opponents. The promoter in Watertown wanted George to put me in with the Canadian.

"I can't do that," George said. "Robinson's mother doesn't know he's fighting. If he gets cut, I'm in trouble."

That made a good excuse. And it was true. Mom still thought I was taking these trips for the ride. But actually, George was negotiating. George wasn't putting these shows together for a hobby. This was his business. He was making as much as $300 a week out of these amateur shows. That made him a big man in Harlem in those years. Eventually, he agreed to let me box the Canadian kid the next week.

"That," he told the Watertown promoter, "will give you a little time to build up the crowd."

When we arrived the next week, the whole town was excited. I had fought in Watertown before, and the people there knew me and naturally they knew all about the Canadian kid. When we got into the ring, there must have been several hundred people yelling and jumping around. For Watertown, that was a huge crowd. But the crowd didn't bother me. I was more worried about my opponent's punch. I didn't want to get cut, because then I'd be in trouble with Mom and she was a lot tougher than any kid boxer. I decided to put some pressure on him right at the start. I walked out and threw some punches, getting him on the defensive, and then I threw a good left hook and he went down.

". . . eight, nine, ten," the referee counted.

I couldn't believe it. I had never knocked out anybody before. When the referee raised my hand, I was jumping around and yelling at George, "I knocked him out! I knocked him out!" And when I came down the steps from my corner, Jack Case, the sports editor of the paper there, looked up at George.

"That's a sweet fighter you've got there," he said, "a real sweet fighter."

"As sweet as sugar," said a lady at ringside who had over-heard Case's remark.

In his paper the next day, Case referred to me as Sugar Ray Robinson. That's how I got my nickname. In sports, a good nickname is important. Like Babe Ruth. When people talk about the Babe, that's all they have to say, everybody knows who they mean. It got to be that way with me. Sugar Ray was enough. There was only one. And that's what I mean about being a blessed man. The mix-up over my name was a blessing. Sugar Walker Smith doesn't have the same ring. Sugar Ray Robinson is different. Man, it's sweet.

5

Marjie

On the street corners, men stood around the sidewalk all day, every day. Not too many people in our neighborhood were working. Those who were, like Mom, weren't about to give much money to their kids.

The older people kept what little extra money they had for a bottle of gin or for a straight play on a number. The gin let them forget their misery. The numbers racket let them have some hope. Everywhere there were big white posters with a blue eagle on them. Anybody who lived through the Depression remembers the blue eagle. It was the symbol of the National Recovery Act, which was supposed to create jobs. Not many Negro people got the jobs.

Some kids my age took to stealing ladies' purses or to mugging somebody. I took to girls.

In those Depression years, a girl was happy if a guy took her for a walk. If a guy had a little money on him, great, but a girl didn't expect him to spend any money on her because nobody had any money. At night we'd meet in the candy stores or on the stoops and try to think of something different to do. Sneaking a cigarette was a big thing then. So was sipping a bottle of beer. I had no taste for either one. And besides, they each cost money. I guess that's why we didn't know anything about heroin or marijuana. I don't remember ever seeing or hearing about a dope-pusher. Too expensive. But girls were free. At night we'd usually end up in somebody's house, dancing to radio music, and if their parents weren't home, we'd do more than that. Other times we'd steal some potatoes and roast them in a fire over in Morningside Park, near Columbia University. When the fire died out, the party was over, except for those who had wandered off.

When you didn't have any money, a guy knew right away when a girl liked him for *him*, but money helped.

I discovered this when I began to make a little money on my trips with George. I was going with a girl named Joan and one night I took her to Coney Island. We went on the roller coaster and a few other rides and we had hot dogs and sodas. We had gone there before, but the only thing I had been able to afford was a stroll along the boardwalk. This time I even paid the subway fare, a nickel then.

"Junior," I remember her saying, "that's a waste of money. We can sneak in."

That's the way we always had done it before. We'd stand where the change-booth man couldn't see us, and when we heard the train coming, we'd leap over the turnstiles and we'd be on the train, pulling out of the station, before he could catch us.

"I know," I told her, "but sneaking in is for kids. When you got the money, you should pay it."

She soon spread the word that Junior had a few coins and suddenly there were more girls talking to me. Not that I discouraged them. Around this time I had learned to drive a '28 Ford, one of the cars George used for us. I didn't have a license but I had money for gas, and that was better than a license. The girls loved to ride in that old car. It always needed gas, but I never let on to them.

"I like to keep the tank full," I'd say to the man in the gas station, "but it don't need but a gallon."

In those days, a gallon didn't cost much more than fifteen cents, if that, and I'd hand the man a quarter, like a big spender. The girls fell for that one every time. None of them bothered to look at the gas gauge.

"And tomorrow," I'd tell them, "maybe we can go to the movies."

Man, a little money went a long way. But my money wasn't making any impression on the girl I wanted it to. Her name was Marjorie. She had beautiful black skin. She had moved in across the street and I used to sneak looks at her when she walked by, but I never made a play for her until one night at a dance the Socialistic Dukes put on in their store-front clubhouse on Lenox Avenue. Our guys were known as the Midtowns. We wore blue-and-white warm-up jackets. There was H. D. Mays and Robert Chaney and Sonny Leacock, and our leader, Bull Johnson, and there was Shake, the kid I had the street fight with.

"Smitty," Bull Johnson said to me on the way to the dance, "you got somethin' on you?"

He meant a razor or a knife, but I never carried anything like that and I said, "Not me, man."

"You're makin' a mistake," he said. "You know there's always trouble over at the Dukes."

There always had been. The leader of the Dukes, a tall skinny guy, had a reputation for having cut three or four guys but he never had bothered me. Nobody tried to rough me up, probably because I was a boxer, so I always thought that I didn't need any weapon to protect myself. But there were times when I wished I had something on me, like that night.

The dance had started nice enough. The lights were low. Nobody had the money for much electricity, anyway. And the music was good. Just three pieces, but those cats knew how. The big song then was her name, "Margie," and Jimmy Lunceford's band had made a hot record. It was a lindy hop, a jitterbug. That's when I noticed Marjorie. Her skirt was swinging high, and man, I couldn't keep my eyes off those slim black legs of hers.

I noticed something else, too. Some of my guys, the Midtowns, were in a huddle against the wall. That had to mean trouble. They served soda at the dance, but there were always some guys who sneaked in beer or gin, and, man, that's trouble in a bottle. I knew what was going to happen. I had been through it all before. Somebody would take a swing at somebody else and then somebody would have a razor in his hand and by the time the cops got there, somebody would be holding his cheek, trying to stop the blood where the razor had slashed him.

"Hey, honey," I said, walking over to Marjorie. "Remember me? Junior, from your block?"

She nodded and smiled and we moved out on the dance floor and started jitterbugging. We danced and danced, and I kept looking at her legs, and when the music stopped, I bought her a soda.

"Marjie," I said, flashing my eyes behind her, "I don't like the look of things. Let's get home."

She agreed. And after we left, the trouble started, or so I was told the next day. By that time, I was in love. Or thought I was. There was something about that girl. From that night on, I was with her every chance I got. I had money in my pocket, and I was able to show her a good time. I took her to the movies and to the dances. And she liked me. She was always doing little things for me. That's how all the trouble started.

Her father, as I remember, worked in the post office, a good steady job in those days. Her mother worked, too.

One noontime Marjie was home from school for lunch. I was home from school, too. But not for lunch. I was always home from school. I had just about stopped going to Cooper Junior High. I was walking down the block when I heard her voice in the front window of her family's third-floor apartment.

"Hey, Junior," she yelled, "want some lunch?"

When I looked up, she waved an empty plate at me, and I wasn't about to turn down that invitation. She started fixing lunch for me almost every noontime. And one time she didn't go back to school for her afternoon classes. We snuggled up on the couch in her living room, and that was the day I was her first guy. It got to be a regular thing. But one day several months later, when I walked into her apartment for lunch, she wouldn't look at me.

"What's the matter, honey?" I said.

"Oh, Junior," she said, and her eyes were glistening, "I haven't had my sickness this month."

"What are you talking about?" I said, and, man, that's how dumb I was.

"I'm gonna have a baby, Junior," she said, and she was crying now. "I'm gonna have *our* baby."

"You sure?" I said.

"The doctor told me," she said. "I went to the doctor."

"Oh, man," I said.

I was in real trouble this time. And I did what I had always done in an emergency. I went to Marie. She knew Marjie, but Marie couldn't save me as she had when the kids used to chase me.

"You've got to tell Momma," Marie said.

I didn't want to tell Mom, but I knew I had to. When I did, Mom didn't get excited. I could tell she didn't like it, but she seemed to understand there was nothing she could do now, except try to make the best of a bad situation. The next day, she went to see Marjie's mother and father. I was there too. After a few words, she got down to business.

"My boy will marry Marjorie," she said.

"No," Marjorie's father snapped, out of pride, I guess.

"But the baby has to have a name," Mom said.

"Your son is not marrying my daughter," her father said. "Please take your son and leave, Mrs. Smith."

"You're making a mistake," Mom told him.

Several days later, Mom went back to see Marjie's parents. This time she convinced them that we should get married, in order to give the baby a name, but that we wouldn't live together.

"In that case," her father said, "all right."

And that's what we did. We went down to City Hall and took out a marriage license. We had a quiet ceremony at a little red-brick church in the neighborhood. After the wedding, I never even kissed my bride. She walked away with her father and mother. I went back to our apartment with Mom. I was married, but I was the saddest bridegroom in the world that day. I loved that girl, but with her pregnant we never had a chance. Instead of being able to love each other, we were like two criminals being led away to different cells.

Several months later, on September 25, the baby arrived, a boy. His name is Ronnie and he has been a skater in the Roller Derby. Not long after his birth, my marriage to Marjie was annulled.

Before the annulment, I had to cool my love life in Harlem. But when we had to stay overnight on the trips to the bootleg fights, it seemed that some girls always knew where to find us. Sometimes we even went as far as Montreal, a good place for girls.

By this time, George Gainford wasn't always with me.

Sometimes he would arrange shows in different towns on the same night. He'd drive one group to one town, then he'd put me in charge of the other group going to the other town. That was a big deal, being the group captain, as George called it. George liked to put me in charge because I always came back with the money he had been promised. Most of the people who put on those shows were always trying to gyp me out of a few dollars. They'd cry about how they lost money and all that, but I'd cry even louder about how we needed that money to eat and how, if I didn't have all the money that George was expecting, I'd be in trouble.

It got so that I was carrying a lot of money for George. When we got back to Harlem at two or three o'clock in the morning, I'd go into Bickford's Cafeteria on 116th Street and Seventh Avenue where George was waiting.

"You got all the money, Robinson?" George would say.

He was even *calling* me Robinson now. Walker Smith, Jr., was a forgotten man.

"I got it all," I'd say, stacking the dollar bills.

"All right, Robinson," he'd say, "have yourself a meal. On me."

And I would. Hot dogs and beans. Every time.

"That ain't a fighter's food," George always warned me, "that's junk food."

"But I'm winnin' on it," I'd tell him.

He had no comeback for that. I couldn't lose. I was a big attraction wherever I went. I was learning things, too, like never to trust anybody. One night George took me over to Jersey City. I didn't want to go, because I had an infection in my left ear. It was like a boil, just to touch it hurt something awful. But it wasn't as obvious as a boil, so the doctor never noticed it. And George knew there wasn't anybody over there who could give me much trouble. It fig-

ured to be an easy pay night for both of us. Before the
fight George was talking with the man who had the Jersey
fighters.

"The kid I put in with Robinson," the Jersey man said,
"he's got to get killed. Can you go easy?"

"Tell you what," George said, "Robinson's got a bad left
ear. If your kid stays away from the ear, Robinson won't
hurt him."

"You got a deal," the Jersey man said.

George told me what they had arranged. It was all right
with me. But when the bell rang, that kid ran across the
ring and let go a right hand at my bad ear. He didn't hit
it flush, but he grazed it, and, man, it burned. So did I.
The deal was off now, so I hit him a couple of good combinations and he went over on his back. Another knockout.

The next time, I made my own deal. There was a show in
West New York, which is really in New Jersey, that Duke
Stefano had arranged for the Italian Sports Circle there.
Duke knew his business. He later became an assistant
matchmaker at Madison Square Garden. But his problem
that night was getting an opponent for Johnny Delsanno,
who had been the 1938 Diamond Belt featherweight champion.

"I want to put him in with Robinson," Duke told
George.

"With Robinson," George moaned, and nobody ever
moaned as convincingly as George. "Your kid will kill Robinson."

"C'mon, George," Duke said, "you know better than
that."

"Delsanno," George groaned. "He's the best around. I
can't let a young fighter like Robinson take that punish-
ment."

"All right, George," Duke said, "I can get you fifty dollars extra for it."

"Well then," Gainford said, "maybe the experience will be good for Robinson. He needs that tough competition."

"That's what I've been telling you," Duke said.

They hadn't realized it, but I had overheard the entire conversation. When George told me who I was fighting, I gave him the same treatment he had given Duke.

"I can't fight Delsanno," I told George. "He's too good for me."

"Now, Robinson," he said, "he's got experience, but he's not as quick as you, he can't punch like you."

"George," I said, "I got to have fifty for myself."

I got it, and I got the decision. That was the first time I had negotiated for myself. George hadn't realized it, but he had taught me all I knew. On those bootleg trips when I had been his group captain, I had discovered that he had been making more than I thought he deserved. When I got ten dollars for a fight, that was only a small part of what George had been paid to provide the fighters. George was clearing up to $300 a week that way, and in those years, that was real big money. After that, I negotiated for myself whenever I knew I had the promoter over a barrel. Instead of ten, my take might be as high as the full fifty-dollar fee, and after a few weeks, the money was filling Marie's shoe. I kept putting money in it and I always knew how much was there. Every time I put some more in, I counted it. Not that I was checking on Marie. I trusted her. I just enjoyed counting all those green bills. To me, that was all the money in the world. One night, I remember, I had $910 in Marie's shoe. But the next time I counted, it was less than $900.

"Hey, Lard," I yelled, using my old nickname for Marie. "What's goin' on with my money?"

"Junior," she said. "I needed an outfit for the party. I didn't think you'd mind if—"

"Didn't think I'd mind!" I shouted. "Look, Lard, this is my money, not yours. Didn't think I'd mind! Maybe I wouldn't have minded if you had asked me, but Lard, you just *took* it. You took my money."

"Whose money?" roared a voice in the doorway, Mom's voice.

I froze. So did Marie. Mom had come in. With all the noise we were making, we hadn't heard her. But she had heard us. Especially the part about money. She was making twenty dollars a week sewing at the Champion Coat and Apron Supply. Man, money was her whole life.

"Whose money?" she repeated, even louder this time.

She had me. "My money," I said, tossing the dollar bills on Marie's bed.

"Where'd you get this, Junior?" she said.

"Boxing," I said. "Boxing upstate on George Gainford's amateur shows."

"Boxing!" she shouted. "Fighting!"

"Yes, Mom," I confessed. "But look, there's not a mark on me. And I've won all my fights."

She glanced at my face, then she looked at the money.

"How much have you got there, Junior?" she said. "How much have you made fighting?"

"Close to nine hundred," I said.

Her jaw dropped. I don't think she had ever seen $900 in her life. She sat down on the bed and her fingers sifted through the money.

"All this from fighting," she said.

"And I'll make more, Mom," I said. "I can make lots more. Let me keep fighting, Mom. Please, Mom."

She reached up and ran her fingers over my face.

"You really don't have a mark on you, do you?" she said.

"Well, maybe you can keep fighting, but if you start to get cut up, I'll have to make you stop."

"Don't worry, Mom," I said, "I'll be all right."

In the confusion, I never thought to mention to Mom that I was fighting under another name. I wasn't trying to keep it from her. I just didn't think to do it. But one day she was thumbing through the *Daily News* when she saw my picture connected with the Golden Gloves.

"Junior," she called, "what's this?"

She showed me the picture and under it, the words: Ray Robinson.

"That's you, Junior," she said. "That's my child."

I didn't know what to say.

"That pimple on your left ear," she said. "That's you, but what's this about Ray Robinson?"

I had to tell her then.

"Imagine that," she said. "Well, all right, Robinson, I guess you must be pretty good to have your picture in the paper."

I thought so, too.

That was the first time my picture had been in any newspaper, and it made me feel like I was somebody. All the other guys on the block were scrounging around, not really accomplishing anything, but man, I had my picture in the *Daily News*. I was special. The other guys knew it, and so did the girls, but the little kids really made me feel it. Some of them would be around the block all the time, waiting to carry my equipment bag or just to talk to me, the way I'd hung around Joe Louis when I was a little kid in Detroit. Man, I was proud. So proud that I wouldn't let my knickers slip down my legs.

In those days, guys wore knickers until they were old enough to get a job. But knickers had a way of sliding below your knees and looking sloppy.

Now that my picture was in the newspaper, now that I was somebody, those knickers had to be tight around my knees and my shirt had to be tucked in. I had to look good all the time. I was the best groomed dropout in the neighborhood. I had wanted to quit school, but Mom was against it. I pleaded with her, a mistake I've suffered for ever since, but at the time school seemed to be more trouble than it was worth. I was getting home late at night from my fights, and in the morning I just couldn't get up. When I talked to her about dropping out of school, she went downtown to ask advice from a doctor she had taken us to when we lived in Hell's Kitchen. He was Dr. Vincent Nardiello, a small Italian man with a pencil mustache. Mom knew he was around boxing. He worked for the New York State Athletic Commission and for Madison Square Garden. He knew all the fighters, and he had even heard about me as an amateur. He even knew my two names.

"I doubt if your son ever will be a good student," he told Mom, "but he might be a very good fighter."

That convinced her. And after that, all she thought about was my career as a fighter. She sewed me new satin trunks, and a new blue bathrobe. And one day when she noticed me shadowboxing in my room, she strolled in to watch.

"Here," she said, "punch at me."

"Punch at you!" I said. "I can't do that."

"Punch, but don't hit," she said.

I had to laugh at that, but I knew what she meant. I'd throw my punches but pull them before they reached her. Other times she'd hold up a pillow for me to punch.

"I'm your punching bag," she said.

I started to call her Punch. Now everybody had a nickname. Marie was Lard, Evelyn was Neck, and Mom was Punch. But even though she was letting me box, and going to some of my fights, that didn't mean I was on my own. One time I was in the poolroom around the corner. Mom wasn't due home from work for a couple of hours, but this rainy night she got off early. I was racking the balls when she came in behind me and slammed me across the back with her umbrella.

"Get out of here, Junior, and stay out of here. And you!" she yelled at the proprietor. "You make sure he stays out or I'll come back and take this umbrella to you."

She shoved me outside onto the sidewalk. Every few feet, she poked me with her umbrella to keep me moving home. The worst part was, some of my guys were watching all this, and some of the girls were there, too. Here I was, a big man in the Golden Gloves, being jostled down the street by my mom. And that was embarrassing, even if Mom had the right idea. She knew that other kids were getting into trouble with the cops.

I got my kicks from dice. Man, I was lucky with dice. By this time Evelyn was married to her first husband, Donald Bristow. They lived with us. One night I suggested to Donald that we go up on the roof and play craps.

"No, Junior," Evelyn pleaded, "please don't."

"What's the matter?" Donald said to Evelyn. "It'll just be a little game."

"You don't know Junior," she said. "He'll win all your money up there."

"Now, Neck," I said.

"Don't 'Now, Neck' me," she said. "You're just too lucky at dice, you know that."

"Hush up, Evelyn," her husband said.

Half an hour later, we were back. I had all his money. All of his and Evelyn's money, for that matter. But she went into an act about how they wouldn't be able to eat until the next payday, so I gave most of it back to her. Those dice were good to me. Another thing about them, they kept me off the streets. I was usually in an alley or up on a roof. The streets were where a kid got into trouble. Some of the other guys thought it was smart to sass a cop. Not me. I thought it was pretty dumb to sass anybody with a gun on his hip. When those cops came around looking for troublemakers, they liked to line up guys against the wall, with their hands up, and empty their pockets. But they never lined me up.

Another reason I stayed out of trouble was that I didn't dare get into it.

I was boxing in the 1939 Golden Gloves tournament, and George Gainford had warned us that anybody who got into trouble with the police was out of the tournament. No appeal. Out, man. Gone. I wasn't about to risk that. I was still a featherweight then, and made the limit at a little less than 116 pounds. My best buddy, another featherweight, named Spider Valentine, was in the tournament, too. We each kept winning, and the night of the city finals we were matched in the old Madison Square Garden. Man, that was a feeling.

Outside, the big marquee lit up Eighth Avenue, and even early, when we had to get there, the spectators filled the lobby. The finals of the Gloves was always a sellout.

Along the curb the mounted policemen were on their horses, keeping traffic moving, and on 49th Street, near the employees' entrance that we used, the cops had put up gray wooden horses to keep the spectators in line. Man, all those people were going to be watching *me*, I thought. And inside, it was even more of a thrill when I came up the stairs on the side of the old Garden and emerged into the aisle leading to the ring.

"All right, all right," one of the gray-uniformed Garden policemen was saying, "let the fighter through."

As I went down the aisle, peeking out from under the towel that George had wrapped around my head, I noticed the faces, dozens of faces turned toward me, studying me as if I was a race horse in the paddock. At the end of the aisle, I followed the policemen to the right, where my corner was, and I hopped up the steps and waited for George to hold the top two ropes apart so I could climb through.

Now everybody could see me, and there was a roar of applause. They knew who I was because my name was on the back of my blue satin robe.

They knew all about me, too. The people who came to the finals of the Gloves always were real fight fans. They had read about me in the *Daily News,* and they had come to see if I was as good as my record. Jogging there in the ring, I couldn't see past the first few rows of ringside. For other sports, like basketball or hockey, the old Garden was lit brightly because of the size of the court or rink. For boxing, the lights are over the ring. Away from it, the spectators seem to be in shadows. And up near the balcony, they're hidden by the cigarette smoke that hangs like fog.

Moments later, there was another roar. My buddy Spider Valentine climbed through the ropes into the other corner.

Spider and I had trained together, done our roadwork together, palled around together. Neither of us wanted to throw a punch at the other, but when that bell rang, we had to, because we both wanted the title. We started throwing them right away, because we were only scheduled for three rounds and that didn't give us much time to pace ourselves.

I caught him with a left hook early and he sagged backward, onto the canvas.

Instead of backing away from him, I moved toward him, and put my gloves under his arms to help him up.

"What are you doing, Robinson?" the referee yelled. "You can't do that."

I wasn't supposed to, I knew that, but I couldn't let my buddy Spider stay there on the canvas. Not that he showed much gratitude. When he got up, he rushed me, his arms flailing, and I had to stick him with a few jabs to keep him away. After the round, Harry Wiley was so angry I thought he'd bust. Wiley, a little fat man, had worked in the Salem-Crescent with me. Since both Spider and I were from the same team, George had declined to work in either corner, so Wiley was in mine.

"The next time he falls," Wiley growled, "you let the referee pick him up."

I couldn't put Spider down again, and after the last round I was worried about the decision.

"The winner, and still undefeated," the announcer droned, "Ray Robinson."

All around me, the people were standing up and applauding, and suddenly, the house lights went out. From the ceiling a spotlight shone on me, and a trumpet blared. I was a Golden Gloves champion. I didn't want to leave the ring. I wanted to stay there and wave to those people all night.

"Let's go, Ray," said Wiley, "you'll be back here soon enough."

The next week, I won the Eastern finals at the Garden and a few weeks later, the Intercity title in Chicago. The next year, I entered the Gloves again. I had put on another ten pounds so I was eligible for the lightweight division. The best part of that was that Spider was still a featherweight. This time we each won our part of these divisions, and we went on to win the Eastern titles and the Intercity titles. By then I was just about the most famous amateur boxer around. Almost every day, a different stranger would talk to George about wanting to manage me when I turned pro.

But we already had a man in mind.

The year before, in the months leading up to the 1939 Golden Gloves tournament, a heavyweight named Buddy Moore was even more famous than I was. Headlines follow a good heavyweight, and he was a good one. He was on the Salem-Crescent team, too, a husky slugger with big shoulders and a round face and a right hand that was flattening opponents the way Joe Louis had as an amateur in Detroit. One day in the gym, I was cooling out when I noticed a white man in snappy gray English-tailored suit, talking to George and watching Buddy Moore hit the big bag.

"Who was that?" I asked George after the stranger had departed.

"That was Curt Horrmann. His family owns a brewery on Staten Island, Rubsam and Horrmann," he said. "That man is a millionaire."

"What's he doing here?"

"He wants to manage Buddy Moore," George said, "and I just might let him. He's talking about a lot of money."

"How about me when I turn pro?" I asked.

"In good time, Robinson," George replied.

After that Curt Horrmann was around every few days. Other people used to wait on him, make a big fuss over him, hang up his coat for him. But not me.

"Hey, Pop," I used to say to him, "there's a coat hook. Hang it up yourself."

Sometimes he would send me to the candy store for cigarettes, but when he would offer me a tip, I'd refuse it. I could've used it, too, but I didn't want his money. He got to like me for my independence, and he got to like me as a fighter. One night he went to Buffalo with us to see Buddy Moore, but when we got there, he was surprised that I was in the main event. Buddy Moore was underneath, in a preliminary.

"How come?" he asked George.

"Because anyplace we go, Robinson fights the main event," George said. "Robinson never has lost."

"Is that so?" he said quietly.

That night Buddy Moore got knocked out by Cyclone Williams. And I almost got knocked out on my way into the ring. Some ring posts have a swinging brass bar to hold a water pail. Usually it's kept against the ropes, but this time it wasn't. As I hopped up the steps to my corner, I slammed my forehead on the bar. Within seconds, there was a lump on my forehead the size of a lemon.

"You can't fight," Harry Wiley said.

Wiley was working my corner. George was back in the dressing room with Buddy Moore and Curt Horrmann, Wiley was worried.

"I won't let you fight," he said.

"Don't you say a word," I snapped.

He didn't like it, but he kept quiet, and I took care of Jimmy Winters, a strong little guy. By that time Curt Horrmann had returned from the dressing room. He forgot about Buddy Moore. Wherever I fought, he was there in his gray English-tailored suit, talking to me and talking to George and slipping me a twenty-dollar bill every so often. I kept calling him "Pop," my boxing pop, maybe because my father wasn't around. Pop's handouts helped. Several months earlier, I had come home one night to find Mom crying.

"What's wrong?" I asked.

"We got a dispossess notice," she sobbed. "We got to find a new place to live by Monday, or the landlord will put our furniture out on the street."

"Ain't we been paying the rent?" I said.

"Not some months," she said. "Some months I missed."

"How about the money I been giving you?"

"I spent some of it," she said, sobbing.

It was too late to do anything with the landlord. I had some money saved up, but he wanted us out. By that Saturday, we were in another place, at 264 West 117th Street, and I had made another promise.

"Mom," I had told her, "someday I'm going to buy you a house, and I'll pay the rent, a pretty house all your own where you won't have to worry about any bills."

She looked at me like I was crazy, but I knew what I was talking about. I knew the money was there if I turned pro. But first, I needed a manager. Curt Horrmann looked like the man. He had the money to bankroll me and I envied his life. He drove around in a big, 16-cylinder maroon Packard, and after my fights in the Gloves, I'd stand on the sidewalk and watch him zoom off to the Stork Club.

"I have a steak dinner there at one-thirty every morning," he once told me, "my only meal of the day."

He was in pretty good shape, but his bank balance was in even better shape.

In the late summer of 1940, he and George agreed that it was time for me to turn pro and that he should be my manager. He had to make a couple of concessions. He couldn't talk to a promoter without George being there, and George had to okay all my opponents. He couldn't sign for a match without my okay on the money. As an amateur with George, I won all of my eighty-five bouts, with sixty-nine knockouts, forty in the first round. I had learned that if I had to get punched, I was going to get as much money as I could for it. In their percentages, Pop Horrmann was entitled to thirty-three per cent as the manager. George got ten per cent as the trainer. I even had my own publicity man. Pop hired Murray Lewin, the boxing writer for the *Daily*

Mirror, to talk me up around the other writers. Everything looked great, but at my age, I needed reassurance.

"Do you think Curt Horrmann is the right manager for me?" I asked George. "I mean for me, for *me?*"

"Robinson, he's the perfect manager. He can come up with a hundred-dollar bill faster than any man alive."

6

The Young Pro

I was jiggling my shoulders as I shadowboxed, trying to get that rhythm flowing through my arms and legs.

I should have been excited but somehow I wasn't. I was loosening up under the bare ceiling light in the same gray-walled dressing room at Madison Square Garden that I had used in the Golden Gloves but on this night, October 4, 1940, I was making my debut as a professional. Now, in the minutes before I would box, I was searching for that rhythm. In some of the bootleg shows there had been a band playing between the bouts, and that music would be blaring as I came into the ring. I always wished they had continued to play while I was boxing. I think I would've boxed better.

Rhythm is everything in boxing. Every move you make starts with your heart, and that's in rhythm or you're in trouble.

Your rhythm should set the pace of the fight. If it does, then you penetrate your opponent's rhythm. You make him fight *your* fight, and that's what boxing is all about. In the dressing room that night I could feel my rhythm beginning to move through me, and it assured me that everything would be all right.

"Now don't be nervous, Robinson, don't be nervous," George was whispering. "Nothin' to be nervous about." George was the one who was jumpy. He always had handled amateur fighters, so in a way he was making his pro debut, too.

"He's a pro, Robinson," he was saying, "he's a tough pro and that means you got to be a tough pro, too."

My opponent would be Joe Echevarria, a club fighter. We were supposed to go four rounds. When an amateur turns pro, he usually begins in a small club and in those days there were a dozen small clubs around New York, but my reputation and my record had enabled Curt Horrmann to maneuver me into making my debut at the Garden. In the main event Henry Armstrong was going to defend his world welterweight title against Fritzie Zivic. My bout with Echevarria was a preliminary—underneath, as they say, meaning underneath the big names on the card. Five other preliminary kids were in the room with me.

"Which one is Echevarria?" I asked George.

"He's in another room," he said. "This ain't like the amateurs where everybody's together. In the pros, they put the opponents in separate rooms."

"I like that. I can talk to somebody now."

Suddenly, a thunderous roar from above, where the spectators were watching the first preliminary, sent a vibration through the room. I knew the sound. Somebody had been flattened. Moments later, I knew he had been knocked out because I heard a voice shout, "All right, Robinson's next, get the kid out here," and George was stuffing a towel around my head and inside the lapels of my blue-and-white robe and he had his water bucket and he was moving me toward the door.

"Don't let this crowd bother you, Robinson," he was saying, "don't let this big crowd bother you."

Outside, as I skipped through the gloomy hallway, jiggling my shoulders to keep that rhythm flowing, I passed the kid who had been flattened. One of his handlers was holding a towel over his left eye, and there was blood on the towel.

"He forgot to duck," George whispered, shoving me up the stairs. "Don't you forget to duck, Robinson."

I was moving down the aisle now, and another roar thundered down through the layer of smoke that hung off the balcony. But as I peeked out from behind the towel, I realized that most of the ringside seats were empty. The main event wouldn't go on for almost an hour. It hadn't been like that in the Gloves because everybody always arrived early, for all the bouts. Some of those fans were there this time, but they were up in the less expensive seats, especially up in the balcony. That's where most of the real boxing fans always were and their roar was welcoming me. I never forgot that.

I was tingling now with excitement as I went up the wooden steps and bent to go through the ropes.

In my corner, I kept moving, afraid that rhythm would vanish if I stopped. During the instructions from the referee, my shoulders were swaying and my feet were shuffling, anything to keep that rhythm flowing, and when I turned to go back to my corner, George was talking to me and so was Wiley, but all I was thinking about was something that Jack Blackburn had told me. Blackburn was Joe Louis's trainer and when I had met him a few months earlier, I had asked him for advice.

"Chappie," he had said, using the name he called everybody, "just remember two things: keep your hands up and your ass off the floor."

When the bell rang, I was ready. My rhythm was flowing. Echevarria had been around, but when I put a couple of combinations on him, I knew that he wasn't any better than some of the guys I had beaten in the amateurs. In the second round I caught him with a left hook and he went down. It's in *The Ring Record Book* that way: KO2. On my way back through the aisle, another roar emerged from the inexpensive seats. I was happy, but I was annoyed, too —annoyed at those empty ringside seats.

The next time, I thought, *they'll get here early when I'm fighting.*

In the dressing room, Curt Horrmann handed me a wad of bills. When I counted it, I was surprised, because I knew that I was going to get $150, but nobody had taken a cut of it. I had it all.

"Hey, Pop," I said, "you and George got to get a share."

"Not this time," he said. "It's your first pro fight, you keep all the money. I'll take care of George. And after your shower, take this ticket and sit outside with us and watch Armstrong and Zivic. Maybe you'll learn something."

Armstrong was one of my idols, but when the fight ended, Zivic was the new welterweight champion.

Zivic had roughed up Henry around the eyes and he got a fifteen-round decision. On the way uptown that night, I was in a cab with Mom and my sisters when I blurted, "Mom, I want to fight Zivic. I'll fix him for the way he beat Armstrong."

"Junior," she said with that motherly fear in her voice, "I don't want you ever to fight Zivic."

Marie had a different idea. "Junior," she spoke up, "you can take Zivic any time you want to."

"Hush up, Marie," Mom said. "Don't you encourage him to fight Zivic. Junior ain't nothin' but a boy and you want him to get in the ring with a man like Zivic. Why, Zivic would gouge Junior's eyes out."

The next day, on the train to Savannah, I asked George to get me Zivic.

"Zivic!" he snorted. "You want to be blind at your age, Robinson?"

We were going to Georgia for my second pro fight. I had signed for it even before the Echevarria match had been made. In the Golden Gloves tournament earlier that year, I had flattened a white kid from that area. Down there, nobody could believe that their boy could have lost, much less be knocked out by a skinny Negro. Down there, they wanted a rematch when I turned pro, because he already had turned pro. But in those days a white and a Negro weren't allowed to fight each other in Georgia. Instead, they substituted the toughest Negro fighter they had, figuring he would teach me a lesson. His name was Silent Stafford, a deaf-mute. He could hit, but he wasn't too good at blocking punches, and I knocked him out in two.

Inside of five days, I had two quick knockouts in two professional fights. I was on my way. Better than that, I was soon on my way to Greenwood Lake to train with Joe Louis, who had won the heavyweight title in 1936 from Jim Braddock and had knocked out Max Schmeling in the first round of their return bout.

Pop had arranged for me to be in the semifinal to Joe Louis's title defense with Red Burman at the Garden. At the time, there were no superhighways in and out of New York City. To get anyplace, you had to drive through every town and take your chances with every red light. Greenwood Lake is only about forty miles northwest of the George Washington Bridge, as the crow flies. But the day Harry Wiley drove me up, we didn't have wings. Wiley's old car was coughing and wheezing going over the Ramapo Mountains. When we got there, the sun was setting and with the golden glow on the lake through the pine trees, I thought it was the most beautiful place I'd ever seen. And at that time of my life, it really was.

As much as I enjoyed watching Joe work, I learned even more from his trainer, Jack Blackburn—Chappie, everybody called him that, too.

My first night there, the camp cook put out a dinner of steak, baked potato, green vegetables, salad, and tea, and all I could think of was how George used to tease me that hot dogs and beans weren't a fighter's food. When we were through eating, Jack Blackburn called me over.

"Sit down, Chappie," he said. "I want to go over the rules of the house with you."

Man, he laid down the law. He told me about how the lights had to be out at ten o'clock, and he meant *out*, and how I would be expected to get up at six o'clock to do my roadwork.

"We are here to help you," he said, "but you have to help yourself, too. See you tomorrow morning, Chappie."

"Yes, sir," I said, but as I got up to leave, he reached out and grabbed my right arm and felt the biceps.

"Chappie," he said, "you have to develop those arms a little. Nothing like rowin' a boat to develop those arms. Plenty of boats here to row. You start that tomorrow, hear? Tomorrow night after dinner, that's a good time."

"Yes, sir," I said, peeking at my skinny arms.

The next day, I was up at dawn with Joe for roadwork. At that hour, the lake was even more beautiful. The morning mist was hanging over the lake and the sun was creeping up over the mountains, and the little boy from Brewster Center was really in his heaven, running on the road with Joe Louis. We ran every morning together, Joe and me, with a car crawling along a few yards behind us. In the car was a New York City detective hired by Mike Jacobs, the promoter of the Twentieth Century Sporting Club, to be with Joe before a big fight. Also in the car was Jack Blackburn.

"Speed it up, Chappie," he would yell at Joe. "Those legs got to carry you fifteen rounds."

Even though Joe was flattening almost all his opponents, Blackburn never assumed a knockout. If the fight was scheduled for fifteen rounds, Joe had to be ready to last fifteen rounds. But his legs were ready to carry him that far. One morning they even carried *me*. We were running together when, about ten yards in front of us, a copperhead snake slid across the road.

"Yow!" I yelled and leaped at Joe.

Grabbing him around the neck, I jumped up, anything to get my feet off that road. The way Joe held me, you'd have thought I was a baby. He just held me in his arms, with my arms wrapped around his neck, and he veered to the side of the road away from where that copperhead was, and he kept running. When we were past the snake, he slowed up and let go of me, thinking I'd get down. But he had the wrong man.

"Keep runnin'!" I yelled at him. "Keep goin'."

Behind us, we heard a pistol shot. We turned and saw the detective standing over the snake. He had killed it. The detective kicked at the snake to make sure it was dead. When the snake flopped over, I slid out of Joe's grip. But I didn't do any more running that morning. I got into the car and rode back to the old wooden house where we lived.

"Chappie," Blackburn said to me, "if you cut short your runnin', you got to make it up with rowin'."

Every evening after dinner, I had been rowing him around the lake. He had told me, "As long as you're rowin', I might as well do some fishin'," and he'd grab his pole and a bucket of bait and climb in the boat with me.

"Troll," he would tell me, "that's the best way to fish. You keep rowin' and that bait keeps jumpin'. Troll, the best way."

He had me rowing all over the lake, and he caught a few fish, too—perch and bass and sometimes a pickerel. He loved to have them for breakfast. But one day Joe got me aside.

"Robinson," he said, "you know what Chappie's havin' you row for?"

"What are you talking about?" I said. "That rowing is developing me."

"Man," Joe said, "that rowin' isn't developin' anything but Chappie's breakfast. He'd let you row him across the Atlantic if he was fishin'."

"Well, I don't care," I said. "I *like* to do it. I enjoy doin' it."

I really did. I had my own feeling that Chappie was taking advantage of me. But I didn't mind that. I was young and the way I figured, any time I spent with Jack Blackburn was time I was learning something about boxing because out in that boat, he was always talking boxing. Man, boxing was his life. After our roadwork, we'd take a nap and then we'd have breakfast and Chappie was always asking how you were. How you slept and how you ate and even how your bowels were moving. And in the afternoon, when we'd walk down from our house to the building near the lake where the ring was, Chappie had his eyes on you all the time. Naturally, he was watching Joe Louis more than me. But he always let me know he was there. One time, on a week end, there were a few hundred spectators and quite a few sportswriters up to see Joe work. I had to do my training before Joe came on and when I noticed all those people, the ham in me couldn't resist punching the bag longer than I usually did.

"Say there, Chappie," Blackburn said to me quietly so none of the people could hear. "You are not here to put on a show, you are here to condition your body. Slowly. Properly. To a peak. To be on time."

It took me time to truly understand what he meant: that all your training is timed so that, on the night of the fight, you are at your best. Not the night before. Not the night after. *The* night. And not near your best. Your *very* best. That's why it has always seemed to me that a place in the woods was the best place for a fighter to train. Nowadays, some fighters like to go to the fancy resorts in the Catskill Mountains, and many have had success training there, so apparently it's right for them. Cassius Clay always liked to train in the city where plenty of people could see him. And that was right for him. But over the years I always preferred the woods. The crickets put me to sleep. I enjoyed the card games. We usually played hearts for pennies, sometimes nickels. And if I wanted a little conversation, without temptation, all I had to do was walk into the village, about a mile away, and have a milkshake. Greenwood Lake was like a cowboy town, old wooden stores on each side of a narrow main street. In later years it developed into quite a little resort. But it never got fancy—one reason I always liked it. Another reason was that I almost always had good luck when I trained there.

That first time, I was matched with George Zengaras in the semifinal to the Louis-Burman title bout, and I had to be ready. Zengaras was a tough guy who'd been around, but I got the six-round decision.

About a month later, Pop set up a bout in Detroit for me. Out there, Nick Londos, the promoter at the Olympia, knew all about how I had grown up in Detroit and had moved to New York, and about how my name got changed. When we arrived a couple of days before the fight, he had the sportswriters waiting at our hotel. The next day my picture was all over the Detroit paper I used to deliver. The boy from Black Bottom had returned. Around dinner-time that evening, I was in my room when the phone rang.

"Ray Robinson?" a voice asked.

"Yeah," I answered, "that's me."

"Ray Robinson, the fighter?"

"Yeah," I said, "who is this?"

"It's your pop, Junior."

He was calling from the lobby and a few moments later, he came hopping off the elevator, my real pop, with the same dazzling smile and the same sharp clothes that I had always remembered. I hadn't seen him in more than eight years. He wanted to know all about me, and about Marie and Evelyn, and about Mom. We were still talking when George looked at his watch.

"Time for bed, Robinson," he said. "You can talk to your pop all night *tomorrow* night."

Pop understood, and the next night, after I finished a guy named Gene Spencer in the fifth round, he took me all over Black Bottom with him. He showed me off in res-taurants and bars and in people's homes and on street cor-ners and just the way he introduced me, "This is *my* son," I realized how proud he was of me. At the railroad station the next day, he had to swallow his pride.

"Junior," he said, as the train chugged in, "things have been a little hard for me. I wonder if . . ."

He didn't have to finish the sentence. I had a few hundred dollars in my pocket. I pulled them out and stuffed them into his hand. In the years that followed, he always showed up when I fought in Detroit or Cleveland or Chicago. I al-ways gave him some money whether he asked for it or not. But that first time, when I mentioned to Mom a couple of days later that I had seen him and had given him a little money, her eyes narrowed.

"After what he did to me," she snapped.

"But he's my pop, and if it wasn't for him as well as you, I wouldn't be in this world."

"He didn't treat me right, or you right."

"I can't judge him for what happened between you two," I said. "That's *your* business."

"All these years, we never heard from him," she said, "but now that you're famous—"

"He's still my pop."

I told George to get me a few more fights in Detroit, so that I could see more of Pop, but it wasn't that easy. He and Curt Horrmann, my other pop, had promised Herman Taylor, the Philadelphia promoter, that I would appear in a series of fights for him. I already had three knockout victories in Philadelphia, and he wanted to use me in Atlantic City. Over the next few months, I fought five more times for Herman Taylor and I got to be popular in Philadelphia. Some friends of mine from Harlem called themselves "Sugar Ray's Boosters" and they would get dressed up in blue-and-white jackets, my colors, and take the train to Philadelphia. And the people there adopted me. Herman Taylor, a little guy but a big man in Philly, realized I was a drawing card, so he arranged my first major main event, a ten-round bout with Sammy Angott at Shibe Park, the old ball park now known as Connie Mack Stadium.

Angott held the National Boxing Association version of the lightweight title, but he didn't want to risk it. So the contract stipulated that we both had to be over the 136-pound limit.

In those days, my problem was putting on weight. When I got up the morning of the fight, I got on a bathroom scale we had in the hotel. Pop Horrmann was anxious to know my weight. When the needle stopped at 135, he phoned room service.

"Do you have any bananas?" I heard him say. "Good, send up half a dozen and two quarts of milk."

The weigh-in was only a couple of hours away, so I had to stuff myself with those bananas and milk. When I finished them, I got on the scale again. I was 136½ and I was just about bursting.

"Whatever you do, Robinson," advised George, "don't go to the bathroom until after the weigh-in. Hold that weight."

I was 136½ at the weigh-in, too. I was assured of a good purse, about $6000—my first big payday—and when I got back to the hotel, I put in a call to the Modern Silver Linen Supply Company, where Mom worked. The boss answered. He knew me. Mom bragged to everybody about me, and I had met him a couple of times when I stopped by to take her home after work.

"Good luck tonight," her boss said to me.

"You're the one who'll need the good luck," I told him, "because if I win, you're losing a worker."

"Who?" he said. "What do you mean?"

"If I win tonight," I said, "my mom ain't coming to work tomorrow, and she ain't coming ever again."

"Are you serious?" he said.

"I never been more serious."

By the time Mom got on the phone, her boss had told her about my plan and she didn't know what to say.

"Say your prayers," I told her.

In the ring that night, I needed those prayers. Being in a main event had disrupted my routine. In the amateurs and in my earlier pro fights, I always had fought almost immediately after entering the ring. But in a main event it was different. I had to stand around for several minutes while a few famous boxers were introduced, and then I had to stand still during the national anthem. I liked to jiggle my body in the ring, and I wasn't comfortable standing at attention. Throughout my career, I would have preferred that the national anthem be played some other time.

As it turned out, I had more trouble with it than I did with Angott.

He liked to grab opponents and it took me a round to get used to that, but in the second I caught him with a good right hand to the jaw and he went down. In a heap. I didn't think he was going to get up, but he was next to the knockdown timekeeper and the noise of the hammer on the ring apron woke him up. He grabbed the lower rope at seven and flung himself at me. He clinched for the rest of the round. This was the mark of a smart fighter, something I wasn't then. I kept trying to knock him out with a right hand, instead of setting him up with my jab. Not only did I fail to knock him out, I never put him down again, but I got the decision easy enough.

I took the train back to New York that night, and Mom had stayed up to wait for me.

"No use of me going to bed," she said with a smile. "I don't have to get up early."

She never worked after that. I couldn't yet afford the house I had promised her but a few days later, we moved into a nicer apartment at 940 St. Nicholas Avenue. It had four rooms, for sixty-three dollars a month. That's a real low rent now, but in those days it was pretty fancy. So was our furniture. All my life we had been using battered old furniture, but one day I went to the Michigan store on 125th Street and bought two bedroom sets, a parlor set, and a kitchen set. When Mom saw it in our apartment, she sat down and wept.

"Never another woman who had to wait for her son to buy her first new furniture," she said. "When I married your father, my mother gave us an old bed and chair, and his mother gave us an old bed and chair. I never had the price of new furniture."

I also had the price of my first car, a '41 blue Buick convertible. I had won twenty-one consecutive pro bouts and some of the sportswriters were calling me "the uncrowned lightweight champion." That was nice of them, but it was just words. There was no music, no do-re-mi, with the emphasis on dough. But soon after that, Mike Jacobs was talking with Curt Horrmann almost every day. Mike Jacobs was the promoter of the Twentieth Century Sporting Club, which put on the fights at Madison Square Garden. He had built Joe Louis into a box-office idol and now he had plans for me. He arranged my first Garden main event, with Maxie Shapiro, for September 19, 1941.

I couldn't wait—not for the bout but to see my name and picture on the showcard.

There it was, SUGAR RAY ROBINSON, in big red letters on the yellow and black cards that were all over. In store windows. On high wooden fences. Almost everywhere I looked.

And after the weigh-in, I drove by the Garden in my blue Buick to see something else.

"Look at that," I said to George, pointing to the marquee. "Look at the name up there. BOXING TONIGHT—SUGAR RAY ROBINSON VS. MAXIE SHAPIRO. Isn't that just the greatest thing you ever saw?"

"Watch the traffic, Robinson," George said.

I drove around the block to see it again, and to this day, I can close my eyes and see it. When I close my eyes, I also can see the crowd that night. When I jiggled down the aisle, the ringside seats were filled. The big spenders were waiting for me. Despite all the noise, I could hear Marie shouting, "C'mon, Junior!"

She didn't have to yell long. Shapiro didn't last three.

I hadn't turned twenty-one, but I was undefeated as a pro, with an over-the-weight victory over a world champion, with a main event at the Garden, with enough money to enable Mom to stop working and to afford a nicer apartment and nicer furniture and a new car. But some people around boxing were worried about me.

"You've got to keep working hard to get to the top," Curt Horrmann often told me then. "The title is your motivation."

He didn't realize it, but I had discovered another motivation the previous summer.

7

Edna Mae

In the summer the heat hung in Harlem. Sticky, wet heat without a breeze.

Even when there was a breeze, it seldom got down into our streets. The breeze usually came out of the west, but Harlem is on the eastern side of Manhattan Island, in a valley below Morningside Heights and farther uptown, below Coogan's Bluff behind the old Polo Grounds, a valley in the sun. The breeze blew across into the Bronx, but it never dropped down where we needed it. The streets were like a steam bath and inside the tenements, with their greasy odors, it was like living in a dirty oven.

About the only place to cool off was the Lido Pool, a nice swim club.

I stopped by there almost every day that summer of 1941 after my workout at Grupp's. Not to swim, because I didn't want to confuse my boxing muscles. I just liked to jump in that cold water and jump out—it was better than a shower. And after I cooled off, I liked to stand around checking the girls. One day I was alongside the pool when this doll came strutting along in a white bathing suit, with the prettiest pair of long legs I'd ever seen.

About the best way for her to notice me, I figured, was

for me to do something different. I pushed her into the pool.

She shrieked on her way into the water, and after the splash, she shrieked again. She was safe enough. The water wasn't too deep there, but she was shrieking because she was angry. She didn't have a bathing cap on and her hair was all wet. She had long shiny hair, and when a couple of other guys helped her out of the water, she stood there, shaking her hair and glaring at me.

"I'm awful sorry," I said, smiling. "I didn't see you coming. I hope you're all right."

She never even answered me. She just shook her hair again, spraying me with water, and walked off. I watched her walk all the way. That walk of hers was something else. After she disappeared, one of the other guys around the pool nudged me.

"You know who that was?" he said.

"That was the prettiest girl I've ever seen," I said.

"Man, that's Edna Mae Holly."

"Well, now I know her name," I said. "Where does she live, man? I got to get to know that gal."

"She used to dance at the Cotton Club with Lena Horne," he said. "Now she's at the Mimo Club."

That made it easy. One night about a week later I dropped by the Mimo Club. I was with a few other guys and we were at a table when she appeared in the spotlight on the stage in a little bitty beaded costume. The M.C. had described her as an "interpretive" dancer.

"I don't know what she's interpreting," I said to one of the guys with me, "but I get the message."

When the show ended, I waited for her to come out of her dressing room. I introduced myself and she said, "Mister Ray Robinson, the boxer. I've read about you, Mister Robinson."

"Honey," I said, "I just wanted to apologize again for pushing you in the pool."

"Honey," she said, "if I get a chance, I'll push you in at the real deep end."

I laughed, and she smiled. We talked for a few minutes and she said she had a date, but that didn't bother me. I told her I'd be back at the club the next night. And I was. In fact, I was there just about every night. The nights I couldn't make it, I'd send her red roses. I was really turning it on. One night I was sitting there, watching her dance when I looked around at all the guys staring at her. Even in the darkness of the night club, I could see their eyes glowing. But damn it, I didn't like other guys looking at her like that because I was starting to consider her my girl. Not that I had a reason to think she was mine. She had been giving me a hard time. I used to drop by the club in the afternoon to watch her rehearse, anything to see her. But every time I asked her for a date, she always had something else to do. She was never nasty about it. She used to smile and say, "I'm sorry, but I have another engagement."

I knew what she was doing. She was still getting back at me for pushing her in the pool.

Her attitude made me all the more determined to get her. That determination was good for me, because I was winning most of my fights without much sweat. I had won a decision in Philadelphia from Marty Servo, a tricky little guy who never gave me much of a target, and that put me in solid with Mike Jacobs. He figured that I was too good an attraction for Herman Taylor to have all the time, so Jacobs arranged for me to have a nontitle bout at Madison Square Garden with Freddie (Red) Cochrane, who had outpointed Fritzie Zivic a few months earlier for the world welterweight title.

"Why not for the title?" I asked Curt Horrmann. "I can beat Cochrane."

"That's what Cochrane's afraid of," Pop said. "He wants a payday, but he doesn't want to risk the title. But if you beat him, then he'll have to give you a shot at the title. I want you to train at Greenwood Lake for this one."

"With the birds and the bees," I said.

As much as I enjoyed going up to the big training camp at Greenwood Lake, I didn't like the idea of being away from Edna Mae and giving all those guys at the Mimo Club a chance to make time with her. I thought I was starting to soften her up, but that didn't do me any good in camp. That old wooden house was about as far away as I could get from the action in the Mimo Club. All I did was train and eat and sleep.

One afternoon I was napping before my workout, when some loud voices woke me up.

My room was upstairs, over the kitchen. But it being an old house, there was a vent in the floor so that the hot air from the kitchen stove could heat the upstairs rooms. Coming through the vent were the voices of Curt Horrmann and George Gainford. It was the middle of the week, so I knew Pop must have just come up from New York. From the way he was talking, it sounded important.

"He's sick or something," I heard Pop say.

"He's just duckin'," George said. "He don't want to fight Robinson."

"I know," Pop said, "but the fight's off."

Obviously, Cochrane had pulled out. Then I heard Pop say something that had me wide awake.

"Jacobs offered me Zivic," Pop said.

"Zivic," I heard George say. "You crazy? Zivic's tougher than Cochrane. Robinson's not ready for Zivic. You saw

Zivic with Armstrong a year ago. Zivic's too tough for Robinson right now. I don't want any part of Zivic."

"Jacobs made a good offer," Pop said.

"No offer is good enough for Robinson to fight Zivic," George said. "Zivic ruin Robinson, Zivic *ruin* him."

"Jacobs told me ten," Pop said, meaning $10,000. "I think he'll go to fifteen. He really wants this fight."

"I want it, too," I said.

They spun around when they heard my voice. I had sneaked downstairs while they were arguing.

"Now, Robinson," George started to say.

"Please, George," I pleaded, "I want Zivic. I know his tricks. I know all about his thumbs."

"Robinson," George said, "you a baby in this business."

"Damn it, George," I snapped, "I'm the one who's going to get hurt if anybody does. And *I* want to fight him."

George looked at Pop, then shrugged his shoulders.

"All right," George said, "but if anything happens, don't come cryin' to me. I warned you. I warned you both."

"Zivic," I said, "will be the only one cryin'."

Pop phoned Jacobs and I think he got $15,000 for me. But I'd have fought for free. As soon as Pop mentioned Zivic's name, I thought of what he had done to Henry Armstrong the year before on the night when I was making my pro debut. All that year I had thought about Zivic every so often and about how some day I wanted to humiliate him for Henry. Now I was going to get my chance on October 31, 1941, a little more than a year after I had turned pro. In that time, Zivic had lost the welterweight title to Cochrane, but on experience, he had a Ph.D. in boxing and I was in kindergarten.

"You're making a mistake," Zivic's manager, Luke Carney, told Pop at the weigh-in. "Your boy is an amateur."

During the first round that night, I fought like one, just as George had feared I would. Zivic was a slender little guy, with pale white skin and a pushed-in nose. And he was clever. His style was to move in close to you. When he did, he liked to hook his left behind my head in a clinch and he would hold me high on the neck and yank me toward him. The way he did it, I was butting myself. Whenever it would happen, he would glance at the referee, Arthur Suskind, and pretend that I was roughing him up. But Suskind knew better. All the referees did. They knew what to watch for—his thumbs and the crisscross laces on the inside of his gloves. He would get his laces against the side of my face and rub them against me. That's like having somebody rub you with steel wool.

All these things were happening to me for the first time, and I really was embarrassed because the crowd was more than 20,000, one of the largest in the history of the old Garden.

When the bell rang, ending the first round, I turned and walked back to my corner and I wanted to hide. For the first time as a pro, I had no idea what I was doing. After he planted the stool for me, George hustled between the ropes and sponged my face.

"You know what you're doin' wrong?" he said.

"Yeah," I said, "I'm doin' *everything* wrong."

In a way, George seemed proud of the way Zivic had messed me up in the first round. He had warned me that Zivic was too smart for me. Zivic had proved it. But I knew that there were nine rounds to go. And so did George.

"Don't let him get close," George said. "Keep him away from you with the jab."

I did, and even though he jolted me with a right hand in the sixth, I loosened up and caught him with some good

left hooks. I got a unanimous decision. When it was announced, Pop remembered how Zivic's manager, Luke
Carney, had joked that I was an amateur.

"Is it all right," Pop sneered at Carney, "if we turn
pro now?"

Pop had arranged a party in a big suite at the Hotel
Theresa in Harlem, my first big victory party because it had
been my first big victory in New York. There were about
two dozen people there, drinking and dancing. I was the
guest of honor, but I wasn't having much fun. The others
seemed to be afraid to bother me, but I had an idea to fix
that.

"Hey, Shorty," I called, "do me a favor."

Shorty Linton was around me all the time in those days.
He was my first valet, so to speak.

"What, Ray?" he said. "What do you need?"

"Go to the Mimo Club," I said. "The last show should
be gettin' out about two. And when Edna Mae comes out,
I want you to bring her back here."

"Bring her back?" he said.

"That's right, man, *bring* her back. If you don't bring
her back, don't bring yourself back."

"Suppose she won't come?"

"That's your problem, man," I said. "Just get her up here.
Tell her I got a present for her."

About an hour later, Shorty opened the door to the suite
and stepped back. Edna Mae swirled in.

"What's this all about, Ray?" she said. "What's so important? Your man created a scene at the club. I had another
engagement . . ."

There was that phrase again.

". . . but he wouldn't take any excuse. He said I just
had to come here, that you had a present for me."

"Honey," I said, "sit down and relax."

By this time, most of the people had left the party. After a few minutes Edna Mae and I had a conversation going, our first real conversation, mostly about how pretty I thought she was. And by the time she went home, we were well acquainted. I even knew that she wore a size-four shoe. She had such little feet, and such beautiful legs. After that, she was my girl. She didn't give me any more of that stuff about having another engagement. Her engagement was with me. Not that we set a date to be married. It just seemed we knew that eventually it would happen. But it wasn't easy for us to go together. We had family trouble, from both sides. When I told Mom about her, Mom didn't think that her son should be going around with a night-club dancer, especially one who was two years older than me. Edna Mae was getting the same static because I was a fighter.

Edna Mae had been raised by her aunt, Blanche Holly. Her mother had died of tuberculosis when Edna Mae was three. Whenever I called for her, Aunt Blanche always told me about Edna Mae's background, about how refined she was.

"Edna Mae," she told me once, "is the fourth generation of college-bred in our family. Doctors and lawyers. And her great-grandfather came out of slavery and graduated from Harvard, studied for the ministry, and was the first Negro to be consecrated a bishop in the United States. The Right Reverend James Theodore Holly, an Episcopal bishop."

All that talk about Edna Mae's family didn't mean much to me. I mean, I was in love with Edna Mae, I didn't particularly care where she came from as long as she was going out with me. But her college education helped me. She had attended Hunter College in New York. She always recognized a mistake in my grammar and she told me what I should've said. And she taught me about clothes. She knew the styles, the proper styles, for me as well as for herself. In those years, the zoot suit was popular. The long double-breasted jacket with the wide shoulders. The baggy pants with the tight ankles, known as pegged pants. One night I arrived at Edna Mae's house with what I thought was the last word in style, a green zoot suit.

"Oh, Edna Mae," Aunt Blanche shrieked when she opened the door. "Oh, Edna Mae, look at this."

Aunt Blanche was mortified, but that night Edna Mae showed me that she really had manners. She not only didn't laugh at me, she didn't even smile. She picked up her pocketbook and kissed Aunt Blanche good-by and went out with me. But later that night, she made a suggestion.

"You look so much better in conservative clothes, Ray," she told me. "So much more handsome."

The next day I started to change my wardrobe. I started to woo Aunt Blanche, too, because I wanted her on my side. I would bring her a red rose whenever I called for Edna Mae. Another time I remembered she had said she liked cashew nuts, so I brought her a box of those. After I started doing that, she stopped talking about her family background. She started coming with Edna Mae to my fights.

Mike Jacobs put me back with Fritzie Zivic early in 1942, and this time I knocked him out in the tenth round.

"Junior," Mom told me in the dressing room later, "you ain't a boy no longer. You showed me you're a man."

In my two fights with Zivic, I had earned more than $25,000. When a fighter is making that kind of money, there's always somebody looking to grab some of it, the easy way. Several weeks later, I was training at Greenwood Lake when I noticed three strangers with George Gainford after a workout.

"Who were those guys?" I asked George later.

"Guys from the city," he said, "guys I see on Broadway. Only around boxing, you know."

I knew, but I wanted to know more.

"Well, Robinson," he told me, "one of them asked me to have a drink with them and I told him, 'I'm not a drinking man,' and then he said to me, 'In that case, let's get down to business, Gainford, we'll give you fifty thousand for a good piece of Robinson,' and I told him that he couldn't get a piece of you for half a million, and then the big guy said, 'Be careful, Gainford, or we'll take all of him for nothing,' and I said, 'That we'll have to see.' And that was the end of it. They walked out."

"And they better not come back," I said.

For years, I had heard about how the mob tried to muscle in on fighters, and how they often succeeded. But they weren't going to get me. I knew that if they got me, they'd get my money.

Nothing ever developed from that visit, but a few months later another incident occurred when we were in Chicago.

I was matched with a tough Italian kid, Tony Motisi, and a few days before the fight, George was in his room at the old Grand Hotel on the South Side when his phone rang. The desk clerk informed George that there were three white men to see him. It was a Negro hotel, so three white visitors were unusual.

"I thought they were sportswriters," George told me later, "so I told the clerk to send them up."

Just from the way the three men strutted into his room, George knew that something was wrong.

"One of them took off his coat," George told me, "and he had an automatic in a shoulder holster, but I pretended not to notice. I asked them, 'What's your pleasure, gentlemen?' and one of them said, 'We want to talk something over with you. We don't want your boy Robinson to lose, but we're betting a lot of money on Motisi going all ten rounds, so we want some assurance that we'll win our bet.' And I told him, 'The best advice I can give you is not to bet on Motisi going the limit, because the only way Robinson won't knock him out is if he can't.' "

I hope they didn't bet. Motisi didn't last the first round.

I got a quick $10,000 for that appearance, but it cost me that much. When we got the offer from the Chicago promoter, Curt Horrmann tried to persuade me to ignore it. He wanted me to fight exclusively for Mike Jacobs.

"I'm not fighting exclusively for anybody," I argued. "I'll fight for whatever promoter pays me."

"You're making a mistake," Pop said. "Jacobs can do more for you than all the other promoters."

Maybe so, but I wanted to be able to make moves on my own. I had nothing against Mike Jacobs, but the other promoters around the country also paid me in United States currency. The irony of the breakup was that I paid off Pop's contract with $10,000 borrowed from Mike Jacobs, a loan against my next purse under his promotion.

Pop was out. He had been a good man for me, but we had been having disputes almost from the beginning.

Because of his money, he had let promoters push him around. In some of my early fights, I had discovered that the promoters had paid me $500 although I had demanded that Pop negotiate for $750. He had given me the extra $250 out of his own pocket. That was nice of him, but he was keeping my price down. I wanted a manager who would be tough in negotiations and who would be honest with me. The more I thought about it, the more I came to the conclusion that only one person in the world was capable of succeeding at that: Sugar Ray Robinson.

My decision shocked George. He had assumed he was taking over.

"What's wrong with me, Robinson?" he complained. "Don't you trust me?"

"George," I replied calmly, "I don't want to *have* to trust you."

The intrigue of boxing had soured me on letting anybody else do my business. Not even George, who had been around me from the beginning. George had been involved in the intrigue, too. I remembered how in the bootleg fights he had pocketed most of the money. And even when Pop had been my manager, George was making deals with promoters involving me, like promising to deliver me if he got $200 on the side. I knew I couldn't trust him completely, but I didn't want to start all over with somebody else.

"I want you to stay as my trainer," I told him, "and you can do the negotiating, but I make the final deal."

He didn't like the idea, but he accepted it. In the years that followed, it would create a wall between us. We got along, but we were never really close. He always felt belittled by my distrust, but he accepted it because I was making big money, and as the trainer he was collecting his 10 per cent. Money was easy to make and easier to spend. At the time of my breakup with Pop, I had paid $8500 for a big brick, ten-room house on West 238th Street in the Riverdale section of the Bronx, the house I had promised Mom three years earlier when we were dispossessed from our Harlem tenement. Before we moved in, I spent another $3000 decorating it for her. That was a waste of time. She redecorated it with pictures of me. She once had as many as twenty-three of them all over the house.

Mike Jacobs soon put me to work. He matched me with Jake LaMotta, maybe the toughest fighter of that era. The Bull, he was called.

In the days before the fight, George kept reminding me, "The matador and the bull. You are the matador, LaMotta is the bull. The matador will win if he has the finesse. The matador never wins if he acts like the bull." When the bell rang, I realized that I would have been safer in a bull ring than a boxing ring.

LaMotta had about ten pounds on me, and he knew how to use his weight. He forced me back, or moved me to the side. Despite his strength, I was doing fairly well. I was hitting him consistently, and around the middle of the fight I caught him with a good combination.

I had him along the ropes. He had his head down and I was really measuring him. For one of the few times in my career, my arms got weary from throwing so many punches. I stepped back for a breather. Jake had his head down and his gloves were up around his head, protecting himself. I thought, *man, he has to fall any moment now.* But not Jake, not the Bull. His head popped up and he let go a left hook that almost tore through my stomach. It hurt so much, I had tears in my eyes, like a little kid. I got the decision but I learned that Jake LaMotta was some animal.

Not many guys had gone the distance with me. The decision over Jake had been my thirty-sixth consecutive victory as a pro, with twenty-seven knockouts—too many knockouts, I soon discovered.

Near the end of the year, I went to Philadelphia to box Al Nettlow. I checked into the old Douglas Hotel, where George and I always stayed. It was on Broad Street, across from where the promoter, Herman Taylor, had his office, and it was near Lew Tendler's restaurant. Tendler had fought for both the welterweight and lightweight titles, and his place was the boxing hangout. After the weigh-in, I was standing on the sidewalk outside Tendler's when Frank (Blinky) Palermo motioned me to join him near the newsstand.

"Where's George?" he asked.

"He's over in Herman's office straightening out the tickets," I said.

"Is it all set?" he said, in his gravel voice.

"Is what all set?" I said, not knowing what he was talking about.

"Didn't George tell you?"

"Tell me what?" I said, annoyed.

"He will," he said.

Spinning on his gleaming black shoes, Blinky Palermo strode off. He was a little guy, not much more than five feet tall, but he had a reputation as a big man in the numbers racket around Philadelphia. He acted tough and he looked tough. His sharp, narrow eyes were set above a big crooked nose and thick, heavy lips. His hobby was being involved with boxers, and from his conversation, he appeared to be involved with me. Back at the hotel, I confronted George.

"What's going on with Blinky?" I snapped.

"Well, now, Robinson," he said, "I didn't have an opportunity to tell you."

"Tell me what?"

"Well, now, Robinson, it wouldn't be good for you to knock out this Nettlow."

"Why not?"

"You're knocking out too many guys. Nobody wants to make a match with you any more. The only way we got Nettlow was to agree that you wouldn't hurt him."

"What about Motisi? You wouldn't agree to me carrying him."

"That was different," George said. "They weren't boxing people. We didn't have to do business with them. And another thing, Motisi was a tough opponent. Nettlow will be easy. You need easy guys to keep you sharp, but if you

knock 'em all out, none of 'em will want to box you. We got
to live with boxing people, Robinson, and we got to do
favors now and then. This is one of those favors."

"But what if I *can* knock him out?"

"I agreed you wouldn't—I agreed."

"That's the whole trouble," I snapped. "*You* got no right
to agree to anything. I told you that after I bought out
Pop's contract."

"My mistake, Robinson," he said, "my mistake."

"You see why I can't trust you, George. You see why
now."

"But don't mess me up again with Blinky."

"What do you mean *again?* What else happened?"

"The times you knocked out Jimmy Tyghe."

The previous year, I had knocked out Tyghe twice in Philadelphia.

"Was I supposed to carry him, too?" I said.

"I thought he'd go the distance," George said, "so I kept
quiet. Don't mess me up with Blinky again, Robinson,
please."

"All right, but after this I make the deals."

I didn t want to mess myself up with Blinky, either. I was
content to carry Nettlow for ten rounds. He was a nice little
guy, and I didn't have any reason to measure him. For two
rounds, he was no trouble but in the third he swatted me
with a good right hand and I let go a left hook. It nailed
him on the jaw and he went down.

Get up, I was pleading silently as the referee began to
count. *Get up, Al, you got to get up, man.*

I sneaked a glance at George, but he had one of his hands
over his face—he was afraid to look. Nettlow was moving
but not enough to beat the count and when the referee
waved his hands, George hopped into the ring with my
robe.

"You double-crossed me, Robinson," he growled.

"It was an accident, George, honest," I said.

It really had been, but I knew that George would never believe me after the argument we'd had.

"You tell Blinky it was an accident," he said.

I knew Blinky would be at Tendler's later, and I knew I had to try to explain it.

"It was an accident," I told him. "I just happened to catch him with the hook."

"All right," Blinky said, with a little shrug. "Nothing we can do about it now."

That was the end of the conversation. If he was angry, he didn't show it. In later years, I occasionally agreed to carry an opponent, almost always in what is known as a tune-up fight. I never considered it morally wrong. As long as I was winning the fight, I saw no reason why I had to punish a lesser opponent. I was never a killer, like some fighters. I never enjoyed knocking out a guy who I knew had no chance to beat me. I'm sure guys in the know made some money betting on an opponent going the distance with me, but I didn't bet—I never bet on any of my fights.

My responsibility wasn't to the betters, it was to the spectators.

They're the ones who paid to see me, and I had to be honest with them. If they weren't satisfied, the deal was off. Any time the spectators began to clap, clap, clap—a sarcastic request for action—they got it. Once, I remember, I was in with Izzy Jannazzo, one of Chris Dundee's fighters. He was a clever boxer, and by the second round we were waltzing.

"C'mon, do something," somebody shouted, and soon I heard that clap, clap clap.

I stepped back and threw a left hook that flattened Izzy. Ten seconds later I had my robe on.

I'll always remember Chris Dundee moaning, "Aw, what did you have to do *that* for?"

I did it for the spectators, because the ham in me wouldn't let me put on a bad show if I could help it—the ham in me was always very important. Shortly after the Nettlow accident, I was training in Grupp's one afternoon when the phone rang. It was for me, but I was working on the light bag and George answered it. When he hung up, he was grinning and hopping. That wasn't like George. He usually was much more dignified, much more serious.

"Robinson," he yelled. "*The Ring* magazine just voted you the outstanding fighter of 1942."

The ham in me didn't know what to think. The honor pleased me, but it also annoyed me. I was the year's outstanding boxer, but I wasn't a champion. Not only that, I wasn't even getting a title shot. It didn't make sense. The next day I went to see Mike Jacobs. His office was on the sixth floor of the Brill Building, above Jack Dempsey's restaurant on Broadway. The sidewalk there was known as "Jacobs' Beach," as Damon Runyon called it, because there were always about a dozen managers waiting for Mike Jacobs to use one of their fighters. Up in his office, with a view of Times Square and with the boxing photos and boxing cartoons on the walls, Mike Jacobs made the decisions that affected people all over the country. He had worked with Tex Rickard, the promoter who had built the old Madison Square Garden in 1925, and he had been a ticket broker, a fruit peddler, a steamboat concessionaire. He was a funny-looking old man, bald and with false teeth that clacked, but Uncle Mike knew what was going on.

"I'm the Fighter of the Year," I snapped at him, "and I deserve a shot at Cochrane's title."

Red Cochrane had won the welterweight championship from Fritzie Zivic midway through 1941, but more than a year later he enlisted in the Navy without having defended it.

"He's not available," Mike said, "and pretty soon, you won't be available, either."

"What are you talking about?" I roared. "I'm right here. I'm not going anywhere."

"Yes, you are," he said. "Any day now you'll be getting your Army induction notice."

"My *what?*" I said, stunned.

"You heard me," he replied.

"But how do you know?" I said.

"I know," he said. "I *know.*"

"How much time before I leave?"

"Time enough for a couple paydays," Uncle Mike said, wrapping me around his little finger again. "You're not the type to live on a private's fifty dollars a month. I'll get you LaMotta in Detroit."

"Good," I said, "we'll draw money."

8

Marriage and Mike Jacobs

Across the ring Jake LaMotta was glowering, his round head bobbing on his thick, squat shoulders.

"And in this corner," the announcer droned, turning toward me, "from New York City, Sugar Ray . . ."

All around me in the Detroit Olympia, a roar went up—but suddenly, for the first time in my boxing career, I was unsure of myself. That moment when you're being introduced, man, that's a boxer's moment of truth. You're all by yourself then. It's too late for anybody to help you and what's worse, it's too late to help yourself. That's what worried me. Staring at the canvas and jiggling my body, I heard the applause from my pop and my other old friends in the Black Bottom neighborhood, but that rhythm wasn't flowing. I hadn't trained properly. My Army induction date had been set for three weeks from tomorrow, and I had been enjoying myself. But now, as I looked across at the Bronx Bull, I knew he would make me sorry.

You left all your strength with those girls you were chasing, I scolded myself.

Edna Mae had remained in New York, and I had discovered that there were pretty girls in Black Bottom, too.

And those days you went bowling instead of to the gym, I thought.

In my previous fights, hearing my introduction always gave me confidence. To me, the ring was like home. I was the rabbit in the briar patch, because I was prepared. But this time, the rabbit had been trapped in the open, trapped by himself, and a bull, the Bronx Bull, was about to stomp him.

When I walked out at the bell, Jake stomped me with his first left hook. And he stomped me for ten rounds.

In the eighth round, he did something nobody had ever done to me before. He hit me with a right hand in my midsection and when I doubled up, he let go a left hook to my jaw. For the first time in my career, I had no legs. I sagged through the ropes and onto the ring apron and sprawled there. In my daze, I could hear the referee, Sam Hennessy, counting, ". . . six . . . seven . . . eight . . ."

I made it back into the ring in time, but when the round ended, George scolded me.

"Well, Robinson," he growled, "maybe next time you will listen to me when I tell you you're not trainin' correctly. You wouldn't do anything I told you for this fight, and maybe now you'll believe me because now you're payin'."

I was not only paying in pain, I was paying in embarrassment, in front of my pop and my Black Bottom friends.

I survived the last two rounds, but at the final bell I knew the decision would be unanimous for Jake, and it was. When I heard the announcer's voice echo, "The winner, Jake LaMotta," I wept. After forty consecutive victories as a pro, I had lost. And as I sat there on my stool, with the boos burrowing inside my blue-and-white robe, I made a vow never to get into a ring unless I was in perfect condition, unless I could face my moment of truth.

In later years, I never hesitated to postpone one of my fights if anything interfered with my training. Some of the promoters nicknamed me "Runout Ray," and it annoyed them to have to put off a card. But none of them had to put the gloves on, none of them had to stand in the corner and hear their name introduced in that moment of truth, none of them had to risk their reputation in the ring with another man. And when the fight was *over,* no promoter ever had to apologize for my performance. I believe I gave the promoter and the people their money's worth.

Two weeks later, Mike Jacobs provided me with another payday, a main event in the Garden with Jackie Wilson, who was known as California Jackie Wilson because there was another fighter around by the same name. Jackie was a Negro, and that created a problem for Uncle Mike. In those days, it was unusual to match two Negroes in the main event. I doubt if he had ever done it before, because, I discovered later, he had his publicity man, Harry Markson, phone Dan Parker, the sports editor of the *Daily Mirror,* to get his reaction.

"Dan has nothing against it," Markson reported.

"All right, then, we'll put it on," Jacobs said.

Jackie and I went ten rounds, and I got the decision. I didn't want to overextend myself, because exactly a week later I had a return arranged with LaMotta in Detroit. I used Wilson as I might a sparring partner, and when I got into the ring again with LaMotta, the rabbit was in the briar patch again. My pride had prodded me into training hard this time, and I was rewarded with a ten-round decision.

It was an important victory, psychologically, because the next day, February 27, 1943, I was inducted into the Army.

"Private Smith," I remember a corporal saying that day, and I ignored him until he pointed to me and yelled, "You!"

Suddenly I was Walker Smith again. *Private* Walker

Smith. I had changed names again. I had changed uniforms, too.

Instead of white trunks, I was wearing olive drab, all over. I was in an olive-drab world. The morning I was inducted at the Whitehall Street center near the lower tip of Manhattan Island, our group boarded an olive-drab bus. The bus took us through the Holland Tunnel to New Jersey and down U.S. 1 to Fort Dix. There a sergeant marched us into an olive-drab building where we were issued our olive-drab uniforms. Then he marched us to our olive-drab barracks.

"And when that bugle blows," he growled at us, "I want you on your feet on that company street."

At attention, too. All this discipline was new to me. I had never really had any regular discipline quite like it. I always had floated around at my convenience. But Army discipline was somewhat similar to the discipline a boxer must have when he is in training. I had lived by the clock at Greenwood Lake with Joe Louis. That wasn't too bad, because I enjoyed what I was doing. But in the Army, I wasn't having much fun. At night there were a few laughs with the other guys in the barracks. Other than that, it was toil and trouble. But after a few months, the discipline began to appeal to me. Maybe someday I might be giving an order instead of taking it.

It happened sooner than I expected. After my basic training, I was assigned to the Army Air Corp. I was stationed at Mitchel Field in Hempstead, Long Island, a few miles east of New York City.

Most of the time I had it pretty good. I was coaching the boxing team at the base. But every once in a while, I pulled guard duty like everybody else. One night I was assigned to a guard detail for some planes that were due to go to England the next day. I never found out what the planes were carrying, but it must have been something special because the officer of the day made a point of telling me, "No one is permitted to board these planes. *No one.* No matter how much rank he has."

And wouldn't you know, just after it got dark, an Air Force officer, a chicken colonel, presented himself outside the hangar.

"Soldier," he said to me, identifying himself, "I'm the pilot of one of these planes and I'd like to go aboard. I forgot some of my equipment."

"I'm sorry, sir," I replied, "but no one is to enter these planes. Those are my orders."

"Soldier," he said, and he was annoyed now, "this is ridiculous. I'm ordering you to let me aboard."

"Sir," I said, "if you were a general, I couldn't let you on that plane. I'm sorry, sir."

He spun on his heel and marched off. The next morning, I was ordered to report to the officer of the day. I was sure I was about to be chewed out.

"Private Smith," he said to me, "I want to commend you for carrying out your orders. You're a good soldier."

Even before that, I usually had been able to get a little time off when I needed it. And late in May, I really needed it. Edna Mae was my gal now. In May, she went to Chicago to dance in the Rum Boogie, a club Joe Louis owned. She went in a huff. We had argued about something, a spat, and I called her to make up.

"You're just saying that," she said, "you don't mean it. You don't really love me."

"Honey," I said, "I mean it so much that I'm coming out there to marry you. I can get a pass this week end. I'll be there Saturday morning."

On Sunday, May 29, 1944, in the home of a friend of hers, Ann Helm, we were married.

I returned to Mitchel Field and I moved Edna Mae into a big suite at the Hotel Theresa in Harlem. Not on my Army pay. Mike Jacobs had provided some spending money a month earlier by arranging a fight in Boston, where I knocked out Freddie Cabral in one. Shortly after my marriage, I had an offer to box in Detroit. The promoter there, Nick Londos, guaranteed me $7500, but Uncle Mike had another idea.

"Do me a favor," he said, "and take Ralph Zannelli in Boston."

"But that won't be worth seventy-five hundred to me," I argued. "I got to go where the money is."

"If you don't make seventy-five hundred," he promised, "I'll give you the difference."

I accepted his word and took the match with Zannelli. I won a decision in ten rounds, but the fight didn't draw too well. As I remember, my share was around $6900, about $600 under what Mike had promised me. The next week, I went to see him about it.

"I can't give you that money, Ray," he said. "You should have drawn your seventy-five hundred."

I argued that he had promised me $7500, but he ignored me. He was like a judge pounding his gavel and ordering the next case. When he didn't want to talk to you any more, he would make a phone call. And there you'd be, standing in his office but as far as he was concerned, you had gone. He would be looking out his big windows and talking on the phone to somebody else, anybody else.

I might have forgotten the $600 if it hadn't been for another incident that occurred a few weeks later. Joe Louis and I dropped in to see him, and when we appeared in the outer office, we were hurried into the inner office where Uncle Mike was hiding behind the door.

"Shhh," he was whispering, "be quiet."

"What's going on?" Joe said. "What's all the secrecy?"

"Henry Armstrong is outside," Mike said.

"Hey, good," Joe said, "let's go see ol' Henry."

"No, no, no," Mike said, "not now."

"Why not?" Joe said. "Why not now?"

"He's trying to put a touch on me for five hundred," Mike said, locking the door. "I don't want him to know I'm here."

As soon as we left, I got Joe outside.

"Did you see that?" I told him. "Did you see what Mike Jacobs did to Henry Armstrong? Did you see how he treated him? Henry Armstrong won three titles. Henry Armstrong made big money for Mike Jacobs—but for five hundred, he won't even *see* him. If he treats Henry Armstrong like that, some day he's going to treat you and me like that, too, Joe."

The irony of it was that a few days later Henry Armstrong phoned me.

"Ray," he said, "we'd make a good match. We'd draw a lot of money."

"I could never fight you, Henry," I said. "You were my boyhood idol."

Jacobs apparently had told Henry to call me, because a few days later he mentioned the match to me, too.

"When do you have some leave coming?" he said.

"In August," I said. "I can get a few days off around the end of August."

"Good, how would you like Armstrong?"

"Not me, I'll never fight Armstrong."

"It'll do a lot of money," he said, "and it won't be a tough fight for you—Armstrong is making a comeback. He needs the money more than you do."

And then Mike, shrewd old Mike, said, "He can make more money with you than with anybody else."

He had me. As much as I didn't want to fight Henry, if I

didn't fight him, I'd be costing him money. In the strange reasoning that sometimes develops in boxing, I had to fight him for *his* good, but I knew I couldn't bring myself to hurt him. Two days before the fight, Hype Igoe, then the boxing writer for the New York *Journal-American,* came to see me finish my training at Irvin's Gym on 125th Street. Harry Wiley was bandaging my hands with gauze and tape as Hype took out his pad and pencil.

"Ray," he said, "what about the hero worship you've always had for Armstrong? How will that affect you?"

"You know this business, Hype," I said. "When the bell rings, Henry Armstrong will be there for only one purpose —to whip me. If he didn't think he could, he wouldn't be in there. He won't care that I've always admired him."

"But what about you?" Hype said. "Will you ease up on him if you see him hurt?"

I knew somebody was going to ask that question. I had decided not to hurt Henry, but I couldn't tell a sportswriter that I might carry him. If I did, the New York State Athletic Commission would jump on me.

"Well," I said, trying not to lie to Hype, "you be sure to write what happens. The only guys who ever went the distance with me were the guys I just couldn't knock out."

"That's right," George Gainford interrupted. "You remember his first Golden Gloves final, Hype? You remember how he knocked down that Spider Valentine boy? They were pals for years. Shot marbles together. Did everything together. But that didn't stop Robinson from knocking him down. No room in this business for friendship, Hype. You know that. Not when that bell rings."

When the bell rang in the Garden, I tested Henry with a few left jabs that snapped his head back. Then I threw a couple of right hands to the body, and I could feel him sag.

He really was an old man. I couldn't hurt an old man, but

I couldn't go through the motions either. I'd hit him enough
to get him in a little trouble, but whenever I felt him sag-
ging, I'd clinch and hold him up. I didn't want him to be
embarrassed by a knockdown. Other times, I'd let go a
good right hand, but I'd throw it off-target. Not that I was
fooling anybody. The next day, in *The New York Times,*
Joe Nichols wrote that my right hands were missing "by
such apparently calculated margins that several critics were
moved to observe that Ray was of no mind to punish the
ex-champion unduly." Joe Nichols always was a good re-
porter. After the fight, Hype Igoe was annoyed at me.

"You told me the other day," he said, "that you wouldn't
ease up on Armstrong."

"I didn't say that, Hype," I said with a smile. "I said,
'The only guys who went the distance with me were the
guys I just couldn't knock out.' And I *just couldn't* knock
out Henry Armstrong either."

Hype smiled. "Fair enough," he said.

In the other dressing room, Armstrong said something
that I'll never forget. One of the sportswriters was sympa-
thizing with him and mentioned that it was too bad that
Henry couldn't have been in with me when he was in his
prime.

"No," Armstrong said, "I couldn't have handled Robinson on the best night I ever had."

That was Henry's last fight, but it was worth his while.
We drew 15,371 people, and the gross gate was $60,789.

Not long after that, the War Department in Washington
arranged for Joe Louis and me to go on a tour of Army and
Air Force bases throughout the country. We were to put on
boxing shows for the troops. In the group besides Joe and
myself were our sparring partners, George Nicholson for
Joe and California Jackie Wilson for me, and a trainer,
Bob Payne. We met in Washington before starting the tour.

The week end we were there, I invited Edna Mae to come down from New York and join me.

"Be here Saturday night," I told her, "because Joe and I will be busy until then."

We were going to be busy, all right. We had met a couple of girls the day before. The adultery commandment was about to lose a decision. We told the girls to meet us at the Clore House Hotel on Friday night. When we got there, the girls had checked into their rooms down the hall from ours. Somebody else was there, too: Edna Mae. Sitting in the lobby, with her beautiful legs crossed. And when she saw me, she jumped up and kissed me.

"Honey," I said, "you got here a day early."

"I wanted to surprise you," she said, kissing me again.

"You did," I said, "you sure surprised me."

I had to think fast. I went over to the room clerk and got a big suite for Edna Mae and myself. But I had a problem. The only suite available was on the same floor as the rooms that the Army had provided for Joe and me, on the same floor that the girls were on. That was living dangerously, but I had to take a chance. After Edna Mae and I went upstairs, I excused myself.

"I've got to see Joe a minute," I said.

Then I made my mistake. I had put down two room keys, the one to our suite, and the one to my room, on the desk in the suite. But when I went to see Joe, I forgot them. I didn't realize it, because I didn't need the key to my room. As I came to Joe's room, he was standing in the doorway. And he was laughing. Joe always thought everything was a big joke. Edna Mae perched a few rooms away from the girls we had met the day before—Joe thought that was hilarious.

"Hey, Ray," he said, chuckling, "what you gonna do?"

"Only one thing I can do," I said. "I got to tell this chick

that my wife is here and that I can't see her. I got to tell her
to get lost, that's all."

"You better tell her quick," he said, "because she's waiting in your room for you."

"I'll make it quick," I said, "but if Edna Mae comes out of
our suite, knock on my door. Then I'll know she's in the hallway. But remember to knock, Joe, don't let me down."

"Not me, man," he said.

The door to my room was ajar, so I never thought about
my key. But when I went in, I made sure to close the door.
The chick was sitting on the bed, and I was explaining
things to her when I heard a knock on the door.

"Oh, oh," I told her, "I have to go see Joe."

I hurried to the door and opened it, expecting to see Joe
standing there. Instead, Edna Mae was there. And she had
me. Behind me, that chick was sitting on the bed and Edna
Mae couldn't help but see her.

"Ray," she said, "who is that girl in there?"

Before I could say a word, she busted out crying and ran
down the hall, past Joe, toward our room.

"Joe," I said, "why the hell didn't you knock?"

"I didn't have time," he said, laughing. "She was coming
down the hall so fast, I was afraid to go near your door. I
was afraid to do anything."

"The heavyweight champion," I said, "was afraid to do
anything."

That episode wrecked the week end, but somehow I convinced Edna Mae that it was Joe's fault, not mine. She knew
Joe, and she wanted to believe me, so she accepted my version. But later, on the tour, there was another episode that
I had trouble explaining. Edna Mae had joined me in Los
Angeles. One morning, she went shopping before we left
for the Army camp. In a note, I told her not to wait up for
me that night, because we would be back late from the

camp. In another note, I told a guy I knew to go out to the Circle Bar in Hollywood and pick up a gal who was singing there and meet me at the Chicken Shack. I gave the two notes to Dusty Fletcher, a comedian who later made a hit record, "Open the Door, Richard." But he got drunk and mixed up the notes.

When I got back to the hotel, Edna Mae was sitting in our suite, drumming her fingers on a table.

Her bags were packed. After she told me off, she stalked out of the hotel and took a train back to New York. It must have cost me a couple of hundred dollars in flowers before she forgave me. My troubles with Edna Mae had begun, and only a few months after our marriage.

My troubles in the Army were about to begin, too.

9

Amnesia

One of our next stops on the tour was at Keesler Field, an Air Force base in Mississippi.

When we arrived, a few Negro troops surrounded Joe and me for autographs.

"The show's tonight," I reminded them.

"We know," one of them said, "but we wanted to see Joe and you now because we won't be able to see the show."

"Why not?" I said. "You on guard duty?"

"No," he said, "the Negro troops aren't allowed to mix with the white on this base. Only the white troops will be at the show."

"Isn't this the United States?" I said. "Isn't this America?"

"No, man," one of them said, "this is Mississippi."

I searched out the Special Services officer, a second lieutenant, who was in charge of putting on the show.

"Is it true," I asked him, "that the Negro troops won't be allowed to see our show?"

"Yes, it is," he said, glancing at my new corporal's stripes. "I've spoken up about it before, but I can't match this bar against a star. The general here is afraid to let the troops mix."

"Well, tell the general," I said, "that unless there's a Negro section in there tonight, there won't be a show."

That stopped him. He didn't know what to say. And I didn't know what else to say. So I went back to our quarters. Half an hour later, outside our barracks, a siren was whining, and when I looked out, a shiny jeep pulled up. On the front was a flag with a star on it.

"Oh, oh, Joe," I said, "the general's here."

When our door opened, we hopped to attention and saluted. The general walked right over to me.

"Corporal Smith?" he said.

"Yes, sir," I said.

"I understand that you are giving orders on my base. I want you to know that you are supposed to take orders, not give them."

"I beg your pardon, sir," I said.

"Easy, Ray," I heard Joe whisper.

"We are under orders from the War Department to entertain soldiers," I said. "I don't understand why you or any other officer would take it upon himself to segregate some men and leave the others out. And if the Negro troops here are not permitted to see the show, well, then there won't be a show."

The general pointed his right forefinger at me, but before he could say anything, I kept talking.

"General," I said, "please don't point your finger in my face. That isn't becoming for an officer to do to an enlisted man. Now, sir, if you will permit me to use a telephone, I will call the War Department and I'm sure that they can straighten this out because this is one of the things we talked about in arranging this tour."

"If anybody calls the War Department," he snapped, "I'll make the call, Corporal, not you."

He spun on the heel of his shiny boots and strode out of our quarters. When the door closed, I slumped down on a bed. Joe was standing over me.

"Man," he said, "you gonna get us all put in the guardhouse. You crazy, talkin' to a general like that."

About an hour later, another jeep skidded to a stop outside. This time it was a sergeant who told me that the general wanted to see me in his office. By the time I arrived there, I didn't know what to expect. For all I knew, I might be up for a court-martial. I entered his office and saluted, but his manner had changed.

"At ease, Corporal," he said.

"Yes, sir," I said, surprised.

"Corporal," he said, "*you* have to take orders. *I* do, too. It wasn't my idea to keep the men segregated on this base. If they can die in combat together, they can sit together and watch your boxing show, but my orders were not to have the men on this post mix. When you complained about the situation, it gave me ammunition to have something to call Washington about, so I did. And I received permission for the troops to mix."

That night, everybody, white and black, watched our show at Keesler Field.

But we weren't through with our problems in the South. Shortly after 1944 began, we were at Camp Siebert, near Gadsden, Alabama. On our tour we had entertained more than 600,000 troops at nearly a hundred military installations. I had been promoted to sergeant. We had been alerted that we were to be shipped to Europe to entertain troops there. In order to go overseas, we required advance training at Camp Siebert. The base was so crowded that our group was quartered in a tourist home at Gadsden. One day Joe and I were waiting for a bus to town. Getting a bus was a problem. There were two buses for white soldiers to every one bus for the Negro soldiers. To make it worse, there was a long line of Negro soldiers waiting.

"No use standin' around here," Joe said. "I'm goin' to call us a cab."

He strolled over to where the white soldiers were waiting and disappeared into a phone booth. I strolled over with him and waited. When Joe came out, an MP, twirling a brown wooden billy club, sauntered over to us.

"Say, soldier," he said to Joe, "get over in the other bus station."

From Joe's puzzled expression, I knew that he hadn't understood what the guard meant, so he asked, "What you talkin' about?"

"Soldier," the MP snapped, "your color belongs in the other bus station."

"What's my color got to do with it?" Joe said. "I'm wearing a uniform like you."

"Down here," the guard said in his 'Bama drawl, "you do as you're told."

I never saw Joe so angry. His big body looked as if it would explode at that MP. But knowing Joe, I realized that he was trying to control himself. Then the MP made a mistake. He flicked his billy club and poked Joe in the ribs.

"Don't *touch* me with that stick," Joe growled.

"I'll do more than touch you," the MP snapped.

He drew back the billy club as if to swing it at Joe. When I saw that, I leaped on the MP. I was choking him, biting him, anything to keep him away from Joe. I wrestled him into the grass. But before Joe had a chance to get at him, a few more MPs ran up and separated us. The new MPs might really have roughed us up, but some of the soldiers were shouting, "That's Joe Louis, that's Joe Louis," and the MPs didn't know what to do then, so they lined us up.

"Call the lieutenant," one of them said.

When the MP returned from the phone booth, we were taken in a jeep to the jailhouse. I thought sure we were going to be locked up. No matter how justified I thought I had been, I had assaulted an MP. But soon after we arrived at the jailhouse, a chicken colonel rushed in. He questioned me about the incident, and then we heard him bawling out the MP. The next thing we knew, we were free. But the word had spread to the troops that we had been beaten up by the MPs.

"Please do me a favor," the colonel said. "Ride through the company streets in a jeep to show that you're all right."

We did, and soon after that, we completed our training at Camp Siebert. Joe and I had a few laughs in the South, too. Once we were in Jacksonville, Florida, and we were staying at a place called the Two Spot, a night club with a few rooms upstairs. We had adjoining rooms, for privacy when we needed it. Among other things, we had a case of Coca-Cola. I drank it instead of water, and Joe drank more of it than I did. One night, we were down to our last bottle. I hid it out on my window sill, for two reasons. One, to have it cold in the morning. Two, to hide it from Joe. The next morning, Joe busted into my room.

"No more Cokes?" he said, seeing the empty case.

"No more, man," I said. "You drank it all up last night. Your turn to buy the next case."

Just then, he noticed the Coke on the window sill.

"You holdin' out on me, Robinson," he said. "Just for that, I'll take your last one."

As he reached out on the window sill, I leaped out of bed.

"C'mon, man," I yelled, "I was savin' that one."

"Savin' it for me," he said, with his big laugh.

"Damn it, Joe," I said, angry now, and I grabbed his right arm.

I was trying to wrestle the bottle out of his hand. He

shoved me away. That made me angry and foolish. I threw
a punch at him, a welterweight throwing a punch at the
heavyweight champion. He blocked the punch, and swatted me with his left hand. We started to wrestle. The bottle
crashed to the floor and smashed. Still squirming around,
I slipped on the spilled Coke and gashed my right foot
on a chunk of glass. I didn't realize I was bleeding. I
thought it was Coke on my foot, but Joe saw the blood.

"C'mon," he said, "you got to get to a hospital."

When I glanced at my foot, our brief bout was over. But
for a few seconds, I had held my own with Joe Louis. He
helped me get dressed, then he picked me up like a baby
and carried me downstairs to a cab. At the hospital, I hob-
bled into the emergency room.

"Right this way," the nurse said, "the doctor will be with
you in a minute."

The nurse was a doll. When Joe saw her, he forgot about
me. He followed her outside, to her office, and leaned
against the doorway, talking to her.

"Hey, Joe," I yelled, the blood all over my foot, "what
about me?"

"You be all right, Ray," he said. "The doctor's on the way
to stitch you up. This little lady told me so herself. Another
nurse is on the way, too, because this little lady goes off
duty now. And she wants me to take her home."

"Take *her* home!" I roared. "How do *I* get home?"

"After you get stitched up," he said, glancing toward a
corner of the room, "you can take that cane. You'll make it,
man."

And off he went, with that doll of a nurse.

Laughs like that were typical. Blowing money was typical, too. Joe had big money then. I had been doing pretty
good, too. My share of the Armstrong fight, as I remember,
had been about $20,000. I had given Edna Mae some for

whatever she needed, and Mom some for her expenses. But I kept the rest, which was maybe as much as $15,000, I don't remember exactly. Whatever it was, neither Joe nor I liked to carry money on us. We made our trainer, Bob Payne, our treasurer. He always had a supply of big bills on him in a gold money clip. Joe or I, or both of us, would hit him for a hundred, sometimes a few hundred, every few days. One morning I asked him for a C note.

"You're gonna have to hock this," he said, handing me the empty money clip, "because that's all that's left."

We were flat. We had gone through maybe $30,000 in six months. And we had done it as easy as if it was thirty cents. Picking up tabs, buying presents for chicks, tipping big. But we knew there was more money where that had come from. Mike Jacobs would always stake us. He would give us an advance against our future fights. That was his insurance that we'd fight for him. After we had been transferred to Fort Hamilton in Brooklyn, where we were to ship out for Europe, we visited Uncle Mike. And not just to say hello. To put the touch on him, as Henry Armstrong had tried to do. But we had a future, so Mike obliged.

Just like that, Bob Payne's money clip was full again. And we were finding ways to spend it.

Soon after that, on the night of March 29, 1944, I was playing poker with Joe and some other guys in our barracks at Fort Hamilton. In one hand, I had four jacks. From the way Joe was betting, I knew he had a good hand, but I was going all the way with my jacks.

"I call," Joe said.

"Four jacks," I said, reaching for the pot of bills.

"Four queens," Joe said.

I was so disgusted and so frustrated, I spun out of my chair and headed for the latrine, which was downstairs. When I neared the head of the stairs, a flight of maybe a dozen steps, I tripped. Olive-drab duffel bags, stuffed with gear, had been scattered all over the barracks floor. I don't remember whether I tripped over one of the duffel bags or not.

All I remember is falling downstairs.

The next thing I remember is realizing I was in a hospital somewhere. I was in bed and I was wearing a white smock. In the next bed was a red-headed patient.

"Hey, man," I said, "where am I?"

"You're in Halloran General Hospital," he said. "On Staten Island."

"Where's Joe Louis?"

"I don't know where Joe Louis is," he said, "but I know you're in for ten years."

"Ten years!" I said. "What are you talkin' about?"

"You're a garrison prisoner like me," he said, "and I'm in for ten years. You must be, too."

I hopped out of bed and ran into the hall.

"Nurse!" I yelled. "Nurse, nurse!" and a nurse hurried out of an office down the hall. When she saw me, she trotted toward me and gently held one of my arms.

"Sergeant Smith," she said, "how do you feel?"

I had a headache, but right then, I wasn't too concerned about that.

"What am I doing here?" I asked her.

"You're a patient here," she said.

"What's the matter with me?"

"You've had an attack of amnesia," she said. "You haven't been able to remember anything about the last week."

"The last *week!*" I spouted. "What *day* is this?"

"April fifth," she said. "Friday, April fifth."

When I put it together later, I realized that I had tripped down the barracks stairs the previous Friday, March 29. As for what happened in between, my only knowledge has been supplied by my Army medical record. My fall downstairs apparently resulted in a complete blackout for the rest of the evening of March 29, as well as for all of March 30 and all of March 31. At 0120, on April 1, I've been told I was taken to a hospital in New York City by a stranger who had found me ill in the street. From there transferred to Fort Jay Hospital on Governor's Island, off the lower tip of Manhattan.

My condition at the time is described in a neuropsychiatric note compiled at Halloran General Hospital, by R. L. Craig, Captain, on April 7:

> This 22-year-old colored pugilist was hospitalized at Fort Jay at 0340 on 1 April 1944 in a confused, disoriented state, complaining of headache and dizziness and thrashing about in bed. He was unable to give any information about his past life or the events leading up to his hospitalization, and he failed to recognize relatives [Edna Mae] and friends [George Gainford] who visited him. Physical and neurological examinations were essentially negative, there being no evidence of any recent head injury. It was noted that on 28 March 1944 he had been referred to the Station Hospital, Fort Jay, for an electroencephalogram, at which time he had given a history of headaches and dizziness off and on since 1939 and had complained of irritability, inability to stand noises, insomnia, inability to concentrate, and "being in a fog of forgetfulness." The EEG was interpreted as "abnormal and consistent with a post-traumatic cerebral disturbance." He was transferred to this hospital on 4 April, 1944, and on admission he was described by the nurse as "very confused, repeating questions over and over"; at that time he was regaining fragmentary memories but he remembered nothing since 28 March 1944. When interviewed the following morning he was fully alert and rational and showed no memory defect except for the period from 29 March to finding himself in this hospital.

Captain Craig recommended that my "amnesia should be explored under sodium amytal," the truth serum.

Sodium amytal was given intravenously, but according
to the summary of Captain S. Stromberg, it "could not penetrate the block to cause him to reveal how he left Fort Hamilton and by what motivation." In another report, Lieutenant V. H. Gill's opinion was that I seemed "upset" that I
wouldn't be able to accompany Joe Louis on the trip to Europe.

"I do not believe," Lieutenant Gill wrote, "that this patient is a malingerer."

I prefer to accept Lieutenant Gill's medical opinion rather than Dan Parker's. In his sports column in the *Daily
Mirror* on April 7, he wrote that "Robinson is in a bit of a
pickle. Leaving the ship which was to carry him overseas
with a group of other boxers to entertain the fighting men
on foreign fronts, Ray was picked up by the military police
after the ship had sailed and now awaits court-martial."

There is nothing in my Army record that mentions me
"leaving the ship." As far as I know, I was never even on the
ship. I was never court-martialed.

On June 3, 1944, I received an honorable discharge as a
sergeant, but the stain of Dan Parker's column was on me.

10

A Crown, a Café, and a Coroner

D-Day, the beginning of the historic invasion of Normandy, occurred three days after I received my honorable discharge. On the front pages of the newspapers were shaded maps with arrows pointing to where the Allied armies had advanced.

In my return to civilian life, I had the feeling that there were arrows pointing at me, too—arrows pointed by people who had remembered Dan Parker's column.

His column had branded the word *deserter* on my forehead. One afternoon that summer, I stopped in to see Mike Jacobs but he was in conference and I had to wait in the outer offices of his Twentieth Century Sporting Club. Among the other visitors that day was a little man in a brown suit, somebody I had seen around for years but had never been introduced to, and I had never known what his name was.

"You may be a good fighter," he said, glaring, "but you don't fight too good for your country."

"Mister," I said, holding my temper, "the United States Army handed me an *honorable* discharge."

He was the only one who ever challenged me with words, but dozens of others challenged me with their eyes and some do to this day. I'll stand on my Army record.

But soon I was boxing again. I was in Washington to

fight Billy Furrone. I was in the ring, waiting for the introductions, when I heard a big commotion behind me. People were standing up, applauding and shouting, and when I looked back, Sergeant Joe Louis was shuffling down the aisle. He had a big white box under one arm and a doll on the other. As he got nearer, he opened the box and waved a mink coat at me.

"Who's that for?" I asked him later.

"My baby," he said, squeezing the girl with him.

"How much was it?"

"Four thousand," he said, laughing.

"Where'd you get all that money?"

"I got an advance on *your* purse, from Goldie," he said, meaning Goldie Ahearn, the promoter.

"I'm only gettin' seven thousand," I whined.

"So he told me," Joe said, laughing and squeezing his girl again.

I finished Furrone in two.

I had won six consecutive bouts, and I was anxious for a shot at the welterweight title, but Mike Jacobs kept stalling me. His argument was that I'd make more money without the title because I'd have more fights. Years later, I discovered that he didn't want me to win the title because he knew I'd be that much more demanding as a champion.

"Robinson is impossible now," he told Harry Markson, his publicity man. "Imagine dealing with him as a champion."

He kept me busy, and he kept me in paydays, but he didn't keep me happy. I didn't need money. I needed glory. Eventually, he had to give me a title shot, and in the summer of 1945 I signed for a title bout. Marty Servo was the welterweight champion. I knew I could handle him. I had outpointed him twice before I went into the Army. But he had received a shot at the title before I did because he had a shrewd manager, Al Weill, who had outmaneuvered me with Jacobs.

Al Weill was known as the Vest, because he was a sloppy eater. But he was not a sloppy thinker, except once.

In later years, Weill was the matchmaker for the International Boxing Club when Rocky Marciano was a heavyweight contender. Just about everybody in boxing knew that Weill was an undercover manager for Marciano. But the New York State Athletic Commission was unable to prove it until Weill himself made a mistake at the weigh-in for Marciano's fight with Harry (Kid) Matthews. Marciano had arrived but Matthews was late, and Robert Christenberry, the chairman of the commission, was impatient.

"Where's Matthews?" Christenberry said to Weill, the matchmaker.

"I don't know," Weill said. "All I know is *my* fighter's here."

That afternoon, Christenberry demanded Weill's resignation. Weill then managed Marciano to the title. In his years managing Servo, he had to be even shrewder because Servo couldn't put lumps on an opponent's head as Marciano could. Servo was just another good fighter, but Weill knew how to move him. Freddie (Red) Cochrane had taken the welterweight title into the Navy with him in 1942. When he was discharged three years later, he was used up. He was thirty and out of shape. I was the obvious challenger—to me, anyway—but not to Al Weill, and not to Mike Jacobs, who guaranteed Cochrane $50,000 to defend his title against Servo.

In the fourth round, Servo was the new champion. Again, I was the obvious challenger.

This time Servo wanted a payday without risking his title. Weill set up a nontitle bout with a middleweight who was becoming a big drawing card, Rocky Graziano. Servo got his payday, about $40,000. He also got a badly busted nose when Graziano finished him in two, but he still had to defend his title. Weill mentioned just about every welterweight who was breathing as a better opponent, but Eddie Eagan, the chairman of the New York State Athletic Commission, ordered that Servo defend against me.

After we signed for the bout, I went to Greenwood Lake to train.

One day, we had a good crowd for my workout. When it ended, I was in the back room, where I showered and changed, when two white strangers strolled in. No sportswriters were around that day, so the strangers had me all to themselves. Nobody introduced them to me, but that wasn't unusual. Whenever I'd be training, there'd be dozens of people around that I might never meet formally. I was putting on a sweater when one of the strangers, in a pearl-gray fedora, moved in closer to me.

"Robinson," he said, "you can make an easy twenty-five thousand cash if you don't fight Servo."

"Don't fight Servo?" I replied. "Man, all I want to do in the world is fight Servo."

"Now take it easy," he said. "All you have to do is say you can't make the weight."

"Get away from me," I snapped.

Soon after that, the fight was off anyway. Servo had his bad nose pushed in by one of his sparring partners. Al Weill decided to retire Servo. I was back where I had started as the uncrowned champion. But Eddie Eagan, the commission chairman, was in my corner. Eagan announced that there would be a fight to determine the new welterweight champion.

"Ray Robinson has to be one of the contestants," Eagan said, "against a worthy opponent."

The trouble was, of the boxers who wanted the bout, Eagan didn't consider any of them worthy. But one day Ernie Braca, a tough-talking guy who managed Tommy Bell, went to see the commissioner. He was hoping to put Bell in with me for the title.

"No," Eagan told him, "the press won't like it."

"What press?" Braca said smugly, like a man with an ace up his sleeve.

"The sportswriters," Eagan said.

"Commissioner," Braca said, "may I bring in three gentlemen I have waiting outside?"

"Who are they?" the commissioner asked.

"Three sportswriters, and you know them well," Braca said. "Lewis Burton of the *Journal-American*, Lester Bromberg of the *World-Telegram*, and Ed Van Every of the *Sun*."

The sportswriters told Eagan that they considered Tommy Bell to be a worthy opponent.

When Braca walked out of Eagan's office, he had the okay for the bout. But he didn't have a contract. He had to have *me* for that. When Mike Jacobs talked to me about money, he wanted me to get the same percentage as Bell. No way I would agree to that. I was the attraction, not Bell. Mike Jacobs knew it and eventually I got what I wanted— 30 per cent, as I remember, compared to 25 per cent for Bell. But in the days leading up to the fight, Bell would be quoted as saying how I didn't deserve more money than he did, and how he'd prove it to me.

"What about what Bell is saying?" one of the sportswriters asked me.

"That's not Bell talking," I said, laughing, "that's Braca talking."

Looking back on it now, I was taking Tommy Bell lightly. I had outpointed him in a ten-round decision early in 1945 and I assumed I could handle him again. He was a lanky guy, a good puncher and a good fighter. Or so I thought.

But when the bell rang, I couldn't get off. I was doing enough to win most of the early rounds, but I wasn't flowing, I was struggling. In the seventh round, Bell hit me with a left hook to the head that put me on my nose. Really. My face was on the floor before my ass was. But I was up at seven. The knockdown woke me up. It made me realize that I couldn't fool around with this guy. In the eleventh round, I put him down with a combination. From then on, I dominated him. When the bell ended the fifteenth round, I felt that I'd get the decision.

"I'm the champ, George," I told Gainford in the corner, "God Almighty, I'm the *champ.*"

"Don't get your heart set," he said, cautious as always. "They got to say that you are."

Minutes later, Harry Balogh, the ring announcer, was holding a microphone and blaring, ". . . the new world welterweight champion—" and even though he was only a few feet away, I could hardly see him. My eyes were filling up with tears. And I could hardly hear him. My ears were almost bursting with the noise. On the floor of the Garden, behind my corner, dozens of people had gathered there to wait for the decision. When Balogh pointed to me and announced, "Ray Robinson," they were jumping and shouting. Mom was there, and Edna Mae, and so was Marie, because I heard her yell, "Junior is the champ!"

The most noise seemed to come down out of the balcony —a steady roar, like a waterfall, splashing all over me.

Unless you've been in that ring when the noise is for you, there's no way you'll ever know what it's like. The noise is different when you're under the waterfall, as I was, just like the difference between being under Niagara Falls and being on the cliffs overlooking it. That night, December 20, 1946, I didn't want to get out of the ring. I was hopping around and hugging everybody and enjoying the sound. Because the sound wasn't the same as it had been at my other pro fights, or at the Garden when I won my Golden Gloves titles. The cheers were a thrill when I won the Gloves, but I always had the feeling that the spectators were saying, "Good for you, kid, but let's see the rest of the bouts." This time there were no more bouts. They were cheering for me, the world champion.

"Clear that aisle," George was yelling at the Garden cops, "we got to get the champ out of here."

I felt like telling George to let the people have their fun, because nobody was having as much fun as I was. But in a few moments, one of the cops was saying, "Okay, let's go," and I was going down the wooden steps and through the aisle, with George and Harry Wiley holding me, and down the stairs to the gloomy gray hallway where the dressing room was, and all the time people were shouting, "The champ, the champ, the champ!" and the ones close by were reaching out to touch me, my hair soggy with sweat, and my whole body drained of energy, but, man, it was wonderful.

After all those years of being bypassed, after sixty-three pro fights, at last I was the crowned champion.

The only trouble was, my throne room wasn't ready. Up on Seventh Avenue, between 123rd Street and 124th Street, my café, Sugar Ray's, wasn't quite finished. I had purchased the building a few months before. It had to be renovated. The target date was the night of the Bell fight. I wanted to open my café with a celebration.

"No way we can have it ready until Christmas Eve," the foreman had told me. "Sorry, but there's no way."

About two hours after I won the title, I drove up outside my café. Inside, the workmen were installing the lights behind the bar. I had them working almost around the clock to finish it for Christmas Eve. And when I walked in, with Edna Mae, they cheered and called me "Champ."

"No time for that," I said, laughing, "you can't stop to cheer, you got to keep putting in those lights."

"Hey, Champ," one of them said, "the sign's hooked up. Turn on the sign. It lights up like Coney Island."

I turned the switch and went outside. Above me, in red neon, SUGAR RAY'S lit up the avenue. Man, my own café, with my name on it. Everything was starting to come together the way I'd dreamed when I was a kid. Winning a title. Owning a business.

I had invested nearly $100,000 in purchasing the site of the café, and the two flats next to it. I had put about $10,000 more into fixing it up.

I almost blew the Bell fight over it. Every time the workmen needed me, I drove down from Greenwood Lake to make the decision myself. Whenever I did, George started to scream that I wasn't training properly. I knew I wasn't. Nevertheless, I wasn't about to let anybody make a decision on Sugar Ray's except Sugar Ray. And now the lights were flashing on Seventh Avenue, my name in lights.

"Let's celebrate, anyway," I told Edna Mae.

"Celebrate with who?" she said, glancing around.

"The workmen," I said.

Rushing inside, I got out a couple of bottles and put them on one of the new wooden tables. No tablecloth. No glasses, but there were some paper cups around. I found a Coke somewhere, and one of the workmen poured drinks for Edna Mae and the other men.

"To Sugar Ray's," one of them said, lifting his cup.

"To Sugar Ray's," I said, raising my bottle of Coke.

It was one of the nicest celebrations I've ever had. It must have inspired the workmen because they got the café finished in time for Christmas Eve, and then we had another celebration. With glasses this time. Man, I was really living. Listening to the jingle of that cash register, and listening to that sweet sound of people calling me "Champ." But now that I had the title, I had to defend it. That didn't mean that I was going to be one of those champions who only fights for the title. That's the quick way to being an ex-champion. George Gainford always had told me that a fighter had to keep busy, had to stay sharp.

"And now that you're the champ, Robinson," he said to me one day, "you got to do the same thing. Don't change your pattern. Keep the feel of the ring."

I had three easy nontitle fights, and I was about to go against another middleweight, Georgie Abrams, when a welterweight title bout was arranged. The challenger was Jimmy Doyle, a nice little guy out of Los Angeles. The date was May 30 in Cleveland. But Abrams mussed up the schedule. He mussed me up, too. I got the decision without too much trouble, but Abrams cut me over both eyes. The Doyle fight was only two weeks away. George called the Cleveland promoter, Larry Atkins, and told him that it would have to be postponed. The next day, Atkins announced a new date, June 10. I got on the phone.

"That's still not enough time," I told Atkins. "You've got to make it the end of the month."

Atkins agreed, but when Tony Palozolo, a one-legged guy who was called Crutchy and who was Doyle's manager, heard about it, he started hollering that I was trying to duck the fight. That's typical of managers. They like to talk a good fight. It annoyed me that anyone would think I was ducking an opponent. If I had wanted to duck him I never would have signed to fight him. Anyway, Atkins made June 24 the new date. That satisfied me, and it quieted Palozolo.

As for Doyle, I had nothing against him. I had seen him

around New York when he fought there a few times. He was a humorous guy, a good mimic. He always had everybody laughing. And he was a good fighter, a bulldog type, always coming at you.

About fourteen months earlier, Doyle had been through a bad experience. He had been knocked out by Artie Levine, a Brooklyn middleweight. He had to go to the hospital with a concussion, but he soon recovered.

I knew about Artie Levine. Six weeks before I outpointed Tommy Bell for the title, I boxed Levine in Cleveland. He clipped me with a left hook to the jaw that flopped me like a fish in the fifth round. Or so I've been told. I really have no recollection of what round it was. All I remember is George talking to me in the corner.

"Robinson," he was growling, "you got to come on to beat this guy."

"Plenty of time," I told him. "I'll get him. There's plenty of time."

"Plenty of time!" yelled George. "The *eighth* round is next, Robinson."

"The eighth?" I said, squinting at him. "I thought it was the fourth."

That's how Artie Levine could scramble your brains. I got through the eighth round, but in the ninth he staggered me again with another left hook. After that round, George lectured me.

"Watch his left hook, Robinson," he advised. "Stay away from his left hook."

The ten-second warning buzzed for the final round, and George hustled to get out of the ring. Behind me, old Soldier Jones, who was also working in my corner that night, leaned between the ropes.

"Gamble, son," he whispered. "Now's the time to take a gamble."

With less than a minute to go in the final round, I dug a left hook into Levine's midsection and he sagged against the ropes. I had him now and I battered him. He was counted out while seated on the lower rope, with nineteen seconds to go. I had been luckier than Jimmy Doyle.

After Doyle recovered from his concussion, he won a decision from Ralph Zannelli and another from Danny Kapilow. Among the welterweights, Doyle was as qualified a challenger as there was around. When I got to Cleveland, I stayed at the house of a buddy of mine, Roger Price.

And it was there, the night before the fight, that I had a dream, a premonition.

In the dream, Jimmy Doyle was in the ring with me. I hit him a few good punches and he was on his back, his blank eyes staring up at me, and I was staring down at him, not knowing what to do, and the referee was moving in to count to ten and Doyle still wasn't moving a muscle and in the crowd I could hear people yelling, "He's dead, he's dead," and I didn't know what to do. Then I woke up.

I tried to get back to sleep, tried to continue the dream so Doyle would be all right, but I couldn't close my eyes.

In the morning, when I got up, I told George Gainford about the dream. But George didn't want to hear about it.

"Forget it, Robinson," he said. "That's a dream, that's all. Don't have it on your mind. Nothing's gonna happen."

That's not the way I was thinking. I considered the dream a warning. At the weigh-in, I quietly told Larry Atkins, the promoter, about it.

"I don't want to fight Doyle," I told Atkins. "I don't want anything to happen."

"Don't be ridiculous," he said. "Dreams don't come true. If they did, I'd be a millionaire."

"Damn it, Larry," I said, "I'm going to tell the commission that I'm not fighting."

"Are you crazy?" he said. "You've already postponed this fight twice. You're not going to say a word. And if I ever asked the commission to put off the fight, they'd think *I* was crazy."

As much as I didn't want to go through with the fight, I decided to do it after being persuaded by a priest whose name I've forgotten and who was summoned by the commission.

That night, when the bell rang at the Cleveland Arena, I hadn't forgotten about the dream, but it wasn't on my mind as much. Doyle kept coming at me. I was winning most of the rounds, but none of them were easy because he knew how to fight and he had guts. In the sixth round and in the seventh, his left hook had me backing up. In the eighth round, I saw the opening I had been waiting for, and I went for it. I threw a double right hand, first into his belly, then to his head. He sagged a little but he kept coming at me, and he started to throw a right hand when I beat him to the punch with a good left hook to the jaw. Lewis Burton of the *Journal-American* later wrote, "Doyle fell back rigidly, pivoting on his heels as if they were hinged to the canvas. He cracked against the floor in three parts, his seat, his shoulders, and finally, like the snapping end of a whip, the back of his head." I stood over him, transfixed, seeing my dream come true, horribly true.

At the count of four Doyle stirred. One of his hands reached for an imaginary rope, but he slumped back.

At nine the bell rang, ending the round and stopping the count. The referee, apparently not realizing how seriously Doyle was hurt, yelled at his handlers, "Pick him up, the fight's not over!" The first handler to get to him cupped Doyle's head in his hands and looked around, frantic.

"It's damn well over!" he shouted at the referee. "Get the doctor in here."

I didn't know what to do. I had knocked out guys before, dozens of them. But in those fights, I always had a good feeling, a conquering feeling when I saw them being counted out, maybe because I could see that they weren't really hurt. But now, with Doyle stretched out and his eyes blank, I had that empty feeling you get when something in your life is really wrong, and all I could think of was the dream.

"Get a stretcher in here," the doctor was shouting now, "and call an ambulance."

He might as well have been talking into a microphone. His voice carried all through the building because his voice was the only sound in it. The spectators were hushed, standing around quietly, staring into the ring, waiting for Doyle to move, to show some sign of life, some sign that he was regaining consciousness. When the Arena policemen hustled into the ring with the stretcher, he still hadn't moved.

You warned me, God, I was thinking, *you told me. Why did I let everybody talk me out of it.*

"C'mon, Robinson," George was saying gently, almost guiltily, "let's get to the dressing room."

Minutes later, we were informed that Doyle was on the way to St. Vincent Charity Hospital.

"I think they're going to operate," one of the sportswriters said. "He may have a blood clot."

By the time that Edna Mae and George and I got there, Doyle had been given the last rites. Father James Nagle, the priest who administered them, tried to console me.

"It's not your fault," he said.

"I hit him, Father," I replied.

"One of the doctors just told me that when he was knocked out by Levine, he suffered cerebral damage that probably wasn't apparent until now."

"But I'm the one who hit him, Father."

"You're supposed to hit him," Edna Mae said softly. "Just like he was hitting you."

"But he's hurt, I'm not," I said.

We waited around for a few hours, long after the operation, but he still hadn't regained consciousness. We went back to Roger Price's house, but I didn't sleep at all that night. Edna Mae stayed up, trying to console me. The next afternoon Jimmy Doyle died. About an hour later I got a phone call. The coroner, Samuel Gerber, had ordered an inquest. I had felt bad because I had been the one who hurt Jimmy Doyle, who put him in the hospital, who killed him. But now, with an inquest, it was as if I were a criminal and that annoyed me. So did the coroner. He didn't seem to understand.

"Why did you pick Doyle to fight?" he asked me.

"Pick him!" I said. "I didn't pick him. He picked me. I had something he wanted, my title."

"Did you intend to get Doyle in trouble?"

"Mister," I said, trying to hold my temper, "it's my *business* to get him in trouble."

Harsh words, I realized later, but true.

My harshness seemed to make the coroner understand what boxing is all about. The idea is to hit your opponent, to batter him if necessary. If you don't, he'll hit and batter you. Every so often a boxer dies. Whenever that happens, some people like to shout that boxing should be outlawed, that it's unnecessarily brutal. Most of the time the shouters are politicians who know it's an easy way to get their name in the newspapers. But an occasional death doesn't mean a sport should be abolished. If that were the case, auto racing should be abolished. So should football.

Not that my harsh words made me feel any better about Jimmy Doyle's death.

For weeks, I had trouble sleeping. Whenever my mind wasn't occupied, I'd see Doyle's blank eyes staring up at me from the canvas. I had written a note to his mother in Los Angeles, but I wanted to do something more for her. One of my next fights, with a little Filipino named Flash Sebastian, was on an American Legion card at the Garden. My end was going to be something like $25,000. I told the Garden to send half of it to Mrs. Doyle. But that night I had another scare. In the first round, one of my punches flattened Flash Sebastian.

"My God!" I heard one of the sportswriters yell as Sebastian lay still, "this guy may be dead, too."

Thank God, he came to a few moments later. If he hadn't, I would have been tempted to quit boxing. As it was, I waited two months before my next bout. I went to Los Angeles and went ten rounds with my old Army sparring partner, California Jackie Wilson, in another benefit for Doyle's mother. She got $6500 this time, enough to open a trust fund for her at the Union Trust Company out there. It paid her fifty dollars a month, as I remember.

It wasn't much, but it was something. After that, I had other things on my mind when I went to bed.

11

The Flamingo Cadillac

I like to sleep with my wife's arms around me, and with my head snuggled into her neck. But these nights, I was sleeping alone. Edna Mae and I hadn't been getting along. After several spats, I moved out of our apartment and went to live at Mom's house. I also got myself a new chick, quite by accident. One night in my café, I was strolling around, greeting the customers, when I noticed this long pair of legs. The rest of her was all there too. I guess I was staring.

"Hi," she said to me, "I'm Dolores."

She introduced her girl friend, and her girl friend's boy friend, but she was unescorted. We got to talking and she told me that they lived in Yonkers.

"I go up there all the time," I said, "to drive golf balls at a range."

It wasn't a line. I really did. I had begun to play golf. And there are no country clubs in Harlem. No driving ranges either. Dolores knew the one I went to in Yonkers.

"It's not far from my home," she said.

"Is that so?" I said. "I was just about to drive up there tonight to hit a few."

"Oh, could you take us home?" she said.

"Better than that, baby," I said, "I'll take you to the driving range and then I'll take you home."

"But I don't know how to play," she said.

"Baby," I said, "let me be your golf pro."

By the time I got her home that night, I had her phone number. The next day I called her. We soon got to be a twosome. She was young and pretty and had beautiful legs. My being an athlete, a world champion boxer, really seemed to turn her on. But we had to sneak our good times. Once we drove up to a lover's lane overlooking the Harlem River, not too far from the old Polo Grounds. After we parked, we were strolling toward a hot-dog stand when a cab stopped behind us.

"Ray," a voice called out.

The door of the cab swung open. Edna Mae stepped out and strode toward us.

"Ray," she said, "won't you come home?"

"Come home for what?" I said. "We're separated."

"Ray," she said, "who is this girl?"

"None of your business," I said. "We're separated and I can be with whoever I want. And don't start any commotion here, Edna Mae. I don't want any embarrassment for this girl, or for you."

Edna Mae turned away, and she was weeping.

When I glanced at Dolores, her eyes were filling with tears, too. *Man,* I thought, *now I got two dames crying on me.* The cab took off, with Edna Mae in it. We turned back to my car. Dolores didn't know what to say. She wasn't much of a talker. She was more something to look at, an ornament, but I knew she was hurt by this scene and I had to cheer her up.

"Baby," I said, "I'm going to Greenwood Lake tomorrow. I want you to come up and stay there with my sister Marie."

She was delighted. So was I. My sister Marie had come

to know her, and Marie took her under her wing in camp. Marie loved anybody who loved me. I was training to defend my welterweight title against Kid Gavilan in Philadelphia. I had outpointed him several months before in New York, but it had been a tough ten rounds. His bolo punch made him dangerous. In a title fight, he had five more rounds to throw that bolo. He not only was aggressive, but you could hit him with everything and still not knock him out. To complicate things, I had to make the 147-pound limit. The weight itself was no problem, but maintaining my strength was. When you have to make weight, you get dehydrated. Your salt content is affected. When my sweat would drip onto my lips, it would be stale instead of salty. And your sugar content drops. You don't have as much pep. Several days later, when Dr. Vincent Nardiello visited me, I had an idea.

"Doc, what's that stuff you give people intravenously to give them strength when they're sick?"

"Glucose," he said. "It's got sugar and salt in it and it goes right into the blood stream."

Dr. Nardiello was the commission physician who had advised Mom to let me be a boxer a decade earlier. In the years since, he had become one of my closest friends. I trusted his opinion not only on medical matters but on almost everything.

"Let's try something," I said to him. "I'll make the weight a week before this fight and we'll try the glucose."

The way it worked out, Doc put a bottle of glucose into my arm about six o'clock one morning, eight hours before my afternoon workout. The eight-hour span was important. The day of the fight, I'd have about eight hours between two in the afternoon and the ten o'clock bell. The day I experimented with it at camp, I was full of pep and fire in my workout.

"That settles it," I told Doc Nardiello, "that's the first time I've had any real strength up here."

After the weigh-in at Philadelphia, the glucose dripped into me again. I outpointed Gavilan easily.

Six weeks later, I had another important fight, with a Bronx middleweight, Steve Belloise, at Yankee Stadium, my first bout under the promotion of the new International Boxing Club. Two years earlier, Mike Jacobs had suffered a stroke. Without him, the Twentieth Century Sporting Club gradually collapsed. Another organization, the Tournament of Champions, assumed control for a short time, but the International Boxing Club soon took over. Jim Norris, a multimillionaire from Chicago, had bankrolled the IBC. One of his aides was Truman Gibson, a Negro attorney from Chicago whom I had met when I was in the Army. They wanted me to sign an exclusive contract. I refused, but they offered me Belloise, hoping that eventually I'd be persuaded. I stopped Belloise in the seventh round. Some boxing people consider it the best fight I ever made. I never thought of it that way, but maybe that's because I had something else on my mind.

"Did you know," one of my aides, Pee Wee Beale, had mentioned to me one day in my café, "that Edna Mae is pregnant?"

After a few days of wondering what to do, I knew there was one thing I *had* to do—see her. I walked in on her at our apartment one afternoon. One look and I knew it was true.

"Is the baby mine?" I asked.

"Of course it is, Ray," she said. "I'm due in November. Count back yourself."

"Then why didn't you tell me before we separated?"

"Because I didn't know it then," she said. "I wanted to tell you myself, but after the incident up at the river when you were with that girl, I decided not to."

"I wish you had."

We moved across the room toward each other, and I held her for the first time in several months. With her pressed against me, I could feel where the baby was, *our* baby, after six years of marriage.

"I'm sorry, honey," I said.

"I'm sorry, too," she said.

Now I had another problem—what to do with Dolores. I needed advice and whenever I needed that, I always went to Marie.

"You put that baby there, Junior," she said, "and now you got to take care of it. Dolores will just have to understand."

It wasn't that easy. When I told Dolores about it, she started to cry and she kept saying over and over, "I never loved anybody before, and now you're leaving me." It was a bad scene. I couldn't argue with her. I had romanced her and led her on, and with me being separated, I guess she thought that eventually we'd get married. The baby changed all that. I don't know if Dolores ever really understood. I never saw her after that.

I moved back in with Edna and watched her get plumper and plumper. She never looked so pretty. The way a woman's face fills out when she's pregnant makes her look prettier than ever. But she never believes that. She's just thinking about how big her stomach is. A couple of weeks before the baby was due, I had a fight scheduled in New Orleans.

"I can call it off," I told Edna Mae.

"Don't be silly," she said, "you go ahead. I've got a couple of weeks to go."

I knew better than she did. Down in New Orleans, they liked to have fights on a Sunday afternoon. Around noon that day, November 19, 1949, just when I was about to leave for the arena, the phone rang.

"Ray," I heard Edna Mae's doctor say, "make way for the new champion. Your son came out fighting."

My son. My second son really, but somehow this was different. When my other boy was born, more than a decade earlier, I hadn't really known what it was all about. I was just a kid then myself. I wasn't able to appreciate the miracle of a birth. To be honest, that first child had created more problems than happiness for me, and for Marjie. But this time it was different. We had a name all picked out if it was a boy. Ray Junior. That afternoon in New Orleans I was all charged up. I knocked out Vern Lester in the second round.

When I got back to New York, I hurried to the Sydenham Hospital. The nurse brought my son to the window of the glass-enclosed nursery, but I shook my head.

"That's not my baby," I said, "he's got too many wrinkles."

The nurse was nodding and pointing to a tiny name tag on his wrist. It was my son, no doubt about that.

"He's got more wrinkles than George Arliss," I told Edna Mae.

When the baby and Edna Mae came home, it was the start of a new life for us, a better life. Until then, I had always been involved in my boxing, and, if I wasn't busy with that, with my café. I hadn't been much of a family man.

With my son in his crib, I had a reason to be home more, to watch him develop, day by day, week by week, month by month, even though I was frightened of him, like the day Edna Mae went shopping and left him with me.

Suddenly he started crying, that quick "Whaaa, whaaa, whaaa," the way little babies cry.

I didn't know what to do. I'd never been alone with him before. Edna Mae had said she'd be back soon, but the little guy wasn't waiting for his mother. I gave him his Teddy bear, hoping it would soothe him, but that didn't work. I didn't dare pick him up. I had never picked him up.

"Whaaa, whaaa, whaaa," he was shouting, even louder.

I went to the next apartment where an older lady lived and asked her to try to calm the baby while I phoned the doctor. When she took a look at little Ray, she laughed.

"What's so funny?" I asked.

"Mister Robinson," she said. "He just has to have his diaper changed. Didn't you change his diaper?"

"No, ma'am, I can't do that."

She took off the wet diaper, powdered him, put on a new diaper, and he started cooing instead of crying. By the next day, that lady had spread the story all over the apartment house of how I wanted to call the doctor when all the baby needed was a clean diaper. I never did learn how to diaper him. I always made sure that if Edna Mae went out, there was somebody available to change him if he had to be.

As much as I loved the baby, I had to be away from him every so often. My business was boxing, not baby-sitting. Shortly after little Ray was two months old, I had a series of four nontitle fights in less than a month. One of them was in Miami, always an uncomfortable area for me. Except for those incidents in the Army, I had never challenged any racial restrictions. And the only reason I did it then was because it involved other men. Personally, I always preferred to go my own way. If anybody didn't want me around, the hell with them, I didn't need them either. But down there, Walter Winchell, the famous columnist of the old *Daily Mirror*, invited me over to the Beach, where he was staying at the Roney Plaza.

"Sugar Ray," he announced on the phone, "I'm going to show you Miami Beach."

That was nice of him, but I was uneasy. I knew that Negroes were supposed to be off the streets of the Beach by sundown. I also knew about the signs in front of many of the places there. One sign read: NO NEGROES, JEWS, OR DOGS. On our tour that night, I hesitated when I spotted the sign.

"Walter," I said, "we're not supposed to—"

"Forget it, Sugar Ray," he barked. "You're with me, you know."

"Yeah, but you're Jewish."

"I'm Winchell," he snapped.

In we went, to be treated like kings, but I was uneasy anyway. I knew I wasn't wanted. Another day he took me to the Hialeah race track. At the time the track had a strict rule segregating Negroes in the grandstand. Not being a horseplayer, I wasn't aware of the rule. I had simply followed Walter into his clubhouse box. During the afternoon, I had my binoculars on the flamingos in the infield pond more often than on the thoroughbreds. With their pink feathers and pencil-thin legs, the flamingos are Hialeah's trade-mark.

"Walter," I said, pointing at them, "how do you think that pink would look on a car?"

"You're crazy," he said.

"No, I'm very serious," I said. "That color on a convertible with a black top. Beautiful, man."

"Watch the horses," Winchell said.

The more I thought about that color on a car, the more I liked the idea. After I returned to New York, I went up to Hartford one night for a boxing banquet. Willie Pep's manager, Lou Viscusi, was there wearing a flamingo-pink tie.

"Lou," I said, "I got to have your flamingo tie."

"It's not flamingo," he said, "it's fuchsia."

"Man, I don't care what color you say it is, but I got to have it."

"*After* the dinner," he said.

"Sure," I said, "after the dinner. I'll see that you get it back in a couple of days."

"Keep it," he said. "My wife made me wear it."

The next day, with the tie in my pocket, I went to see Larry Mandras, a Cadillac salesman in the Bronx. Since 1941, I had purchased a dark blue Buick convertible every year, but this year I had ordered my first Cadillac, a white Eldorado convertible. When I entered his showroom, I was holding the flamingo tie.

"What's that thing?" he asked.

"Larry," I said, "can you paint my new car this color?"

"Are you crazy?"

"Man, I ain't crazy," I said. "I just want my new car painted this color. It's my car, ain't it?"

He was laughing and he said, "You really want to be exclusive, don't you?"

It hadn't occurred to me quite that way before, but now I liked the idea even more. The paint job couldn't be done in his shop, so we drove to a Cadillac garage on Fifty-sixth Street and Eleventh Avenue in Manhattan, a few blocks from where I had lived as a kid in Hell's Kitchen. When we walked in, Larry was holding the fuchsia tie.

"Can you mix up a batch of paint this color?" he said to the foreman, Ernie Brian.

"This color?" Ernie asked, his eyes wide. "For a car? You want *this* color on a car?"

"*This* color," Larry said, winking at me.

"Well," Ernie said, "I'll give it a try."

Ernie disappeared into a workroom to mix some shades. After a few minutes, he emerged with a spray can. He strolled over to where part of an old fender was hanging on a wall.

"Let's see how this looks," he said, spraying the fender.

"Man, that's it!" I yelled. "You got it. That's the one."

On the way back to Larry's showroom, he reminded me that a custom paint job would be extra on the bill.

"How much is extra?" I asked.

"About three hundred dollars," he said, sounding as if he wondered if I'd be willing to go that high.

"For an exclusive color," I said, "that's a bargain."

When my car arrived, it was not only exclusive, it was a symbol. When people think they recognize a celebrity, they hesitate a moment. But when they saw me in that car, they didn't have to hesitate. They knew. There was only one like it—Sugar Ray's pink Cadillac. Most people called it pink, but to me it was always more than pink, it was flamingo pink.

At first the car was an even bigger attraction than I was. Its paint job made it the most famous car in the world.

"Mister Robinson," a man from *Life* magazine said to me on the phone one day, "we'd like to come up to your café tomorrow and shoot some pictures of your car."

"In color?" I asked.

"Of course," he said. "In black and white it would be a waste of space."

12

Jim Norris

The world was moving for me. My pink Cadillac had made me the talk of the town, and my café was booming.

Whenever my car was parked in front of my café, the grownups liked to drop in for a drink or for some fried chicken. They knew that if my car was out front, I was inside and they wanted to talk to me about the color and, more than anything else, about how much it had cost. The kids stayed outside, staring at it and reaching over to touch the pink fenders or the black leather seats. That car was the Hope Diamond of Harlem. Everybody had to see it or touch it or both to make sure it was real. And to most of them it literally was the *Hope* Diamond because if skinny little Walker Smith could come off the streets to own a car like that, maybe they could too.

I'd had other nice cars but this one had soul—almost two decades before soul was popular.

At night, I loved to look out the window of my café and see that car glowing with the reflection of SUGAR RAY's in big red neon lights. Nearby my doorman would be helping people out of cabs under the big blue-and-white awning the width of the sidewalk. And there were always some fancy people arriving, like Frank Sinatra or Jackie Gleason or Nat

King Cole or Lena Horne, or some of the big sports names, like Joe Louis or Jackie Robinson. Between me and my famous customers, my café attracted people from all over because in those days Harlem was nicer. People were safer there, and women enjoyed coming to my café because it had rules.

One of the rules was that a man had to check his hat and his overcoat or raincoat. Nothing makes a place look worse than for a man to be standing at a bar in his hat and coat, like someone waiting for a bus. I enforced that rule, personally sometimes. One night I was talking with some friends when this cat in a wide-brimmed hat and a double-breasted overcoat breezed by the checkroom.

"Sir, sir," the hat-check girl called, "you have to check your hat and coat."

"Not me, baby," he said. "I like to wear my hat and coat. I'll keep 'em on."

As he sauntered toward the bar, I spun around and grabbed him by the collar of his coat.

"Hey, old buddy," I said, forcing a smile, "didn't you hear what the young lady said about your hat and coat?"

"Yeah, sure, Champ," he said, recognizing me, "but I was only gonna be a minute."

"A minute or an hour, we have a policy here about checking your hat and coat," I said. "You wouldn't want to tread on the policy of the café, now would you?"

"No, sir, Champ," he said, removing his hat and coat.

Another time I got the word that two leaders of the Harlem underworld had arranged to meet at my café to settle a feud. I made sure I was at the door that night. When they walked up, I took them aside.

"Do me a favor," I said, "don't make any trouble here. And you'll be doing me a bigger favor if you have your meeting somewhere else."

They did, quietly. My café had a good reputation, and I wanted to keep it that way because I had too much at stake. In addition to my café, my businesses dominated the block between 123rd Street and 124th Street on the west side of Seventh Avenue. When the café began to make money, I had opened Sugar Ray's Quality Cleaning, Edna Mae's Lingerie Shop, and George Gainford's Golden Glover Barber Shop. Next to my café was my office, with RAY ROBINSON ENTERPRISES on the big plate-glass window. All my enterprises were making money, and I was spending it.

Edna Mae owned a full-length ranch mink coat, a Russian lynx coat, a Persian lamb broadtail coat, a platinum mink jacket, a platinum mink stole, and a silver-blue mink stole—about $30,000 in furs.

I needed a big closet, too. I had about twenty-five suits, a dozen sports jackets, a couple dozen pairs of slacks, a couple dozen pairs of shoes. I even had three tuxedos. And then there were all my sports clothes. Drawers full of shirts and sweaters, dozens of them. And whenever I played golf, I liked to wear plus fours, the old-fashioned knickers that Gene Sarazen always wore. I had half a dozen pairs of them, in different colors, and the long socks to go with them. Whenever I wore the plus fours, I thought about how as a kid I had kept my knickers pulled up tight around my knees after my picture had been in the *Daily News*.

I had thought I was somebody then, but I really was somebody now. I had everything I wanted—except the middleweight championship. I had held the welterweight title for more than three years, but there were no more real challengers I could make any money with. My future was as the middleweight champion, but I was being ignored by the new promoters at the Garden, the International Boxing Club with Jim Norris as president. They had maneuvered Jake LaMotta into a title shot. I had outpointed Jake in four

of our five bouts, but he had better connections, like Frankie
Carbo, an accomplice of Frank (Blinky) Palermo, my old
Philadelphia acquaintance. Every so often Palermo would
be around the Garden or at the gym, trying to approach me.

"As good a fighter as you are," he told me once.

"What do you mean—as good a fighter as I am?"

"As good a fighter as you are," he said, "if somebody
could just *talk* to you."

"Talk to me about what?" I asked.

"Oh, you know," he said, winking.

And then I did know, but I smiled and walked away.
They were able to *talk* to LaMotta, and he listened. Carbo
and Palermo had arranged in 1947 for LaMotta to lose in
the Garden to one of Palermo's fighters, Billy Fox, a fix that
LaMotta confessed in 1960 during the Kefauver Committee
investigations. When the IBC took over, Carbo moved in as
Norris's unseen adviser. And since Carbo had no control
over me, he ignored me. Instead, he obtained a title shot for
LaMotta with Marcel Cerdan, the middleweight champion.
LaMotta bulled him around and when the Frenchman
couldn't answer the bell for the tenth round, Jake LaMotta
had the title.

I was worse off now. I had to wait for LaMotta to give
Cerdan a return bout, under their IBC contract.

The date was set, but LaMotta asked for a postponement.
Another date was set, but on his way over from Europe to
continue training, Cerdan was killed in an airplane crash
in the Azores, a tragedy that France mourned. Cerdan had
been its hero. His death, ironically, would affect my career
later on, but at the time it meant that LaMotta couldn't
avoid me any longer, except that he did. He agreed to an
over-the-weight match at the Garden with Robert Villemain,
another Frenchman, and lost it. Several months later he
still hadn't signed to defend his title.

I deserved the shot, and I was griping so much the IBC people must have thought I was ready to come in on their terms.

I got the word that Jim Norris wanted to talk to me about the situation. In their takeover, the IBC had set up its headquarters on the second floor of the Garden in gloomy, old-fashioned offices with smoked-glass partitions, roll-top desks, and high, dusty windows. Norris's office overlooked the corner of 50th Street and Eighth Avenue, and when I strolled in, he greeted me with a big smile and a big handshake. Handsome, with black hair above his tanned, rugged face, Jim Norris was a multimillionaire who had grown up in Chicago, where his father made a fortune in the grain business.

With his money, Jim Norris was able to make a hobby out of sports. He owned race horses. He owned the Chicago Black Hawks hockey team. He had been around boxing before he bankrolled the IBC.

Strangely, for someone on such a high economic and social level, for someone who had attended the best prep schools and Hamilton College, he liked to be around mob guys. His fascination for them began when he was twenty-four. One day he was robbed of $1000 by three masked gunmen outside his elegant North Side home in Chicago, but a few days later at the race track a tall, slender man with a mild manner handed him a wad of bills.

"Your money, kid," the man said.

The man was Golfbag Sam Hunt, reputedly a notorious killer during the Al Capone era, who liked to carry his machine gun in a golf bag. After the return of the money, Norris and Hunt got to be friends. Norris often arranged boxing and hockey tickets for Hunt, and he would later say, "It was hard for me to believe that Hunt did the things that he has been charged with." After he moved into the IBC, Norris trusted mob guys like Carbo and Palermo, who eventually would destroy him with their plan to monopolize boxing. But that first day in his office, I was anxious for a title shot.

"You know I deserve it," I said.

"Ray," he said, "if you would, well, not exactly team up with us, but if you would let us handle you and take care of you, we could do a lot for you."

"You mean fight exclusively for you?"

"That's right," he said. "You're a great attraction and we could get you a shot at the middleweight title. That's what you want, don't you?"

"Not under those conditions."

"What's the matter with them?"

"If I'm good enough to deserve a shot at the title, I deserve a shot. It shouldn't have to depend on whether I fight exclusively for you or not."

"You're not being smart, Ray."

"I'm smart enough to know what's going on with your television money, the way you and the sponsor decide how much I'm worth without me having anything to say about it, and the way you have to cut in Madison Square Garden Corporation."

"That's our agreement," he said, "Madison Square Garden Corporation gets half of our television revenue."

"Then you must have an agreement with yourself, Jim, because you are Madison Square Garden Corporation. You got control of it and what you're saying is that if you sell the television rights for $100,000, right away $50,000 goes to Madison Square Garden Corporation and you and I talk about the other $50,000, isn't that right?"

He looked away. He knew that I had him, but he didn't give up. In the weeks that followed, he had George work on me.

"Robinson," George said to me one day, "you can't fight

this man, he's too powerful. He controls Madison Square Garden, the Chicago Stadium, the Boston Garden, the Detroit Olympia, all the big indoor arenas in the country. If you're gonna make any money indoors, you got to work for this man. You like to think the world is on the up-and-up all the time, but it ain't. Robinson, sometimes you got to play ball with the man who owns the ball."

"Maybe other people do," I said, "but I don't."

"What makes you different, Robinson?" he said.

"Because of the way I believe in God," I said. "My faith in God has carried me this far and it will carry me through Jim Norris. I know it's hard for you to understand, but the way Norris wants to do it is wrong."

Soon after that, George agreed with me because Norris had turned on him.

"Ray," Norris said to me at another meeting in his big office, "we want you to get rid of Gainford. If you do, you can call your own shots with us, anything you want."

"What's the matter with George?" I asked.

"We want him out of boxing," Norris said. "We don't like the way he's operating. He's involved with Kid Gavilan, and he's working too many angles. We want him out of boxing, and you're the man who can put him out."

"Not me."

"Why not?"

"Because he hasn't done anything to me, that's why. This man has been with me since I was a boy, and you want me to get rid of him so that you can open the road for me in boxing. No chance."

"But you don't trust him," Norris said.

"I don't trust him as a manager, but I trust him as a trainer because he knows me better than anybody else, and as for trusting people, you are the man I don't trust."

By that time, the Pennsylvania Athletic Commission had

vacated the middleweight title because LaMotta hadn't defended it. I was matched with Villemain in Philadelphia. I
outpointed him and I was the holder, as Frank Graham
wrote in the *Journal-American,* of the middleweight championship of "the narrow world within the confines of the
Commonwealth of Pennsylvania." After all those years of
fighting middleweights, I was a middleweight champion
but the title wasn't worth as much as my purse, which came
to slightly more than my $25,000 guarantee.

In my next title fight, my purse would be $1. That's not a
mistake, one dollar.

Several weeks earlier, one of my boyhood buddies had
died of cancer—Spider Valentine, the skinny little guy I had
helped up after I knocked him down in the 1939 Golden
Gloves. I had to do something for Spider. I phoned Walter
Winchell, who was the chairman of the Damon Runyon
Cancer Fund. I offered to donate my purse from a fight to
the fund in memory of Spider.

"You'd really do that, Sugar Ray?" Winchell said.

"Yes, sir," I replied. "My whole purse. But if it'll make
you feel better, you can give me a dollar."

"I always thought you were a tough man with a buck."

"It depends what the buck is for, and I want to do this
for cancer research."

We had a deal, but we didn't have an opponent.

I wanted to defend my welterweight title. None of the
welterweights had filed a challenge with the New York State
Athletic Commission, but I remembered that one day when
I had been training for the Villemain fight, I had two visitors, a Jersey welterweight named Charlie Fusari and his
little manager, Vic Marsillo. I knew Marsillo. He had handled George Costner, the one who thought he was *the*
Sugar, and he had been after me to box Fusari. On a radio
show one night, I heard him say, "Where has Ray Robinson

been hiding lately? Charlie Fusari will fight him anyplace
on any date he names."

The next time I saw Vic, I told George, "Don't let Marsillo get away. Sign him. Give him twenty-five per cent.
Give him thirty per cent."

The day they had visited me, Marsillo had done all the
talking. He had tried to sell me on a bout with Fusari. I
joked with him that day, but when we needed an opponent
for the Cancer Fund fight, I thought of Fusari and contacted
Marsillo. We agreed to put it on at Roosevelt Stadium in
Jersey City, on August 9, 1950, but before the match was
announced, Winchell phoned me.

"Ray," he said, sounding worried, "I've had quite a few
calls from people who tell me that I shouldn't trust you,
that you'll run out on the fight, that I shouldn't pledge the
fund on you. What do they mean by this?"

"Walter," I said, "don't believe those people. Believe *me.*"

Throughout my training, I had difficulty losing weight. I
had been 155 against Villemain. Now I had to get down to
the 147-pound welterweight limit.

At weigh-in, when I stepped on the scale, it registered 147¼.

"You've got two hours," one of the commissioners told
me, "to take off four ounces."

It is not as simple as it sounds. I sat in a steam box for
half an hour, then I had a quick rubdown. When I got on the
scale, only three ounces had disappeared. After another
steam and another rubdown, I was one ounce under the
limit. I've often heard that I really weighed over the limit,
and that Marsillo agreed to overlook it if I wouldn't hurt Fusari. Another version is that Marsillo, who knew all the tough
guys in New Jersey, had warned me that if I knocked out
Fusari, I'd go home in a coffin.

Neither story is true, but I had agreed to carry Fusari.

It was Marsillo's idea. I had no objection. I didn't want

to unload on Fusari because I didn't want to risk another
Jimmy Doyle episode. I had lost my "killer instinct" that
horrible night in Cleveland. Another reason was that I
wanted to put on a good show for the Cancer Fund, to give
everybody their money's worth, fifteen rounds. All of Winchell's pals on Broadway had bought tickets. Even the President, Harry Truman, was represented by his daughter,
Margaret. The 25,000 spectators hadn't come to see a quick
finish. They had to be entertained, so I toyed with Fusari.
He was a nice guy, a blond Italian, and although I knew I
was doing enough to win the rounds he began to think I
wasn't as good as he had feared.

"Turn me loose," he told Marsillo before the fifth round.
"He's not much. I can take him out. Let me open up."

"No, no," Marsillo said, realizing the deal would be off if
Fusari got bold, "if you open up, we may close quick."

Wise advice. In the ring, I could hear Marsillo shouting,
"Keep moving, keep moving," meaning for Fusari to keep
moving away from me. And he did. The trouble was, I had to
chase him in order to earn points. In New Jersey, the referee
is the only official. There are no judges. The referee, Paul
Cavalier, scored thirteen rounds for me, one for Fusari, and
one even. The next day Barney Nagler, writing in the *Bronx
Home News,* described the fight as "the greatest carrying
job since Momma Dionne." Years later, when Teddy Brenner took over as the matchmaker at Madison Square Garden, he once asked me what had been my toughest fight.

"The one with Fusari," I said.

"Fusari!" he howled. "You've got to be kidding. Fusari
never touched you. That had to be the easiest fight you
ever had. How can you say it was your toughest fight?"

"Because," I said, "I had to fight fifteen rounds for me and
fifteen rounds for him."

It was also my proudest fight. More than $100,000 went to the Cancer Fund, nearly $50,000 from my share. The next Sunday night Walter Winchell, in his staccato voice, opened his radio show with "Good evening Mr. and Mrs. North and South America, and all the ships at sea, this is Sugar Ray Winchell. . . ."

It was my last fight as a welterweight. It had been too difficult for me to make 147 pounds.

I had the Pennsylvania middleweight title, and I defended it twice—a first-round knockout over José Basora, a lanky Puerto Rican, and a twelfth-round knockout over Carl (Bobo) Olson, a Hawaiian I would get to know better. During these months, Lew Burston, who imported European fighters, was advising me to go to Europe for a few fights.

Burston had been after me for years, but I had put him off. This time he was persistent.

"You'll have a good time, you'll make good money, and you'll add to your reputation."

"But who would I fight for?" I said. "I don't know any of the promoters over there."

"They know you," he said, "and they'll take good care of you. Charlie Michaelis in Paris. Jack Solomons in London. But let me give you some advice. Don't take it easy on an opponent, like you did with Fusari. Knock him out as quickly as you can. In one round if possible. Let the European boxing fans see you at your best. They won't give you anybody we're interested in bringing over here. There are enough decent fighters to give you all the action you want, and you'll be well paid for belting them out. With your style and your punch, you'll be a hero there to the people and the sportswriters. Mark my words, you'll be a hero."

Despite my record, one defeat in one hundred seventeen fights, I had never really been a hero.

"Maybe I will go at that," I told Lew Burston. "You contact the promoters."

Several days later, I was in Harry Wiley's gym, working on the heavy bag, when the phone rang. George answered it, then he put down the receiver and walked toward me with a big grin on his big face.

"It's for you, Robinson," he said.

"Well, who is it?" I said, annoyed that he should be interrupting me. "Can't you answer it?"

"It's person to person," he said.

"Didn't you ask the operator who was calling me?"

George grinned again. "She just said, 'Paris calling.'"

13

Paris

The huge black hull of the *Liberté* dwarfed the yellow taxis at the entrance to the French Line pier on the Hudson River. Inside in the baggage area my man Chops, one of my detail men whose real name was June Clark, was tying thick red string on the handles of our luggage.

"What's that for?" I asked.

"So we know which bags are ours," he said. "This way it'll be easier to spot them when we disembark."

"How much luggage do we have?"

"With the clothes trunks for you and Edna Mae," he said, "it makes a total of fifty-three pieces. I counted them."

"That's why I need you, Chops."

We were about to sail for France. Charlie Michaelis, the promoter who had called me from Paris, had arranged a series of fights for me. He also had arranged for four round-trip tickets on the *Liberté*, for me and three others. I didn't want to ask him for any more tickets, he had been generous enough, but I had been used to traveling with as many as a dozen people. Years later, Barbra Streisand would sing about "People . . . people who need people." I'm one of those people.

"Four is enough," George had said. "You, Edna Mae, me and Wiley."

"No good," I had told him. "Everybody is going, just as if we were going to Philadelphia."

"Do you know how much money that's going to cost you, Robinson?"

"Money is for spending, George. Money is for having a good time."

On the pier with Edna Mae and me that day were my sister Evelyn, George and Wiley, Honey Brewer, June Clark and Pee Wee Beale, and my barber-valet, Roger Simon. Several others were there to see us off, including Mom and Marie, who were going to take care of little Ray. Scattered around the baggage area were our fifty-three pieces of luggage, each one marked with red string.

"Leave it to June," said Evelyn, "to think of the red string."

June Clark had been with me for a few years. His mother had prayed for a daughter, and when he arrived, he got the name that had been picked out. He grew up to be a hot trumpet player but he came down with tuberculosis and he spent several years in a sanatorium. Eventually, he was released with an arrested case of T.B. Soon after that, I met him and I took to him right away.

"Get rid of him, Robinson," George advised me. "You might catch T.B. from him."

He was worth the risk. He had a way of producing a spiritual feeling within me. Wherever we were, he would be the first one to find the nearest church. It didn't make any difference to me what kind of a church it was. I always believed that God was inside all of them. In addition to that, he was a mother hen when I was in training. He never closed his eyes until I went to sleep. He was with me all the time because he wasn't married. Fred (Pee Wee) Beale was, so he had to check in at home, but Pee Wee was like a secretary. He introduced me to Biblical literature. He introduced me to astrology, not that I believed in it.

"You are a Taurus, you were born under the sign of the bull," he once told me.

"You got it wrong," I said, laughing. "You got me mixed up with Jake LaMotta."

Whenever I made fun of Pee Wee's horoscopes, he'd pout for a few days. He took them very seriously, the way Roger Simon handled my clothes. As soon as Edna Mae and I got into our stateroom on the *Liberté*, he had our clothes unpacked and hung up. On our way up the gangplank we had been conspicuous. It wasn't usual for nine Negroes to be sailing on the *Liberté*, and sailing together.

"The boxer, Sugar Ray Robinson," I overheard one of the stewards say in awe, "and his entourage."

I liked that word *entourage*, a French word meaning attendants. I didn't consider them attendants, I considered them friends, but *entourage* sounded classy. I began using it every so often and so did the others. In the years to come, anyone with me would be considered a member of my entourage.

The voyage was pleasant. The Atlantic was calm. None of us got seasick.

"Monsieur," one of the ship's officers informed me as we neared England, "when we stop at Plymouth, I understand that several newsmen will come aboard to interview and photograph you."

I was expecting maybe half a dozen, but the several turned out to be forty-eight. I know, I counted them.

When we docked at Le Havre, France, more than a hundred reporters and photographers clomped up the gangplank to greet me. After they were through, I rang for our steward.

George shook his head. "Robinson," he said, "the crew left hours ago."

"Hours ago!" I said. "We only docked here an hour or so ago."

"Robinson," he said, "it was five hours ago."

"Monsieur," said Charlie Michaelis, the big bald promoter with the gentle manner who had come down to meet me, "I never saw Paris so excited about the arrival of a sports champion. You may not realize it, but you received a welcome worthy of Charles Lindbergh."

When we arrived in Paris later that day, the manager of the Claridge Hotel made a big fuss.

"Monsieur Rahbeanson," he said, "we save our most beautiful suite for you and your wife."

White furniture, in French provincial. White walls. Velvet-tufted upholstery. And a view overlooking the Champs Élysées. The others in my entourage had adjoining rooms. We had about half a floor to ourselves. Man, it was a long way from Black Bottom.

The next morning George, Wiley, June, and Pee Wee took a walk with me before breakfast. Instead of returning to the hotel to eat, we decided to stop in a small restaurant. We didn't order anything fancy. Omelettes mostly, as I remember. When we were finished, the waitress put the bill on the table. She had figured it in francs, but at the time I had no idea how to figure it.

"How much is that in American money?" I asked her.

After studying the bill for a few seconds, she said, "Forty-five dollars."

"For breakfast! Five people!"

She smiled. "Oui, monsieur."

"Pay it, Robinson," suggested George, "but let's learn the rate of exchange."

I paid it and left a five-dollar tip.

"Merci, monsieur," she gushed.

I learned later that morning how many francs equaled a dollar, but I seldom had to get involved in figuring it out. At the Claridge, our meals went on the bill, and when we weren't eating at the hotel we were the guests of honor at a luncheon or dinner. One of our first nights, we were invited to the show at the Lido, next door to the Claridge.

"You go without me, Ray," Edna Mae said. "I don't feel like a show."

She had been to Europe before we were married, and every so often on this trip she would remind me of her previous visit. That always annoyed me, because I liked to take my girl someplace different for the *first* time, as I was doing for everybody else in my entourage. That night Edna Mae went shopping while I went to the Lido. The nude chorus girls fascinated me. When the show ended, the manager invited us backstage.

"Look at that," I said, nudging George, "look at that chick."

Backstage, the nude chorus girls were swirling past us, on their way to their dressing rooms.

"And look at that one," I said, noticing another. "Man, oh, man."

"Too much temptation here, Robinson," said George. "Let's go."

Another night we cut out for Pigalle. In one of the joints there, we were watching the nudes parade around when a midget appeared at our table. He knew who I was, the way everybody did there. My picture was in the paper every day.

"Monsieur Rahbeanson," he said, "do you speak French?"

"I'm trying," I replied, "but I'm still an amateur."

"Then let me be your interpreter," he said. "I speak both English and French fluently. My name is Jimmy Karoubi."

"You got a deal, Jimmy," I said.

I assumed he meant that he'd interpret for us the rest of the night in his bistro, but when we got up to leave he had his coat on and he went with us. He showed us Paris that night and when we went back to the Claridge, he was still with us.

"I am your interpreter forever," he said, bowing.

Jimmy Karoubi became the tenth member of my entourage. He was with me all the time, not only as an interpreter but as a good-humor man.

"Why do you keep him around?" Edna Mae asked me.

"Because he makes me laugh," I tried to explain.

Not many people ever understood why I liked to have somebody like Jimmy with me. In boxing, everything is so serious—the training, the mental preparation for the fight itself—that a fighter has to be able to relax in his spare moments. Every good fighter needs a good jester to keep him laughing, and Jimmy Karoubi was very important to me in Paris because we were on the move all day every day. There was always an appearance I had to make somewhere. One day the sportswriters had a luncheon for me, and Maurice Chevalier was there, his eyes twinkling. Another time we stopped at a bar owned by Georges Carpentier, the "Orchid Man," who had fought Jack Dempsey in 1921 for the heavyweight title. And when we weren't on the town, our suite was filled with visitors. Every time I turned around a waiter was holding a tray and saying, "Champagne, monsieur."

There was even champagne at the weigh-in with Jean Stock.

"Monsieur Rahbeanson," one of the boxing commissioners announced, "it is a custom in Paris for the contestants to have a glass of champagne after the weigh-in."

Stock wasn't waiting for a glass. He was drinking it out of the bottle.

"Here, monsieur," the commissioner said to me, "let me fill your glass."

I was really on the spot. I didn't want to do anything that might offend anybody, but I had to do something to pass it off. Jimmy Karoubi was at the other end of the room, so I turned to George, whose French was better than mine.

"George," I said, "what do I do? If I drink this champagne, the fight is going to be *now*."

Almost everybody in the room understood English, and they burst out laughing. George explained to the commissioner that I didn't drink. I was off the spot. When they gave the toast, I raised my glass, but that was all.

"Don't waste that stuff, Robinson," whispered George. "Save it for me."

That night, when I arrived at the Palais des Sports, I had another surprise. The doors had opened at six o'clock. Several thousand spectators were in the balcony with bottles of wine, big cheeses, and big loaves of bread.

"Most of them come directly from work in the factories," explained Charlie Michaelis. "They're having their dinner."

When I emerged from my dressing room later on, the Palais des Sports was filled with 17,500 spectators. As I strode toward the ring, they rose and gave me a standing ovation.

"Hey, Robinson," George whispered to me, "you better be good. They are *expecting* you to be."

Jean Stock was a tough middleweight, but I remembered what Lew Burston had told me about finishing off my opponent as quickly as I could. In the second round I put him down twice. When he got up, he was groggy but he came at me again. All around me the people were shouting for me instead of him.

"Finish him, Robinson!" George was yelling.

I hit him with a combination and he went sprawling

again, and from his corner, a towel came flapping into the
ring. The referee never even started to count. He waved his
arms, and all the people were roaring louder than before.

I didn't know what to do, I had never been accorded
such an ovation.

"Take a bow," I heard Wiley say. "You ought to take a bow
for this kind of hand."

And that's what I did. I bowed four times, once to each
side of the ring.

Lew Burston had been correct. I was a hero, for the first
time in my career. For all my success, I had never really been
a hero in the United States where Joe Louis was the boxing
idol. But now, as I bowed and waved, my skin tingled. All
around me the people were on their feet, some of them waving their wine bottles but most of them applauding. But the
sound of their ovation was different from what I was used
to.

"You are an *artiste*, like a musician or a dancer," Charlie
Michaelis had told me, "and you will see, the people will
react to you as an *artiste*."

And that, I realized now, was how their applause
sounded, as it would at Carnegie Hall or at a ballet, and applause with respect in it, and it was wonderful. And as I
moved through the ropes and down the steps of the ring, I
heard some of them yelling, "*Le sucre marveilleux.*"

"What are they saying?" I asked one of the sportswriters.

"They are calling you 'the marvelous Sugar,'" he replied.

In my dressing room, while the sportswriters and the photographers swarmed around me, I recognized a familiar
face, Robert Villemain, the Frenchman whom I had defeated earlier in the year for the Pennsylvania middleweight
title. With him was his manager, Jean Brettonell. Seeing

them, Charlie Michaelis pointed at Villemain and then at me.

"My next big match," he said with a laugh.

He later confessed that he had been joking, but everybody took him so seriously that within five minutes we had set the terms and the date, December 22. He had already arranged two other bouts for me, with Luc Van Dam in Brussels, Belgium, on December 9 and with Jean Walzack in Geneva, Switzerland, on December 16.

"Come to my office tomorrow," Charlie said, "and you can sign the contract for the Villemain bout and the other two."

"I don't need a contract with you, Charlie," I said. "Your word is good enough for me. I'm sure you won't cheat me."

I had absolute faith in him. His gentlemanly manner had impressed me. He wasn't like Jim Norris or Mike Jacobs or any of the other American promoters I had come to distrust. Charlie Michaelis didn't try to con me, didn't make any wild promises. His matchmaker, Gilbert Benaim, was the same way. I believed in both of them.

In dozens of fights for them over the years, I never had a contract, and I never needed one.

I got by Van Dam and Walzack without much trouble. I remember knocking out Van Dam in the fourth round. As he lay sprawled on the canvas, his wife jumped out of her seat behind his corner and angrily shouted, "Get up, get up," as if she were waking him up in the morning. But he couldn't quite get up soon enough. Walzack was tougher. I had to go ten rounds with him. Afterward he had lumps all over his head, but I couldn't knock him out. By that time, there were only six days to the Villemain fight, perhaps the biggest boxing attraction in the history of France.

The day the match had been announced, the owner of a men's clothing store marched into Charlie Michaelis's office.

"Monsieur," the visitor said, "I want to buy half the tickets in the Palais des Sports for the Robinson-Villemain match. You gentlemen do not understand what it is to properly promote a boxing match. I will do it for you."

"You want half of *all* our tickets?" Charlie said.

"Exactly," he said. "I will sell them in my store, all nine thousand of them."

"They'll cost you fifteen million francs."

"I'm aware of that. I have my check."

While the visitor wrote out a check, Charlie phoned the Palais des Sports' lawyer to make sure it was legal for him to sell 9000 seats to one person. It was. The tickets were delivered to the man's store the next day. When the other 9000 tickets were put on sale at the Palais des Sports, they were bought up in less than two days. To the public, all the tickets appeared to be gone. The next morning, hundreds of people descended on the men's clothing store. The aisles were in turmoil. Outside, the weight of the crowd threatened to smash the plate-glass windows. The owner in great anxiety made two phone calls—the first to the police for protection, the second to Charlie Michaelis.

"Will you take your tickets back?" he asked.

"What's wrong?" said Charlie, not knowing the situation. "Aren't they selling?"

"They're wrecking my store," he moaned.

The next day, the tickets were put on sale at the Palais des Sports and within a couple of days they were gone. When Villemain and I entered the ring, the sellout crowd had set a gate record for the Palais des Sports of 30 million francs, the equivalent then of about $85,000. Villemain weighed 164, four pounds over the middleweight limit, so my Pennsylvania title wasn't in jeopardy. I tried to take him out early, and almost succeeded, but he hung on until the ninth round.

I put him across the ropes with a left hook and when he got up he was so dazed he couldn't defend himself. I pounced on him, hoping to finish him off quickly, but he stayed up for more than a minute until I caught him with another left hook. He sprawled on the canvas, but scrambled to his feet. This time the referee stopped it.

All around me, the spectators were shouting louder than when I had knocked out Jean Stock.

"You are a legend here," Charlie Michaelis told me later. "In a month, you are Mr. Boxing."

I had my fifth fight three days later, on Christmas, in Frankfurt, Germany. Our hotel, the Frankfurter Hof, was surrounded by the rubble of buildings that had been bombed during World War II. In the hours before the fight, a dozen German children stood under my window and sang Christmas carols. That night, I took out Hans Stretz in five. In a span of twenty-nine days, I had won five bouts, four by a knockout. I had pocketed nearly $50,000, and I needed every penny. My entourage had run up a big bill at the Claridge, and Edna Mae had been shopping. Her tab at Schiaparelli's and Jacques Fath's was very big.

Meanwhile, two important developments had occurred in New York.

First, the IBC surrendered to public opinion and agreed to give me a shot at Jake LaMotta's middleweight title, without my having to sign an exclusive contract. And second, the Boxing Writers' Association had voted me the Edward J. Neil Memorial Plaque for having "done the most for the sport during the year." My contribution to the Damon Runyon Cancer Fund in the Fusari fight had been a major factor in the ballot. In his story in The New York Times, Joe Nichols referred to it as my "grand gesture." About fifty grand.

Over in Paris, both developments added to my popularity.

The day we boarded the *Liberté* in Le Havre for our return voyage, Charlie Michaelis saw us off.

"And when you take the title from LaMotta," he said, "return to see Paris in the spring."

"We'll be back," June Clark assured him. "I'm keeping the red strings on all the bags."

14

Mister Gray

In my best tuxedo, I was sitting on the dais at the Boxing Writers' Dinner in the Waldorf-Astoria, waiting to recite my acceptance speech for the Neil award, when Jim Dawson of *The New York Times*, the toastmaster, began to read several telegrams from people who had been unable to attend.

"Here's one Ray will really appreciate," Dawson said. "It reads: 'SEE YOU FEBRUARY 14 IN CHICAGO. MAKE SURE YOU'RE THERE.' It's signed JAKE."

My title bout with Jake LaMotta, the Bronx Bull, had been scheduled—with our long romance in mind—for Saint Valentine's Day, but several days later, I discovered that Jake wasn't the only one interested in my participation. For a change, I was training in Pompton Lakes, New Jersey, where we lived in an old white wooden house. We were sitting around late one Sunday afternoon when the phone rang. I normally let George or Wiley or June or Pee Wee answer the phone in order to intercept the pests. But they were playing cards, and rather than bother them I picked up the receiver.

"Hello," I said, disguising my voice.

"Is Ray there?" asked a strange voice.

"Who wants him?" I said, not letting on it was me.

"Mister Gray."

Around boxing, Mister Gray was a name that Frankie
Carbo used as an alias. He had gray hair and he had a gray
reputation as one of the mob guys who organized many of
the IBC matches. I had never had anything to do with him,
but I had seen him around and I had no reason not to talk
to him.

"Yeah," I said now in my normal voice, making believe
somebody else had answered the phone, "this is Robinson."

"Ray," he said, "Mister Gray wants to see you down by
the gate. I'll be there in about five minutes. You be alone."

Near the road in front of our house was a big wooden
gate, but before I could reply, the line went dead. When the
man known as Mr. Gray wanted to see somebody, it was a
command performance. Or at least he thought it should be.

I knew about his reputation, but at the time I didn't know
how really bad it was. When the Kefauver Committee investi-
gated boxing in 1960, Paul John Carbo's police record
showed twenty-two arrests—seventeen for such offenses as
grand larceny, felonious assault, vagrancy, suspicious character, and violation of New York boxing laws, and five for
murder. Three of the murders involved gangsters, one involved a Philadelphia beer baron, the other a taxicab
driver.

Carbo was a familiar figure around boxing. He often
ordered Jim Norris and Truman Gibson of the IBC to use
certain fighters. Carbo was the underworld czar of boxing.

Carbo's phone call had surprised me. He often had
greeted me with "Hiya, Champ," in the aisles of the Garden,
but that had been the extent of our association. Not knowing what he wanted, I was willing to grant him the courtesy
of seeing him. What the hell, he always had been courteous
to me. Slipping out of the house while the other guys continued their card game, I strolled down to the gate near the
road. Moments later, a big black Buick sedan slowed to a

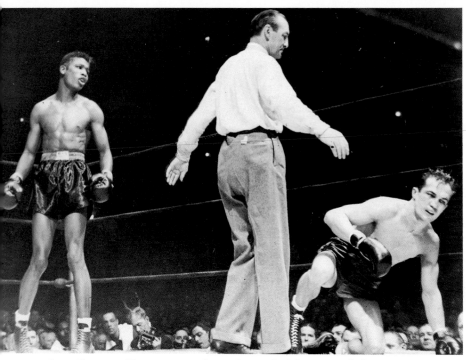

Sugar Ray stops Fritzie Zivic in the tenth round of their non-title bout, New York, 1942.

A right to the kidneys saw Kid Gavilan on his way during their world welterweight title fight in 1949.

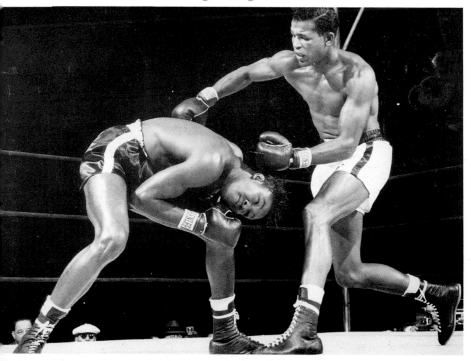

Preparing for his fight with Randolph Turpin at Earl's Court on 10 July 1951. *(Popperfoto)*

A clinch in the closing stages of the fight, which saw Turpin bring the world middleweight championship back to Britain. (*Popperfoto*)

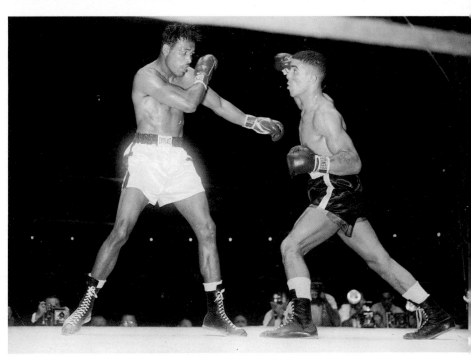

Turpin's 64-day reign as world champion ended in New York when Sugar Ray defeated him with a TKO in the tenth round. (*Popperfoto*)

Between 1942 and 1951 Sugar Ray fought the Bronx Bull, Jake LaMotta, six times, taking the world middleweight title from him on 14 February 1951. (*Associated Press*)

Sugar Ray and Joey Maxim *(right)* sign the contracts for their fight to take place in June 1952. *(Popperfoto)*

With his long-standing friend, Joe Louis.

The 41-year-old champion was outpointed by Terry Downes at Wembley in September 1962. (*Popperfoto*)

With Edna Mae and 13-year-old Ray junior. (*Popperfoto*)

In the best of spirits: Sugar Ray dances in the London rain in September 1962, and greets his wife to be, Millie, in Geneva in October. (*Popperfoto*)

Offering British boxer Billy Walker a little helpful advice. (*Popperfoto*)

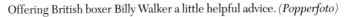

Sugar Ray and Fabio Bettini in Rome, 28 November 1964. *(Popperfoto)*

Acknowledging the cheers of his fans after outpointing Yolande Leveque, Paris, 1964. *(Popperfoto)*

A farewell salute from four boxers who gave Sugar Ray some of the toughest fights of his career on his retirement on 10 December 1965 in New York at the age of 45. *From left:* Randolph Turpin, Gene Fullmer, Sugar Ray, Carmen Basilio and Carl 'Bobo' Olson. *(Popperfoto)*

stop. Into the chill of the winter evening stepped Frankie Carbo, his hundred-dollar black shoes gleaming, a knife pleat in his black pants, the collar of his black cashmere overcoat up near the gray hair, and his black eyes shining from under his gray fedora.

"Ray," he said, "I represent the Bull."

"Yeah," I said, realizing that he was referring to LaMotta.

"I got a deal for us."

"What kind of deal?"

"I want you and the Bull to have three title fights. You'll win the first. He wins the second. The third is on the level."

"You mean I take a dive in the second?"

"Either that or you don't put out," he said. "Just so the Bull wins. He'll let you have the first one. In the third, you're both on your own, on the up-and-up. The best man wins that one."

"You got the wrong guy," I said.

"Three fights is a lot of money."

"You give the Bull a message," I snapped. "You tell the Bull to keep his hands up and his ass off the floor. You tell him to be sure to do that when the bell rings."

Without waiting for him to answer, I spun and headed back to the house.

Halfway there, I heard one of his car doors slam. The wheels skidded on the snow as the Buick pulled away. I must have made myself clear because I never heard from him again before the LaMotta fight and he never approached me after that. Not many guys turned him down, so maybe he respected me for it. The last time I saw him was in 1966. I was working a night club in Atlanta. One afternoon I did a special show at the Federal penitentiary there.

"Hiya, Champ," a voice called.

"Mister Gray," I said, smiling.

He had been convicted in 1961 of conspiracy and extortion concerning a world welterweight champion, Don Jordan, who was not involved. Sentenced to twenty-five years in prison and fined $10,000, Carbo had begun his stretch at Alcatraz, but now he was in Atlanta. In his prison suit, he was really Mr. Gray. After my show, I chatted with him for a few minutes and when I was about to leave, he said, "Say hello to the Bull for me."

At the time, LaMotta was the only man to hold a victory over me, the ten-round decision in Detroit when I was about to go into the Army in 1943. I had fought him four other times and got the decision each time, even though he dropped me twice. I had never knocked him down, but neither had anybody else. Not even when he dumped that Garden main event in 1947 with Billy Fox. That night Carbo was believed to have collected $35,000 in bets, but Jake refused to be knocked down. He pretended to be defenseless against Fox and the referee stopped it in the fourth round, but he was on his feet.

"I never been off my feet," he liked to brag, "and I never will be."

When he won the title, he had been presented a championship belt by *The Ring* magazine—a red-white-and-blue-ribboned belt about six inches wide with a big gold-plated buckle.

"He likes it so much," his wife Vicki complained, "that he wears it to bed."

He wasn't wearing it to bed in Chicago. He was training hard, I was told. Shortly after I arrived there, we were at a contract-signing luncheon and, for one of the few times in my career, I tried to psych an opponent. I wanted to create a doubt in his mind that he wasn't training as hard as I was, and as we sat near each other on the dais of the luncheon, munching on roast beef, I called over a waiter.

"Would you ask the chef," I said, "if I could have a big glass of beef blood?"

Jake glanced over to me, puzzled, and the waiter appeared a little puzzled, too.

"You mean the gravy, sir?" he said. "I'll get you some extra gravy right away."

"No, not the gravy," I said. "The actual blood, the blood in the meat before it's cooked."

"You're crazy, Robinson," Jake said.

"I drink it all the time," I said. "Jack Blackburn told me about it years ago when I used to train with Joe Louis. It's my secret weapon, Jake. It's what makes such a skinny guy like me so strong."

"You're outta your mind," Jake said.

"You'll see," I said, glancing at the waiter. "As soon as he brings it, I'll let you have some."

"Not me," he snorted. "I don't want that stuff."

Moments later, the waiter returned with a tall glass of beef blood. Jake thought I had been joking, but I actually had been drinking beef blood regularly for more than ten years and I still drink it today. It's one of the most nutritious things you can put in your system, and that day in Chicago I sprinkled it with salt and pepper and offered some to Jake.

"Keep it," he said.

"All right," I said, raising the glass with a flourish, "when I'm still dancing in the last round and you're dragging, you'll know why."

And I gulped it down.

Our last previous fight had been six years earlier, in 1945. He was the champion now, and that always makes a man a better fighter psychologically, but there was no way for Jake LaMotta to change his style.

"He's still the Bull," George kept reminding me, "and you're still the matador."

My only concern was LaMotta getting the decision if the fight went fifteen rounds. His man Carbo had a way of influencing a decision, so I knew I had to stop him to be safe. George knew it and so did Wiley and they were worried, but I wasn't. I knew I was ready, and as George taped my hands in the dressing room in the cellar of the Chicago Stadium, I was so relaxed I was almost falling asleep.

"You all right, Robinson?" George said.

"You look *too* cool," Wiley said. "Anything the matter with you?"

"No man should be this cool," George said.

I had to laugh. It was the most important fight of my career at that point, going for the middleweight title, but damn, I *knew* I was prepared for this one. I felt that I was going to be on time in the ring. I knew that it was all going to come together and I felt that I was going to be the new middleweight champion, and I was laughing when I turned to George and Wiley.

"I did my work," I said. "I don't feel I have anything to be worried about with Jake."

It's a marvelous feeling. You only get it a few times in your career, that absolute confidence in winning, but I had it that night. Upstairs in the ring, when the bell rang, I never felt better. One look at Jake shuffling at me and I knew that Carbo had delivered my message. Jake had his hands up and, looking at his face, I knew he was determined to keep his ass off the floor. He had his lumpy round head against his chest and he was rushing me as if I was waving a red cape at him. He never had been fast, but he was slower than he had been six years earlier. That made him an easier target. By the tenth round, my jab had puffed his fat face and I had hit him with quite a few body shots. His punches had lost their zing, but he stood there, wobbling a little, and defied me to put him down.

"You can't do it, you black bastard," he was growling, "you can't put me on the deck."

Near the end of the thirteenth round, I was battering him when the referee, Frank Sikora, stepped in and waved his arms.

In his story in *The New York Times* the next day, Jim Dawson wrote that LaMotta had been "in a state of utter helplessness in a struggle that developed into a slaughter," but Jake would never have agreed. As the referee led him away, he continued to protest. When he realized the fight had been stopped, he peered through his puffed eyes at me and his bloody lips parted in a sneer.

I knew what he was thinking, *You didn't put me on the deck, Robinson. You got my title, but you didn't put me on the deck.*

I was the middleweight champion, but I had to share my joy with my respect for Jake. I couldn't take my eyes off him. He was on the stool in his corner, his leopard-skin robe thrown over him. His handlers were all around him, but he was snarling at them and waving them away. The doctor was checking him, but Jake wanted no part of him. On his way out of the ring, he ignored the hands reaching up to help him down the steps. In his dressing room, I was told later, he had to gasp for breath as he spoke to the sportswriters.

"That's all, that's all," the doctor ordered. "Get a tank of oxygen in here."

The doctor gave him oxygen for half an hour. He wasn't able to leave the stadium until nearly two hours after the fight. But despite all that, it never occurred to him that the doctor had made the proper decision in signaling the referee to stop the fight.

"Robinson never hurt me," he was quoted as saying a few weeks later. "I almost knocked Robinson out in the eleventh."

Jake LaMotta hadn't lost. Something had happened to keep him from winning. Jake LaMotta was a gladiator, too, when he wanted to be. Soon after that Charlie Michaelis phoned me about returning to Paris. I told him that my entourage would be even larger this time.

"My golf pro will be coming," I said, "and this time I'm going to bring a couple of sparring partners with me. George's wife, Hazel, will be coming, too. Can you line up a few fights beginning the end of May?"

"On one condition," he said, laughing.

"What's that," I said, surprised.

"That you bring your pink Cadillac with you."

"On the boat?"

"Of course," he said. "I will pay the shipping charge."

15

The Grand Tour

The first morning at the Claridge, I was having poached eggs in my room when the phone rang.

"Monsieur Rahbeanson," the man at the front desk said, "please come downstairs immediately. The police are here to talk to you."

"The police?"

"Oui, monsieur. Your car has created a traffic jam in front of the hotel."

"I'll be right down," I said.

Through the window, I could hear the blare of police whistles. Glancing out, I noticed a clog of cars on the Champs Élysées. In their capes and round hats, the Paris policemen were waving people to keep moving, but without much success. Some people were getting out of their cars and walking over to stare at my car, along with several dozen pedestrians who surrounded it. By the time I got downstairs, one of the policemen was in the lobby waiting for me.

"Monsieur," he said to me, "your automobile is an exquisite color, but do not park it on the Champs Élysées, merci."

"The people will get used to it," I said. "It was like this in New York before the people got used to seeing it."

Actually, there had never been this much commotion in

New York, but I was trying to soothe him, and I honestly believed that the people in Paris would ignore my car after a day or two. But they didn't. Whenever it was parked outside the Claridge, it created a traffic jam. The policemen pleaded with me to keep it in the garage, but I hadn't brought it across the Atlantic to hide it. After all, I had my reputation as an *artiste* to maintain, and that car was the symbol of my reputation.

I loved to drive it around Paris with the top down and the radio on loud, and me wearing a beret.

One day we were riding near the Eiffel Tower when a policeman whistled and waved for me to stop.

"Oh, Monsieur Rahbeanson," he said, realizing it was me, "I'm sorry, but you have no license plate."

He meant French license plates. I explained that I had been busy and hadn't had time to get them.

"Oui," he said, "and you will not be here too long, eh? About a month? For that you won't need them."

He was the only policeman to notice that I didn't have license plates. The others must have been staring at the color, and wherever I went, if there was a policeman around, he escorted me. I was more of a hero this time than during my previous visit because of my victory over Jake LaMotta. To the French, he was a villain. He not only had dethroned their idol, Marcel Cerdan, but if he hadn't postponed their return bout, Cerdan wouldn't have been on the plane that crashed.

"Don't you see," Charlie Michaelis told me, "now that you have dethroned LaMotta, you have avenged Cerdan's death."

Being a hero in France had its surprises. At a night club once, I was in the men's room, standing at a urinal, when I noticed a middle-aged woman stroll through the door.

"Your autograph, monsieur," she said.

I was in no position to sign her menu.

"At your convenience," she suggested.

I must have autographed thousands of menus in the night clubs. I never ordered any food in any of them because I never would have had an opportunity to eat it. I was on the go every night. One time I remember I wore a white tie and tails to a benefit for retired comedians at the Palais de Chaillot. We raised three million francs. Another time I was at some club and Martine Carol, the blonde French actress, was there.

"Dance with her," the photographers pleaded.

"If she wants to," I said. "You go ask her."

They did, and she did, and the picture made all the Paris papers the next day. I was the biggest celebrity in Paris. Every time I walked out of the hotel, it was like leading a parade. People swarmed around me and trotted behind me, and when I got into my car, some of them even hopped on bicycles and rode behind my car. My little man, Jimmy Karoubi, had moved in the moment I arrived and he went everywhere with me. And over my shoulder, George was trying to be my watchdog, especially when I was stuffing myself with French bread.

"You can't fight with all that bread in you, Robinson," he kept saying. "That bread's too doughy."

It wasn't too doughy, it was too good. I had never been much of a bread eater, but French bread was something else. I liked it with grape jelly on it, and I'd eat almost a loaf of it at every meal, something I never did at home.

I was there for a good time, and also as an ambassador for the Damon Runyon Cancer Fund.

I had several checks, each for $10,000, to donate to cancer committees in various nations throughout Europe. In Paris I was to make my presentation to Mme. Vincent Auriol, the wife of the president of France. The day of the ceremony I put on my flamingo tie, Lou Viscusi's tie to match my car, and a soft gray suit. When we drove away from the Claridge, George looked at me.

"Robinson," he said, "do you know where to go?"

"No," I replied, "I thought you knew all that."

After going back to find out our destination and creating another traffic jam near the Arc de Triomphe, we got to the Latin America House late. Half an hour late. When we strolled into the fancy salon, gilded in gold and silver, about fifty people were waiting for us—elegantly dressed women in diamonds and furs, dignified white-haired men in black suits. None of them was smiling. To make things worse, when I reached into my pocket for the $10,000 check, it wasn't there. While I waited for George to get it from Pee Wee, I stalled for a time with a speech, in French.

Maybe that was what saved me. I stumbled through the syntax, but at least the guests realized that I was trying to speak their language, and they started smiling.

After my speech, Justin Godart, the president of the cancer campaign in France, made his speech. I didn't understand it, but every so often I heard him mention my name and when he finished, all the people applauded and as I presented the check to Mme. Auriol, I forgot myself and lapsed into English.

"Now," I said with a wink, "I get to kiss Mrs. President."

And I did, on each cheek, while she laughed and blushed.

"Encore, encore," the photographers pleaded, "encore."

Mme. Auriol, a wonderful lady, smiled as I kissed her again.

About a week later she was at ringside when I fought Kid Marcel, the welterweight champion of France, for the benefit of the cancer campaign. I finished him off in five rounds. That same week I outpointed Jean Wanes in Zurich, Switzerland.

Shortly after we returned to Paris, we had a visitor, Jack Solomons, the London boxing promoter.

"You handle this guy," I told George. "Don't accept anything less than a hundred thousand for a fight with Turpin."

Randy Turpin, the son of a British Guianan soldier and an Englishwoman, was the European middleweight champion. Solomons wanted to match us for the world title in London in early July, but when George mentioned my figure of $100,000, Solomons walked out.

"We don't need him," I said. "There's plenty of other guys to fight, and I won't have to risk the title."

"Yeah," George agreed, "I just had a call from somebody who wants us to fight in Turin, Italy, next month. He's over at the Lancaster Hotel, and he asked me to come over to see him anytime this afternoon."

"What's his name?"

"His last name's Agnelli, he's from Turin."

"A promoter there?"

"I don't know," George said, "I don't know who he is, I never heard of him."

"Is he a phony?"

"I'll find that out, Robinson, with my first question."

About an hour later, George returned.

"You won't believe this, Robinson," he said. "I went in to see this man Agnelli and he's in a beautiful suite, but he's dressed like a bum, a sweater and slacks, a shirt with no tie. I figured I'd test him right away, so I tell him, 'Mister Robinson has to have a twenty-thousand-dollar guarantee to go to Turin, and not only that, he has to have it in American money the day before the fight.' Agnelli shrugged and said, 'That's no problem, I'll go to the American consulate here and have my check authorized. Wait here. Have a drink.'

"In a few minutes, Robinson, he's back with the certified

check for twenty thousand, but I had to test him again. 'Mister Robinson,' I said, 'has to have additional money for expenses—the train fare for all the people with him, their hotel rooms and meals while they're in Turin.'

"He was a little annoyed at that. 'Of course, Mister Gainford,' he said, 'I had assumed that. The railway tickets, Paris to Turin round trip, will be delivered to you tomorrow at the Claridge if you will tell me how many you will need. When you arrive in Turin, check in at the Principi di Piemonte Hotel. Your rooms will be waiting, your meals will be provided.' "

"George," I said, "who is this guy?"

"You know the little Fiat cars, Robinson?" he said. "This man Agnelli owns the plant in Turin where they're made. He's the Henry Ford of the Fiat cars."

"And who do I fight?" I asked.

"He said for us to work that out with Charlie Michaelis. Any decent opponent. The date is July first."

"It's too good to be true," I said.

My grand tour of Europe was now complete. I had four bouts scheduled within twenty-two days—June 10 in Antwerp, June 16 in Liège, June 24 in Berlin, and July 1 in Turin. The next day, Jack Solomons surprised me. He had returned from London to resume negotiations for a title match with Randy Turpin. He and George were in the room adjacent to my suite.

"You got me beat," I overheard Solomons tell him. "I'll give you the hundred thousand dollars you asked for."

"But the date you mentioned before, July tenth," said George, "we're going to have trouble making that date because we've got a fight July first in Turin."

"It has to be that date," Solomons said.

"Never mind the date," I said, bursting into the room.

"I'll fight Turpin and everybody in England for a hundred thousand."

"That's five fights in thirty-one days," George mentioned.

"The first four will keep me sharp," I said. "You always told me, George, to keep the feel of the ring."

"You really want it," George said.

"I really want it," I said, shaking hands with Jack Solomons.

"July tenth, perfect," Solomons said.

As soon as Solomons departed, George warned me that Turpin would be a tough opponent.

"I'll be ready, don't worry," I said.

"You better be ready, Robinson. And if you're going to be ready, you better start going to the gym instead of to all these receptions."

"The fights will keep me ready."

"None of these fights are going to be fifteen rounds," he said. "Turpin won't be easy to knock out. You may have to go fifteen rounds with him. And they better be fifteen good rounds, because it's in his country and that means they'll be his officials."

"Don't worry, George. I can go fifteen rounds in my sleep."

"That's what I'm afraid of, Robinson. That's exactly what I'm afraid of."

"C'mon, get dressed. We got to go to the club."

I had been invited to speak at a club of American businessmen in Paris. The last previous American dignitary to speak there had been Dwight D. Eisenhower, shortly after the end of World War II.

"What am I going to tell these guys?" I said to George as I weaved my car through traffic.

"Tell them about your life, Robinson," he suggested. "About Detroit and Georgia and Harlem."

I spoke for nearly an hour. When I finished, they gave me a standing ovation. On my way out, one of the club members approached me.

"Mistuh Robinson," he said, with a 'Bama drawl.

"Yes, sir," I replied, put on guard by his accent.

"Mistuh Robinson," he said, "I'm from Alabama, Birmingham, Alabama, and I must tell you that when you were invited here, I resented the idea. But having heard you speak, suh, let me say that I'm proud we're both Americans."

"Well, thank you," I said.

"Thank you, suh," he said.

When we were in the car, George said, "That man from Birmingham, his words went through me, Robinson. I hope you make as good an impression on Turpin as you did on that man."

Several days later, we took the train to Antwerp for a bout with Jan de Bruin.

In the eighth round, I was pounding him with my combinations and he was grunting and groaning. Suddenly, he grabbed my right arm and raised it as he turned to the crowd.

"The winner!" he yelled.

Turning to me, he said, "You are too good for me." He dropped my arm and walked to his corner. He had surrendered. Nobody had ever done that with me before, nor would anybody ever do it again.

Six days later, in Liège, Belgium, I boxed one of my opponents on the previous trip, Jean Walzack. He went in six.

Eight days later, I was in West Berlin for another nontitle bout with Gerhard Hecht at Walbuehne Stadium. In the open-air Sunday afternoon crowd of about 25,000 were a few thousand United States servicemen, but the German spectators out-cheered them in welcoming me into the ring. I was the first world champion to appear in a Berlin ring in twenty-five years. Over in the other corner Hecht was having his robe removed.

"Hey, Robinson," said George, always alert, "he's got a plaster print on his right side. Maybe he's sore there."

Midway through the first round, I aimed a left hook at his right ribs but he spun toward me and it landed near his kidney area. Writhing in agony, he collapsed.

". . . eight . . . nine . . . ten."

The referee, Otto Nispel, had counted him out, but in Hecht's corner his manager was up on the apron, pointing to his kidney area and shouting at Nispel.

"Wait," the referee said, turning to me, "you will have to fight again."

"What are you talking about?" I flared. "You just counted him out. I won."

"Yes, I know," he said, his voice trembling, "but I've got to live here."

All around us, the people were on their feet, shaking their fists at me and shouting angrily. Hecht's agony and the motions of his manager had convinced them that I had thrown a kidney punch. Hecht's handlers propped him on his stool and worked on him.

At the bell for the second round, Hecht wobbled toward me. I hit him a few punches and he went down, writhing again and his face contorted with pain.

"The end," the referee said, pointing to me. "The end."

Suddenly, from out of the upper tier, a bottle soared into the ring. And another, and another. All around us now, the people were whistling, the European version of booing. Over the public-address system a voice was saying that Hecht was the winner on a disqualification. Several more bottles bounced off the canvas, but I didn't wait to count them. George had his arms around me, and he was leading me down the steps from the ring.

"Under the ring, Robinson," he said. "Hurry under the ring."

Although the ring was elevated, it afforded protection from the bottles being hurled toward it. Several of the sportswriters at ringside also had crouched under there, but the people in the first few rows had rushed away from the ring.

"Police!" George yelled. "Get the police in here and get us out."

Instead, the United States soldiers escorted us to the safety of my dressing room. Edna Mae was there, weeping hysterically with a welt on her leg. One of the Germans, realizing that she was my wife, had kicked her.

In the confusion, I hadn't realized the impact of the decision.

"You know, Robinson, you lost," George said. "It goes on your record as a loss."

A loss—the second of my career. When the sportswriters arrived, both George and I complained about the situation. I told them what the referee had said in the ring about having "to live here" and that night, the West Berlin Boxing Commission, after a six-hour meeting, announced that the bout had been ruled "no contest," meaning neither Hecht nor I had won or lost. I hadn't waited for that decision. We got on a military train for Frankfurt as quickly as we could. I vowed never to return to Germany.

Later that week, we arrived in Turin, on the edge of the Italian Alps. In the lobby of the Principi de Piemonte Hotel, the manager had our room keys waiting. Everything had been arranged, as Mister Agnelli had promised, but George wanted to check the details.

"Our rooms and our meals will be paid for by Mister Agnelli, right?" George said.

"That is correct, sir. Signor Agnelli has given explicit instructions regarding that."

"The only things we have to pay for are liquor and telephone calls, right?"

"Yes, sir, Signor Agnelli has made that very clear to us. There will be no problem, sir."

"Do you know Mister Agnelli personally?" George asked.

"Yes, sir," the manager replied, "he owns this hotel."

Our stay was delightful. So was the fight. My opponent was Cyril Delannoit. He didn't last the third round. It was the easiest $20,000 I had ever earned, but it was worth it to Agnelli. I had attracted a crowd of almost 25,000 people.

"Thank you so much for coming," he told me after the fight. "It was my pleasure to have a world champion in Turin."

It was Sunday evening. The title bout with Randy Turpin would be held a week from Tuesday. By the time we returned to Paris and went on to London, I would have less than a week to prepare for Turpin, but I was concerned about something else.

"How can I get my car to London?" I asked George.

"That car!" he shouted. "That's all I ever hear—that car. Stop worrying about that car, Robinson, and start worrying about Randy Turpin."

16

Randy Turpin

When we arrived at the Savoy Hotel in London, several dozen people were clustered around the fancy entrance.

"All ryte, all ryte," one of the English bobbies was telling them, "make way 'ere for Mista Rahbinson."

Inside, the red-carpeted lobby was crowded with sportswriters and photographers. The manager was concerned.

"I don't know what we're going to do, sir," he said to me, his mustache twitching. "We've never had this kind of a scene before at this hotel. We have a very nice reputation here, sir, and all these people appear to be on the edge of getting out of hand."

"Everything will be all right," said George, "if you keep Robinson's room number a secret."

The manager agreed. Edna Mae and I were ushered into a fancy suite, with the old Victorian decor. But instead of quieting the curiosity seekers, our disappearance inspired them. Outside on the street, several of them were staring up at the windows, trying to spot ours. Other people were running through the halls, knocking on doors and hoping I'd answer.

The manager was frantic now. His hotel had been invaded by stampeding spectators.

"Mister Robinson," he told me, "I'm very sorry, sir, but

it is not practical for you to stay here. We will gladly maintain your friends, but you, sir, will have to move to other quarters. I am terribly sorry, but I'm sure you understand that the decorum of the hotel is at stake."

"I understand," I said, "but can you suggest another hotel where I might stay?"

"I doubt if any of the other major hotels would tolerate the same situation," he said. "I suggest that you check with Mr. Solomons. He may be aware of available quarters."

"I'll find something, Robinson," offered George. "Be packed and ready to move. I'll be back as soon as I can."

An hour later, George returned. He had a sheepish look on his big face, but he was trying to appear pleased. From experience, I knew something was wrong.

"I got us a place," he said. "Away from everything, away from everybody. You'll get your rest there, Robinson."

"What's the name of it?"

"It's like a private home," he said.

"Where is it?"

"I don't know the exact address."

"Is it far from here?"

"We got to take a cab anyway, Robinson. We got to travel incognito."

"Stop talking in circles, George."

"You'll only be there a few days."

As we got into the cab outside the Savoy's delivery entrance, George whispered something to the driver. He took us along old cobblestone streets and stopped in front of a pub, the Star and Garter.

"Here we are, Robinson," said George.

"Here?" I snapped. "I'm living *here?*"

"Upstairs," he said. "We got a nice little room on the second floor."

"Not me," I said. "Not in this dump."

"Robinson," he said, "you have become such a famous man that now you're too famous. You disrupt the decorum of the leading hotels and you have to return to the small world. There is no pink marble here, no Victorian architecture. For the next few days, you'll have to be satisfied with what you can get and, Robinson, 'this dump' is all you can get."

"You couldn't find anything else?" I said.

"Only two benches overlooking the Thames."

Inside, it was even worse. The stairway creaked. The door handle was loose. There were plaster cracks in the walls. The two beds were like cots. And above us, a bare bulb stared from the ceiling, its pull-string brushing our heads like a spider web.

"For a week, Robinson," said George. "You can stand it for a week."

"At least it's quiet," I said, trying to think of something positive.

"You'll get your rest," he said. "You'll need your rest for Turpin."

At the moment, the pub downstairs was quiet. But later that night, it was swinging. And the jukebox was blaring. And the customers were yelling and pounding their glasses on the bar. It was like that every night. I never got to sleep until long after midnight.

By the day of the fight, I was exhausted. The weigh-in was at Jack Solomons' office in Picadilly Circus.

Right there, Turpin impressed me. His torso was like an oak tree. If he could box even a little bit, I was going to be in trouble. He weighed a solid 158¾, while I was 154½. Afterward, I was scheduled to have my pre-fight meal, a steak, at a good restaurant a couple of blocks away. But outside, the streets were filled with people.

"You can't walk through that mob," George said. "You need an escort."

Patrolling the street were several mounted policemen. In the confusion of the crowd, the horses were snorting and yanking their heads, but the bobbies knew how to handle them. The captain of the detail was in Solomons' office and George drew him aside.

"It's all set, Mr. Robinson," the captain said. "You walk between our horses to the restaurant."

Reining their horses into two lines about ten feet apart, the bobbies waited for me to get between them. Beyond, the people moved back, making way for the horses clomping along the pavement. Protected by the horses, I walked untouched to the restaurant.

That night I should have had some of those horses between me and Turpin.

Surrounding the ring at Earl's Court was a capacity crowd of 18,000 who had paid about £80,000, then the equivalent of $224,000, a British record. During my introduction I was cheered, out of admiration, but the cheer for Turpin evolved from emotion. Quite naturally, they were rooting for Turpin. He gave them plenty to root for. He had a ruffian style developed as a cook in the British Navy. From the first round, he was all over me, and I couldn't get off.

In the seventh round, we were in a clinch when his forehead smacked against my left eyebrow.

Moments later, I could feel the blood matting the eyebrow and oozing into my left eye. I could tell it was a bad one, not only from the feel but also from the way Turpin was staring at it and aiming his right hand for it. He was trying to open it more. If he succeeded, the referee, Eugene Henderson, might have to stop the fight, but I kept him away with a few stiff jabs.

After the round, George and Wiley worked on the cut in the corner.

"It's bad, Robinson," George said. "Don't let him butt you again."

It wasn't that easy. Turpin was out-punching me. In the clinches, he was jerking his head at me. He was doing well, and I wasn't. At the bell ending the fifteenth round, I knew I was about to lose my title. The referee has the only vote in England and Henderson cast it for Turpin. I wasn't surprised, and I had excuses—that jukebox, for one—but I wasn't going to use them. When the BBC announcer got us together in the ring, I was diplomatic.

"You were real good," I told Turpin, "just like everybody said you were. I have no alibis. I was beaten by a better man."

Better that night, but our contract stipulated that if Turpin won, the rematch would be in New York in September. I was sure I would be the better man there. My only concern was the gash over my left eye. In my dressing room, Dr. Vincent Nardiello examined it. He had come over from New York specifically for the fight.

"You'll need several stitches," he said. "I'll put them in back at your place."

"Do it here," I said. "I might be jostled by the people before I get there."

"What people?" said Dr. Nardiello. "There's nobody waiting for you. They're all outside Turpin's dressing room."

"You lost, Robinson," said George. "Turpin is their hero now. He's the champ."

It hit me then. I hadn't quite realized until that moment that Randy Turpin was the new world middleweight champion. I was the *former* champion. Until that moment, it had seemed like another stop on my grand tour of Europe, but suddenly, it hit me that this had not been an appearance.

"Let's go, Ray," said Dr. Nardiello. "I want to stitch that eye while it's fresh."

Outside, a cab was waiting. It rattled along the cobblestone streets to the Star and Garter. Upstairs, in the darkness of the tiny room, George reached around for the pull-string. The bare bulb lit up the dingy room.

"You've been living in *here?*" the doc asked.

"Don't remind me," I said, lying on my cot.

Opening his black medical kit, he took out a long surgical needle and some flesh-colored surgical thread. He lit a match and held it under the needle, sterilizing it.

"Hey, Doc," I asked, "Don't you have something to kill the pain?"

"Here," he said, tossing me two aspirin tablets, "chew on these."

He draped a towel over my eyes, protecting them from the glare of the bare bulb. Slowly, precisely, he weaved the needle through my skin, drawing the thread tight around it. He did it once, twice, and then I stopped counting.

"All done," he said finally.

"How many did it take?" I asked.

"Eight," he said.

"Will it be all right by September?"

"It should be. Get some sun on it."

"There's good sun at the Riviera," I said, smiling for the first time. "Maybe I'll go down there for a couple weeks."

"Yeah," said George, brightening, "that'd be good."

"You're lucky you're coming," I said, laughing. "You bring *me* to this dump, and now I bring *you* to the Riviera."

"Stay in the sun, Robinson, not in the casino."

I should have listened to George. We stayed at the Carlton Hotel in Cannes. During the day I got the sun on my eyebrow, but at night the casino cut me up worse than Turpin had. Jack Warner and Darryl Zanuck, the movie producers, were vacationing there then. The three of us were regulars in the baccarat game. We'd put up about $1000 apiece every night and we were the bankers. We lost so much that they reserved our seats. They wouldn't let anybody play until we got there.

In two weeks, I lost a lot of money in the casino, but I always considered it an investment. I needed the relaxation.

Strangely, the loss to Turpin hadn't diminished my status as a hero in France. On the beach, the police had to rope off the area where I took the sun. When we sailed on the *Liberté*, I was cheered and embraced. And when we arrived in New York, I was awarded a City Hall reception. In the months before leaving for France, I had become quite friendly with the new mayor, Vincent Impellitteri, who had succeeded Bill O'Dwyer the previous year. Outside the French Line pier, my man the mayor had eighteen gleaming limousines waiting for me and my entourage. Some of the limos already were filled with Mom and Marie and several friends who hadn't made the trip. And on the steps of City Hall, my man the mayor greeted me.

"Our guest of honor," the mayor said, "is *temporarily* the former middleweight champion."

When it was my turn to speak to the 3500 spectators, I promised to return the title to America. My eyes were brimming with tears of happiness at this welcome. Being home made me sure the rematch with Turpin would be different. Home in this country, and home in my training camp. Sometimes your training camp can affect your entire fight, as that dingy room above the Star and Garter had done in London. In contrast, at my camp in Pompton Lakes everything was happening with a smile.

"You got a little money on you?" Wiley asked me one night after dinner.

I knew what he was getting at. For years he had dared to

jump off the wooden dock that jutted into the lake, but he had put a hundred-dollar price on it. I had always laughed him off because he couldn't swim.

"Yeah, Wiley," I said, surprising him. "I got the money if you got the nerve."

"The hundred?" he said. "You really got the hundred? You really mean it, boss?"

"I really mean it," I said, flashing my money clip. "I'm going down to the village for the papers. And when I get back, I want you to be ready to jump."

Returning from the village, I saw our camp people and some strangers around the dock.

"Here comes the boss," Wiley announced. "It seems like the boss finally got a little money in his pocket and I'm jumping off this dock with his money in my hand."

"Now, Champ," Johnny Jenkins, the New York detective, said, "I don't know if I should let this go on."

Jenkins had been assigned by Mayor Impellitteri to watch over the camp. Whenever he got excited, he sniffled as he spoke.

"Now, Champ," he said, sniffling, "suppose something happens to Wiley. You know the Mayor sent me—"

"Johnny," I said, putting a hundred-dollar bill in Wiley's open hand, "you let him go right to the bottom. He's got enough money with him to pay his way in anyplace he finds down there."

"Now, Champ," he said, sniffling again, "you know he can't swim."

Wiley was wearing a pair of old brown pants and a faded yellow shirt, but he had taken off his shoes and socks. Stepping gently to the edge of the dock, he peered into the dark water. He held his nose with his left hand, and his right arm was pointing straight up as his little fat body splashed into the lake.

"I better save him," Pee Wee said, sounding like a hero. "Not yet," I ordered. "Not until he gets to the bottom." The lake was maybe ten feet deep there. Wiley had gone down like a rock, but I knew that he'd bob to the surface. When he did, I let Pee Wee jump in but Wiley was so frightened he put a strangle hold on Pee Wee. As they thrashed around, they both went under.

"Now, Champ," Johnny Jenkins said, sniffling louder, "maybe I better help Pee Wee."

Suddenly, they both popped up. Pee Wee had Wiley under the arms and he was shoving him toward the dock ladder. But when Wiley got to the ladder, he had to pull himself up with his left hand. He had his right hand closed around the hundred-dollar bill, and he wasn't about to open it.

"Nice work, Pee Wee," Wiley sputtered when he got on the dock. "I'll give you the twenty-five when—"

"You'll give him twenty-five!" I roared. "Wait a minute. Pee Wee, I'm fining you twenty-five for a bad job."

"A bad job?" he moaned.

"Yes, sir, a bad job. You didn't get him out quick enough. You had me a little scared."

"Me, too," Wiley grunted.

We laughed about that for days. Any time you can laugh in training camp, you're ahead. But none of us were laughing about Turpin. He had shown me plenty in London. Our problem was trying to solve his style of yanking his head back. But one day my old adviser, Soldier Jones, had the answer.

"Robinson," he said, "if you feint Turpin into yanking his head back, you got him. Because then he can't yank it back no more."

We tried it with a couple of sparring partners and it worked, but that didn't necessarily mean that I was going to take Turpin. I thought I was, but it wasn't a sure thing. That's what Pee Wee couldn't understand.

"Ray," he said, "I got a little money to bet on this one. The odds are good."

The odds had me favored, but at eleven to five, they were a little lower than usual.

"Don't bet," I told Pee Wee. "I think I can beat him, but I don't want you betting your money on what I think."

"Man, you usually don't off me."

"I know," I said, "and I don't underestimate myself. But don't underestimate him, either. He beat me once and now he thinks he can beat me. He might be even tougher this time. I believe that I will win, but it's possible that he will win."

The night before the fight I was in Mom's house, lying on the sofa with my feet in her lap.

"Mom," I said, "you always predict my fights, but you ain't said a word about this one yet."

All the years I'd been fighting, she had always made a prediction on my big fights. And to make her look good, I had always tried to shoot for the round she picked. Not that it always worked out that way, but several times it did. She took her predictions quite seriously.

"Ray," she was saying now, "you're gonna knock out Turpin in the tenth round, but he's gonna butt you, like he did before."

As soon as she said it, she eased herself out from under my feet and went upstairs. I heard the lock click on her bedroom door. She got down on her knees to pray, saying, "God, if I have deceived him in this, if this don't come to pass, how can he trust me anymore?" All the next day she was more worried than usual, but I had my own worries—Randy Turpin. He was built like a heavyweight. I never understood how only 160 pounds were packed into his body. He should've weighed 190.

In addition to his strength, his unorthodox style was baffling. "His jab," Joe Liebling wrote in *The New Yorker*, "was like a man starting his run for the pole vault."

Perhaps my biggest burden involved the pressure of returning the title to the United States. There hadn't been a British-born middleweight champion in sixty years, since Bob Fitzsimmons, and Turpin had inspired several thousand Britons and a few thousand Canadians to make the trip to New York. Thousands more came in from all over the United States, anxious for me to regain the title in what amounted to a patriotic duty. And then the night of the fight, riding up to the old Polo Grounds in my car, the police had to clear the people out of Eighth Avenue so I could get near the stairway leading to the dressing room.

"No more tickets," I heard a voice shouting near the ticket booths. "All tickets are sold out."

It was two hours before the fight, and all the tickets were gone. In the box office, the money counters would add up $767,626, a record for a nonheavyweight bout, and the attendance would be 61,370. And man, they were everywhere. The dressing rooms there were in center field, with the ring at second base, and when I came down the steps onto the field, jiggling and hopping, with a towel hooded around my head, I seemed to be walking into a sea of people. They were in the aisles of the field seats, with the cops chasing the ones who had tried to sneak down near the ring. All around me, in the double-decked ball park, people were looking down at me and applauding and yelling and the closer I got to the ring, the louder their roar.

And then, suddenly, as I climbed into the ring, onto my stage, I looked around at the ringside regulars.

They were all there, Toots Shor and Walter Winchell and Joe DiMaggio, and all the big writers in the press row, and there was a new face—General of the Army Douglas Mac-Arthur, who had recently been relieved of his command in Korea. And damn, now I knew it was a patriotic duty for me to win the title. During the national anthem, I peeked at the general and he was at attention, saluting. To me, having him there was like an order to win.

Through nine rounds, I was slightly ahead but not really in charge. And then early in the tenth, Turpin butted me again and I felt the blood oozing out of the scar from the first fight.

The blood dripped down into my left eye and across my cheek, and I might as well have had a black patch over the eye. That's the way it is when you have a bad cut and the blood is in one of your eyes. You're blind in that eye. Absolutely blind. To protect myself, I had to clinch. When I did, I noticed the referee, Ruby Goldstein, staring at the blood on my face. His concern made me think that the cut might be dangerous enough for him to stop the fight at the end of the round. In my desperation, I feinted Turpin into retreat with my left jab, as I had done to my sparring partners. When he had yanked his head back, I let go a right hand to the face. He sagged, but clinched. Breaking free, I hooked a left to his midsection and smashed a right hand to the jaw that dropped him.

He was on his knees at three, but his left eye was half shut. When he arose at seven, I attacked him again.

Clubbing him with both hands, I battered him across the ring. In the movies later, somebody counted my punches in that flurry—thirty-one in twenty-five seconds. Turpin flopped against the ropes and Goldstein waved his arms, stopping the fight. All around me the people in the ringside seats were on their feet, their mouths open, their hands waving. And in the upper deck, little human dots were waving at me, too.

And when I waved back that night, the blood spun off my gloves—my blood.

With all those people shouting and yelling, Mom climbed up on the apron near my corner and she was screaming, "Baby, I told you the tenth round!" Below her, Evelyn was holding Mom's pocketbook and her skins, her new stone martens. In her excitement, she had forgotten her pocketbook with $130 in it and she had run out from under her skins.

Down at my café, about thirty blocks from the Polo Grounds, most of the rounds were on me that night.

By the time I got there, there wasn't anyplace to park for blocks, except for the spot reserved in front for my flamingo Cadillac. That was a Cadillac night on Seventh Avenue. It looked like an assembly line.

"If you ain't got a '51 Caddy," somebody said in the café, "you got to double-park."

In my little corner of the world, Cadillacs were double-parked. But not for long.

17

The Million and Maxim

Nearly a year earlier, I had begun to think
about retiring. I didn't want to make the same
mistake Joe Louis had. Joe had announced his
retirement in 1948 as the heavyweight champion, undefeated in twenty-six title bouts. In the summer of 1950, the
Internal Revenue Service hit him with a tax lien of nearly
$250,000. Not knowing how else to earn that much money,
he made a comeback. He signed to box Ezzard Charles,
who succeeded him as the National Boxing Association
champion, at Yankee Stadium on September 27, 1950.

Joe lost in and out of the ring. Charles outpointed him.
His purse was less than $40,000.

In his dressing room later, blood seeped from cuts above
each of his eyes. One of his eyes was swollen shut. I was in
there with him, but it was like trying to console an old
blind man. Squinting in pain and embarrassment, he was
unable to put on his pants or locate his shoes.

I bent down and worked his feet into his big shoes and
tied the laces. I helped lead him out of the ball park.

Desperate for whatever money he could scrape together,
Joe continued his comeback. He accumulated eight consecu-
tive victories, including four knockouts. At the time, Rocky
Marciano was on the way up. The match was a natural

from the IBC's viewpoint—the young contender against the old master. It was scheduled for the Garden on October 26, 1951, about six weeks after I had stopped Turpin. In the eighth round, Joe went sprawling from a left hook.

As he hit the canvas, I leaped out of my ringside seat and edged toward the ring.

When he got up, Marciano threw two left hooks that ruined Joe, although he was still on his feet. Marciano threw a right hand that dropped Joe through the ropes and onto the apron. One of his legs was inside the ring, under the lower rope.

I had moved up behind the row of sportswriters, and as Joe was counted out, I jumped onto the apron.

"Joe, Joe, you'll be all right, Joe," I said, holding back my tears. "You'll be all right, man."

The memory of that scene haunted me for weeks. Some people were belittling Joe, saying how maybe he hadn't been that good after all. And someday, I realized, they would be saying the same thing about me if I overextended my career. Even before the second Turpin fight, I had mentioned this to Jimmy Cannon, then a sports columnist for the New York *Post*. We were sitting in the wooden bleachers above the canopied ring at Pompton Lakes.

"When you think I'm through, Jimmy," I said, "I want you to tell me."

"I can't do that," he said. "I can't speak for another man's career."

"Yes, you can, because a fighter is blind when he looks at himself. If you say it, I'll believe it. I don't want to be like Joe Louis was against Charles, or like Tony Canzoneri. Most people don't remember how great Canzoneri was, because all they remember is his last years."

"All right," he said, "I'll be the custodian of your future."

After my dramatic triumph over Turpin, my future glowed.

My café was busier than ever. So was the dry-cleaning shop and Edna Mae's lingerie shop. To get a haircut in George's barber shop, you had to make an appointment three days in advance. I purchased another house for Mom, a few blocks away in Riverdale, and Edna Mae and I moved into the big house on 248th Street. Every few days, I had to appear at a luncheon or a banquet. One day I got a call from Ed Fitzgerald, the editor of *Sport* magazine.

"Ray," he said, "we've selected you as the Man of the Year in sports. We want you to be our guest at a luncheon at Toots Shor's next week."

Man of the Year in sports. Not merely boxing, but all sports for 1951. Quite an honor, and a beautiful luncheon. My man the mayor was there to present me with the big plaque, but before he did, Harry Markson of the IBC told how he had needled George about me getting a plaque.

"After all," Markson said, "George doesn't get any percentage of a plaque, but George told me: 'When a fighter starts out as an amateur, he wants to win medals and cups and plaques. When he turns pro, he wants to win in Madison Square Garden. When he wins in the Garden, he wants to win a championship. When he wins a championship, he wants to make a lot of money. And when he makes a lot of money, he wants to win medals and cups and plaques.' And so," Harry said, "you can see that Ray Robinson has been all around the mulberry patch."

"No, no," George's voice boomed across the room, "you mean all around the cauliflower patch."

Sometimes it was more like a briar patch. I had to go fifteen rounds against Bobo Olson in San Francisco. That led to a match that boxing people had wanted to make for years—me and Rocky Graziano.

You remember Rocky. He wrote a book, too, *Somebody Up There Likes Me.*

Everybody liked Rocky. He was out of the Lower East Side of New York, a real Dead End Kid who walked and talked like one. And punched like one. His three fights with Tony Zale for the middleweight title had been classics. The films should be put in a time capsule. He was knocked out by Zale in 1946. He got off the deck to knock out Zale in 1947. Zale knocked him out again in 1948. Each one had been a war. Now, in the spring of 1952, he was thirty and he was thought to be past his peak. That made me laugh, because I was thirty. Anyway, the week before the fight I was a three-to-one favorite when three mob guys strolled in to see me after my workout at Coulon's Gym in Chicago.

"The big man," one of them said quietly, "wants to see you in the Sherman Hotel this afternoon. We'll take you up."

In those days, it was impossible to be in boxing without mob guys being around somewhere. I knew who they were referring to. Their "big man" ruled the Mafia in Chicago. He often had visited my camps.

"How do you feel, Champ?" he always said.

"I'm fine," I would say, telling him the same thing I told the sportswriters. "I never felt better."

"I just wanted to hear it from you," he'd say.

Over the years, I occasionally received a mysterious gift. Nothing really lavish. Once, I remember, it was a set of golf clubs. Another time, an expensive set of cuff links. Whenever something like that arrived, I knew that the "big man" in Chicago had made a score taking the odds on me to win. When I was told that he wanted to see me in the Sherman Hotel, I was more curious than concerned. We rode over in a cab. When I was ushered into his room, it was like stepping into an old George Raft movie. He was wearing a wide double-breasted black suit and was smoking a fat cigar.

"Ray," he began, "you know I like you."

"Yeah," I said, "we always got along."

"I've got a deal for you, Ray," he said. "If you want it, you take it. If you don't, we'll still get along."

"What kind of a deal?"

"One million dollars," he said. "Cash. One million dollars if you have three fights with Rocky."

"You mean he wins the first, I win the second, and the third is on the level—that what you mean?"

"As easy as that," he said.

"I'm sorry," I said. "That's a lot of money, but I guess I'm too stupid to be anything but a winner if I can help it. You've known me a long time and from the way you spoke, I got the impression that you knew what I was going to say before I got here. But it was nice of you to ask me. Not many people get a chance to turn down a million dollars."

"If you're not interested, that's your business," he said. "If you were, I just wanted you to know that we had something for you. No hard feelings."

No advice to keep my mouth shut either. The "big man" trusted me. I hadn't reported Carbo's attempt to fix the La-Motta fight, and I wasn't about to report this offer. I knew the Boxing Commission rule that a contestant is supposed to report even the offer of a bribe, but it isn't my style to squeal on anybody. The only reason I identified Carbo is because he's in jail. I'm not about to identify the "big man" who talked to me in Chicago. I always considered him to be a pleasant acquaintance—that's acquaintance, not accomplice. He never harmed me, and I'm not about to harm him now.

Graziano was different. He had fifty-two knockout victories, and damn if Zale wasn't rooting for him. During the introduction at the Chicago Stadium, their bond was obvious Zale, his blond hair slicked back above his hard Slavic face, took a bow, then strolled over and touched my gloves. He did it quickly, unemotionally, the way hundreds of other fighters had done it to me.

When he got to the other corner, he grabbed Rocky's gloves and held them for several moments. Then he made a fist with his right hand and clenched it in front of Rocky's face as he spoke to him. I never learned what Zale told Rocky, but his gesture seemed to be saying, "Hit him like you hit me." Whatever he said, Rocky smiled and tapped him on the jaw with a playful left jab.

When the bell rang, Rocky was scowling instead of smiling. He came out of his corner with his curly black hair flopping on his forehead, and with his right hand cocked like a revolver.

While I watched that right hand, he caught me with a good left hook in the first round. He bombarded me in the second. Midway through the third, I pulled my head in toward him to avoid that right hand, but I didn't pull it in far enough. He whacked me on the side of the neck and I went down. Some of the sportswriters claimed that one of my legs had merely brushed the canvas, that it wasn't an official knockdown. None of them had been swatted by that right hand. I was down, and Rocky put me there. When he saw me down, his instinct was to move in for the kill. That was his mistake.

In his anxiety, I nailed him with a left hook to the jaw and a right hand to the jaw. He went down on his back.

Flat on the canvas through the count of five, he started to scramble up at six. At eight, he reached for one of the ropes, but he missed it and tumbled forward on his face.

"... nine ... ten ..."

If the count had continued, he would've been up at eleven or twelve, and I would've found out what Zale had to go through. For a split second, it seemed as if he was going to keep swinging anyway. He had recocked his right hand and he was glaring at me. But when our handlers rushed into the ring, he knew. He dropped his hands, walked over to me, and poked me playfully in the ribs. Moments later, Don Dunphy had his radio microphone in front of us and Rocky leaned toward it.

"Anybody," he said, "who says anything about Sugar Ray is a crumb."

In his dressing room later on, one of the sportswriters asked him how he rated me.

"He must be good," Rocky said, "because he knocked *me* out in three."

The tape wasn't even off my hands that night when Norris started talking about me and Joey Maxim for the light-heavyweight title. But I was playing it cool. I had to act hard to get. Maxim had that shrewd manager, Jack (Doc) Kearns, working for him.

"That would be a fight," George said on the Twentieth Century Limited taking us back to New York. "That would be a *real* fight."

"What do I want to fight him for?" I said. "If I fight Maxim, I have to be fast. If I have to be fast, I have to be 160 while he weighs 175. That don't make sense."

"But if you beat Maxim," said George, "you'd be the light-heavyweight champion. You'd have held three titles."

"That's the trouble," I said. "If I win Maxim's title, then I have to defend it against all those big guys."

"Yeah," George said, with a wink, "you win Maxim's title, you can fight Jersey Joe or Charles, whoever wins."

Jersey Joe Walcott and Ezzard Charles had been matched to fight for the heavyweight title in June in New York.

"You're something, George," I said, laughing. "I don't think you like me. How about the time you wanted me to fight Billy Conn? Now you want me to fight Maxim. And if I win, Walcott or Charles. And don't wink at me. I know you, man, you're serious. I'll tell you what you do, *you* fight Maxim."

"Robinson," George said, "you don't understand. Fighting is your business, not mine."

So was negotiating. The more Norris talked to me about the fight, the more I knew that he'd come up in price. He started out by telling me how it was Maxim's title, how Maxim had to get the most of the money. He should've known better than that.

"Jim," I told him, "you know that I'm the man selling the tickets. Maxim never sold a ticket in his life."

When the contract was signed, Maxim was getting 30 per cent of everything. And so was the challenger—me. But there was something wrong about that fight from the start. Even in camp. One night there, Wiley and Gainford got to arguing about something, and Wiley was really steaming.

"You let me make the decisions!" George yelled.

"You!" Wiley roared. "I got as much right to make the decisions as you do."

"You serious?" George said.

"I have as much right being the manager around here as you do," Wiley shouted.

"You better shut up, Wiley," George snapped.

"No, I won't shut up," Wiley said, his voice getting higher and higher. "I can't fight you, you're too big—"

Jumping to his feet, he pulled out a pistol.

"—but I can shoot you, George!" he yelled. "I can shoot you. And you be sure to always remember that, George."

"Hey," I ordered, "put that thing away."

Until I saw the pistol, I thought it had been just another flare-up.

"Put that thing away," I repeated, "and cool off."

I guess Wiley was kidding, but it shook me up.

"Now look what you done," said Pee Wee Beale, ushering Wiley toward the door, "you got the champ all upset, man. You know that's no way for him to think before a fight."

Never mind that Wiley might have shot George, don't get the champ upset. That was my man Pee Wee.

Most of the time, the toughest thing I had to do in any of my training camps was keep peace between George and Wiley, but this time I had been upset by something else. Several nights earlier, I had dreamt that in the fight with Maxim I was stretched out in the ring, and somebody, a doctor I guess, was bending over me saying, "He's dead, he's dead." And when I woke up, sweating all over, all I could think of was my dream a few years earlier involving the premonition about Jimmy Doyle's death. This time I decided not to say anything about the dream. Nothing. To nobody. Physically, I had trained well for Maxim. I had taken a few B-12 shots to maintain my weight. In the gym I was smooth and fast. But mentally, with the dream and with Wiley pulling a gun on George, I was edgy when Pee Wee drove me into New York for the fight, which was scheduled for June 23, a Monday, at Yankee Stadium.

At the weigh-in at noon in the Madison Square Garden lobby, I was 160 on the nose, Maxim 174¾—a quarter of a pound under the light-heavyweight limit. Outside it was raining.

"The rain is supposed to continue," Jim Norris said, "so it looks like we'll have to put it over to Wednesday."

Ordinarily, the fight would have gone on the next night but the IBC contract with Yankee Stadium had a clause which gave a priority to a baseball game at the nearby Polo Grounds. The Giants were playing the Cincinnati Reds there on Tuesday night. As a result, the next fight date was Wednesday.

"Well," I said, thinking it wouldn't make much difference to me, "I don't have to make the weight, Maxim does."

When we weighed in again on Wednesday, Maxim had dried out to 173, I had dropped even more, to 157½. I was giving away fifteen and a half pounds, but that didn't concern me. I had given away that much to LaMotta once and outpointed him. The important thing to me was that the sun was out.

"And the Weather Bureau assures us it won't rain," Norris said. "It'll be hot, but we'll be all right."

It was 92 on the sidewalk outside the Garden. There was a process server on the sidewalk, too. Some dog in the buildings I owned had bitten an oil-delivery man, and he was suing me for $100,000. The piece of paper annoyed me, but I put it out of my mind. I knew that the piece of paper wouldn't be punching me at ten o'clock that night. More annoying was the heat.

". . . the temperature rose to 96.5 degrees at five P.M.," the voice on the car radio was saying on the way to Yankee Stadium. "That is the highest for this date in fifty-three years. Not since 1899 has . . ."

When I emerged from the third-base dugout at the Stadium shortly before ten o'clock, it was 90 degrees at the City Weather Bureau at Battery Park where there's usually some breeze off the bay. At the Stadium it had to be hotter than that. Ordinarily, I was able to breathe better in an outdoor fight, but when I hopped up the steps into the ring, with all those klieg lights above me, it was like a steam bath. Some of the sportswriters not only had their jackets and ties off, they had their shirts off. Jim Jennings of the *Daily Mirror* was to write of the "conditions which might have made Dante's Inferno seem like a refrigerator." Jesse Abramson of the *Herald-Tribune* put a thermometer on the ring apron. It registered 104.

Maxim was very strong and a good boxer, but my plan was simple enough. I was much faster, and with my speed I hoped to keep him off balance.

My strategy was working. Through five rounds, Maxim was an easy target. The two judges, Artie Aidala and Harold Barnes, gave me all five rounds. The referee, Ruby Goldstein, gave me four, with one even. In the seventh, I stunned him with a right hand to the jaw. But the heat was beginning to get to me. After the ninth, I plopped on my stool.

"I don't know what's the matter, George," I said, "I'm getting sleepy."

"Sleepy, hell," he growled. "You better wake up. That man over there has got two guns on you."

That is the last memory I have of anything that happened that night.

After the tenth round, Goldstein signaled that he could not continue as the referee. On the verge of heat exhaustion, he was helped from the ring. His replacement was Ray Miller. In the eleventh, Robinson jolted Maxim with another right hand to the jaw, but when the bell rang, he wandered aimlessly toward a neutral corner. In the thirteenth, he almost fell through the ropes in retreat from one of Maxim's rare attacks. Later in the same round, while staggering, he missed a sweeping right hand and sprawled flat on his face. When the round ended, he clung to the ropes in a neutral corner. His handlers leaped into the ring and dragged him to his stool. They applied ice-packs to the back of his neck. Smelling salts were waved under his nose. When the bell clanged for the fourteenth, Robinson remained on his stool. Alert to the situation, Dr. Alexander Schiff of the Commission staff hurried to his corner.

"Can you go on?" Dr. Schiff asked.

"I just can't," Robinson answered.

Turning to referee Miller, Dr. Schiff told him that the fight was over. Maxim, on his feet at the sound of the bell, was the winner by a knockout in the fourteenth round, the first time that Robinson had ever been stopped, and the only time that he ever would be stopped. He had been far ahead on the cards of the officials. Barnes had him ahead, 10-3, in rounds. Aidala had him ahead, 9-3, with one even. The original referee, Goldstein, had awarded Robinson five rounds, Maxim two, with three even. Miller had awarded him two of the three rounds that he had refereed. The combined scorecard of the referees had Robinson ahead, 7-4-3. Robinson merely had to last fifteen rounds in order to win by a unanimous decision, and to add the light-heavyweight title to his record.

After several minutes in the ring, Robinson headed for his dressing room, his arms around his handlers.

"The door opened and in he came: a limp, dragging body being supported by a couple of handlers," wrote Leonard Lewin of the *Daily Mirror*, who had been in Robinson's dressing room to observe the first-aid administered to Goldstein and who, in the confusion, had been permitted to remain. "His eyes were rolling and there was no co-ordination in the body they lifted onto the dressing table. Immediately, handlers began whipping the breeze (with towels) over Robby's burning body, trying to fan out the fire under the sweating direction of Dr. Ira McCown.

"The first sign of real life came from Ray when the Commission doctor dug a needle into him. In a few moments he was sitting, but the eyes still gazed blindly into space. Then through the haze, Robby spotted the Mayor [Impellitteri]. He eased off the table and, propping himself on Impy's shoulder, staggered away, pleading with the Mayor:

" 'He didn't knock me out, did he?'

"The Mayor spent a couple of minutes trying to convince Robby that it wasn't Maxim, it was the heat. Then Sugar's handlers, figuring that a cold shower might bring him fully to his senses, attempted to drag him in. Robby wouldn't buy it at first. Then, with a headlock on the supporting Mayor, he slowly headed for the shower and into it—with the Mayor. Impellitteri didn't break away from Sugar until the cold water relaxed Robby's strong grip. And the dripping Mayor sneaked away to join the spectators as the fully dressed George Gainford held Ray under the cooling spray. That restored the bounce to his legs and the life to his eyes. But it didn't seem to offset his incoherent thinking.

" 'The heat didn't beat me, God willed it that way,' Ray told his audience. 'You fellows think I'm crazy. I'm not crazy. I tell you the heat didn't beat me. It was God. He wanted me to lose.'

"By this time his friends must have figured the heat had driven him batty. They requested that Dr. Nardiello take him to a hospital immediately. But when Nardiello approached Sugar, he got the same answer.

" 'I'm not crazy. You fellows only think I am. But God beat me!'

"Now they were hunched around Sugar, fighting to dress him. His wife, allowed in the dressing room in violation of Commission rules only because of the unusual circumstances, was kissing him, doing anything she could to ease his troubled mind," Lewin concluded.

Instead of ordering Robinson into a hospital, Dr. Nardiello decided to let him return home.

"Ray doesn't like hospitals," Dr. Nardiello explained later that night, "and I didn't want to do anything that might frustrate his brain. He might've passed out then, and that could've been dangerous."

Driven home, Robinson was put to bed. With two dozen people in the house, he was "like a poundcake on display," his mother has said.

He had lost more than sixteen pounds, and since he was too weak to vomit, he was not permitted to drink or eat anything. But throughout the night, his mother held small pieces of cracked ice on his lips.

In the morning, my senses returned and, resting there in bed, I thought I knew what had happened.

"Maxim knocked me out," I said, looking around at Mom and Edna Mae and Dr. Nadiello and the others. "Maxim knocked me out, he must've knocked me out."

"No, the heat got you," Dr. Nardiello said.

"Maxim knocked me out," I said, annoyed. "You don't want me to know that Maxim knocked me out."

"No, baby," Mom said, "here it is in the papers."

And there it was, in headlines, how I had collapsed in the heat, and how it had saved Maxim.

"I had him beat, too," I said, almost crying.

"It just wasn't meant to be," Edna Mae said.

"God willed it," I said. "God didn't want me to win. God willed it, just like I dreamed."

"Like what dream?" Mom said.

"The dream I had at camp, but in the dream, I was dead."

"Oh my God," Mom said.

"Stop that talk," Dr. Nardiello said. "You're all right. You lost your strength, but you'll get it back. Rest up today and tomorrow you'll be all right."

"Then tomorrow we go to the movies," I said.

None of them understood what I had in mind.

"Tomorrow, I want to see the movies of the fight," I said. "I want to see what happened."

"As long as it's air-conditioned," Mom said.

The next day we drove downtown to Loew's State theater in Times Square to see the films. Through the early rounds everything was working as I had planned, but as the fight progressed I noticed that my balance was bad. I was punching wildly, something I had never done before, and after the tenth round the referee was changed.

I didn't notice the switch during the fight because I was groggy, but that's where my corner lost the fight for me.

I never heard of a referee being replaced between rounds like that, but neither George nor Wiley protested it. When they saw Goldstein leave and Miller come into the ring, they should have jumped around and yelled at the commissioner to keep the next round from starting. Maybe the commotion wouldn't have accomplished anything, but it would've delayed the start of the next round. And a delay would've given me a little extra time to rest and recoup my strength. At that point, a little extra strength might have carried me through. In the late rounds, I was told later, my water bottle was almost empty. And no one had brought salt pills to replenish my body's supply.

Walking out of the theater, I was disgusted. I had wanted that third title, and I had it won but I had lost. To add to my disgust, I had been knocked out. Not by Joey Maxim but by the elements, by God in a sense because he had created the heat, but no matter how I rationalized it, for the first time in my career the phrase *KO by* was on my record. On my page in *The Ring Record Book* it would read:

June 25 — Joey Maxim, New York . . . KO by 14

The more I thought about it, the more I remembered helping to put on Joe Louis's shoes and how I had led him out of Yankee Stadium. And now people had done that for me, in the same dressing room in the same ball park. In the days that followed I began to think seriously about retiring, because Dr. Nardiello had advised me to take a long rest from boxing.

I had developed a friendship with Joe Glaser, the president of the Associated Booking Corporation, one of the biggest agents in show business. He handled Louis Armstrong and later he would handle Barbra Streisand.

"If you're ever interested," he had told me several times, "I'll book you as a dancer when you retire."

I was interested now. Thinking back to my dream before the Maxim fight, I realized that God had warned me, and I had been foolish enough to ignore him. I wasn't going to ignore him again.

18

Show Biz

One morning several weeks later, I was in my
blue silk bathrobe, having breakfast, when Joe
Glaser phoned me.

"Meet me on the corner outside my office at eleven," he
said. "I've got some big deals to talk to you about."

His office was on the twentieth floor of 745 Fifth Avenue,
a big gray office building across from the Plaza Hotel, but
he knew I didn't ride in elevators and he didn't expect me
to walk up. Instead, we would do our business while driving through Central Park in his car, a big black Rolls Royce
with a chauffeur and soft gray upholstery.

"What's up?" I asked him.

"I've got you booked to open in the French Casino at
the Paramount Hotel on November seventh."

"For how much?" I asked.

"Now, Ray," he said, smiling, "the money isn't what
you're used to, but it's pretty good."

"What's pretty good?"

"It's pretty good for a rookie dancer."

"Joe, what's *pretty* good?"

"Fifteen a week, for four weeks."

"Fifteen hundred?" I said, sadly.

"Fifteen big ones, fifteen thou."

"Man, sixty big ones in a month."

"And after that," he said, breaking into a big grin, "you go to the Sahara Hotel in Vegas, another fifteen a week for four weeks."

"A hundred and twenty in two months."

"Ray," he said, seriously, "I used to handle Bill Robinson, Bojangles, and I know what Fred Astaire and Gene Kelly have been paid for their night-club acts. And you're making more per week than any dancer who ever lived."

When the story broke in the newspapers about my retirement from boxing and my new show-biz career, I got another phone call, from Pee Wee Beale.

"At fifteen thou a week," he said, "there's got to be room somewhere for Pee Wee."

I found room. I had kept June Clark around as my secretary, even though he had never taken or typed a letter. The other members of my entourage had scattered. George and Wiley were searching for new fighters. My sparring partners were working the small clubs or in somebody else's camp. Their standard of living had changed somewhat. No more cabins on the *Liberté*.

My standard of living hadn't changed, but I hadn't expected that dancing would be a tough piece of bread.

In the weeks before my debut at the French Casino, I trained harder than I ever had as a boxer. My dancing teacher, Henry LeTang, kept reminding me that my legs had to be as strong as when I depended on them in the ring. I had to do roadwork every morning, five miles a day. In the afternoon, I was dancing, five hours a day. I'd do my routines over and over. Whenever I made a mistake, the piano would stop and Henry would glare at me.

"You must understand," he liked to say, "that you are telling a story with your feet."

I also had lines to learn. I had to do a patter as the master of ceremonies. I had to tell a few jokes. I kept telling myself that it wouldn't be any different than the time I was a kid dancing for two dollars a night at the Alvin Theater. But by opening night, I was more nervous than I ever had been before a fight. Peering out from the side curtain, I could see the smoke hanging near the ceiling of the night club, just as it did up near the balcony at the Garden. In my boxing gear, I always had felt natural, but now, with a yellow-and-black plaid tuxedo jacket and my face stiff with make-up, I felt strange. George used to slap a little Vaseline over my face, to prevent cuts, but make-up was different. It was thick and pasty, and it made me feel like a girl. When the trumpets blared and I hopped out into the spotlight that sifted through the smoke, my make-up was the first thing that Joe Louis noticed.

"The referee," Joe whispered to Jimmy Cannon, "ought to wipe that off with a towel."

Joe and Jimmy were at a ringside table. So were Milton Berle, Jackie Robinson, Jersey Joe Walcott, and the night-club columnists. In his review, Bob Dana of the *World-Telegram & Sun* wrote that "instead of feinting, punching and counterpunching, all he has to do is turn on his natural charm, dance with vigor and unusual gift for one so new in the game and toss off a few topical gags to win an easy decision." In the *Journal-American*, Gene Knight wrote that I had "won by a knockout," that "his leads for the revue acts were good, his yaks snappy, he was right in there with stiff counters for ad lib jabs from the fans."

My wardrobe captivated them. In my six appearances that night, I wore six different outfits: the yellow-and-black plaid tux, a cream-colored suit, a dark brown suit, a dusty-rose jacket with cerise slacks, a white suit, and midnight blue tails with a top hat.

"The guy is a superb clotheshorse," commented Lewis

Burton, the boxing writer of the *Journal-American*, "but if you are going in for horses, Native Dancer is a better bet." In a serious paragraph, he wrote that "he is a remarkable fellow, capable of making a go of almost everything he tries. Probably if they'd let him stumble along without a set routine, he'd be much more amusing orally than the management now permits."

He meant my opening gag.

"Do you know," I asked my dancing partner and straight man, Joe Scott, "the three quickest ways of communication?"

"No, what?" he answered.

"Telephone, telegraph, and tell a woman."

Not many people laughed.

Several days later, Joe Glaser agreed. "We'll get some new gags written," he said, "and we'll get rid of Scott."

"I want to keep Scotty," I argued.

"Ray," said Joe, "you're paying him a thousand a week and he's not worth a hundred."

"He is to me. I like him around."

That's the way I was. Scotty was a member of my new entourage, my show-biz entourage. I liked him, and if I liked people, it didn't matter how much I paid them. I wasn't worried about making money to pay them. There was plenty of money for everybody, but for the money I always demanded loyalty. Like the time my act was packaged with Count Basie's band and The Dominoes, a singing group. The Dominoes had a habit of arriving late, and one night the backstage valet arrived an hour late. He had been late several times before.

"You got to get here on time," I snarled. "The next time you're late, it's coming out of your check."

His eyes flashed, but I didn't have any more time for him. I was waiting for my entrance cue. As I stood there, the valet moved closer to me, so close that I wondered what he was doing. I looked down at him and there, aimed at me, was the shiny black snout of a .38 revolver.

"You not so tough now," he sneered. "Say it again, Robinson, say what you said before and I'll blow your head off."

I had to think fast. I didn't dare throw a punch. He could have pulled the trigger before I let one go. I decided to ignore him, trusting that he wouldn't have the guts to pull the trigger. At my cue, I strutted onstage as if nothing had happened, but I was wondering if he might be crazy enough to shoot me in the back. His threat had not gone unnoticed. By the time I came offstage, one of the other backstage workers had disarmed him.

"You pulled a pistol on the champ," he was growling at my valet. "Let's see how tough you are *without* the pistol."

He was whimpering and sobbing, and I had to fire him.

Another episode developed one night on a Georgia highway. We were in a big bus, roaring along between one-night stands, when we sideswiped a trailer-truck. Miraculously, our bus careened safely down the highway. The truck skidded into a ditch. The driver was shaken up but not really injured.

"Officer, it was like this," one of our guys, a tall Negro, started to tell the state trooper.

"Now listen, boy," the trooper said sharply, "don't you be telling me nothing. You wait until I ask you. Down here, boy, you don't talk until you are spoken to, and I would say that the town judge will be the first one to speak to you."

"Man, we're in trouble," the head trumpet player said, nudging me.

"Maybe not," I said. "I think I know that trooper, he's got a very familiar face."

Strolling over to him, I stared at his face for a few seconds, nodding my head.

"I know you from someplace, Officer," I said, "and you know me, Sugar Ray Robinson."

"Sugar Ray," he said, "well, how about that? We were in the Golden Gloves together, on the East team in the Inter-city finals with Chicago."

"That's it, man," I said.

When I explained what had happened in the accident, he took down all the details, and sent us on our way.

"No need to keep you here all night," he said.

I enjoyed performing, but I didn't enjoy the traveling. Most of the time we were doing one-night stands and when our show ended, we'd jump into the Count's big bus and ride all night to our next stop. We were hot and smelly and trying to sleep on that bus. But when it was over, I had $70,000 for nine weeks. Then one day when I was back in New York to rehearse a new routine, I was putting on my coat to go downtown and little Ray, who was nearly four, glanced up at me.

"Daddy," he said, "are you going to work?"

That word *work* made me realize that this was the first real job that I'd ever had except for those few weeks in the grocery store when I was a kid.

"Yeah, son," I said, "Daddy's got a job."

The shock was softened by the money and the laughs. My price had dropped a little after the first few months, but I was still making terrific loot. And I never had more laughs. Once I had the act down pat, I didn't have to rehearse too much. When the show ended, my night was my own. And man, something was always swinging.

One night in San Francisco, I finished my act at the Fairmont Hotel and dropped in at a cocktail lounge, the Blue Mirror.

The owner, Leola King, a gal I had known for years, discovered that I was going to play Los Angeles the following week.

"When you're there, Ray," she said, "do me a favor and call up Millie Bruce. When we were kids, we lived in the same neighborhood in Los Angeles and we were like sisters. She'd get a big thrill if you called her and gave her my regards."

"Yeah, Leola," I said, not too enthusiastically, "give me her number."

She wrote it on a paper napkin. I folded it and stuffed it into my wallet. About a week later, when I had been in L.A. a few days, I was invited to a party in the Watts area. Edna Mae wasn't with me, and I thought that Leola's friend might like to go with me. Leola had mentioned that she was pretty, and it's always nice to walk into a party with a pretty girl on your arm. I dug out the piece of napkin, dialed her number, and inside of a few minutes, I not only had a date, I had a chauffeur. It looked like a good night.

She picked me up at the Beverly Hilton, and man, I couldn't believe it. She wasn't pretty, she was beautiful.

"I appreciate your invitation, Mister Robinson," she said, "but I know and you know that you're a married man."

I had heard that from other girls.

At the party, she told me about herself. Her maiden name had been Wiggins, "like Wiggins of the cabbage patch," she laughed. She had been born in Georgia, but she had grown up in L.A. She had been married before, to Herman Bruce. They had produced three children, but they were divorced. Her sister, Mamie, was married to Eddie Anderson, the actor who portrayed Rochester on the Jack Benny show. Millie had performed on the Amos 'n' Andy television show. Most of her conversation involved her boy friend. The way she spoke about him, I knew she was stuck on him, but when the music at the party got groovy around midnight, she snuggled her head into my shoulder. Assuming that was my cue, I pulled her body tightly against mine.

Suddenly, she pushed away from me.

"Ray Robinson," she said firmly but quietly, so no one would hear, "don't you get fresh with me, don't you dare. I'm not one of your girls for a night."

Man, I thought, *this one's different.*

I cooled it for the rest of the party, and she drove me back to the hotel. I got her to promise to call me at the café, if she came to New York.

The next time I was in L.A. I phoned her again, but she explained that she was about to get engaged and that she couldn't go out with me. Fair enough, but she was easy to talk to, and we chatted for nearly an hour. After that I phoned her long-distance every so often, and I always reminded her about my invitation if she ever got to New York.

"I'll remember," she promised.

"But don't come for a few months," I said. "I'll be in Europe with my act for several weeks."

"With your wife?" she said.

"And my sister," I laughed.

We arrived in Europe in late June of 1954. I played a few clubs on the Riviera, but the critics were waiting in Paris. My first night there, the show was bad. So were the reviews. The show got better after that, but critics don't come back. What made it better was the producer's idea to put my rope-slapping act in the show. On my other trips to Paris, the spectators at my workouts had enjoyed my rope slapping more than the sparring.

"Ray," the producer told me, "you've got to put the rope slapping in your act."

"What for?" I asked. "I'm a dancer now, not a boxer. The rope slapping is something I did as a boxer."

"Exactly," he said. "In Europe, people want to see you do what you're famous for."

The next night, I put on a pair of boxing trunks and slapped the rope on the floor and skipped time to it, and the band played at a fast tempo, and the customers thought it was great. So did I. My arms and legs had the weirdest feeling, as if they were doing what they were supposed to do. And every time I did it in the act, I wondered if it would be wise for me to make a comeback.

Several days later, I was sitting around with Edna Mae and Evelyn when I decided to blurt it out.

"I think I might box again," I said.

"No, Ray, no, no," Edna Mae scowled.

"Oh, Robinson," Evelyn said, calling me Robinson as she always did, "why would you want to do that?"

"I'm in good shape," I said.

"But you've been so blessed," Edna Mae said. "You've never been hurt. You might get hurt at this age."

"I won't get hurt," I said.

"But you don't have to box," Evelyn said. "You don't need the money. And you know what people said when Joe Louis tried it, that they never come back. He proved them right."

"I'm not Joe Louis, I'm Ray Robinson."

"You know what I mean," Evelyn said. "They never come back. And they never do."

"*Who* said that?" I asked.

"What do you mean, '*Who* said it'?" Evelyn asked.

"Man said it, right?"

"That's right," she said. "Man said it."

"God didn't say it, did He?" I replied.

"No," she said.

"Then if God didn't say it, it can be done," I said. "I'll tell you what we'll do. You know the little Catholic Church around the corner from here, we'll pray there every night before we go to the club, we'll pray for two weeks, and God will give us an answer. You'll see. When the two weeks are up, we'll have an answer."

We didn't have to wait two weeks. Several days later, our answer appeared in a cable from Anne Harris, my secretary at the café. The cable read: HURRY HOME. BUSINESS GOING TO THE DOGS.

19

The Comeback

In my big years, I never had to think about
money. I always had more than I could spend,
more than I could give away.

My share of the two Turpin fights had come to more than
$250,000. In the Maxim fight I had been consoled with
about $150,000. Some of that went in taxes, some of it to pay
the salaries of my entourage, but much of it I invested in my
various businesses. Shortly after my retirement from boxing,
Dun and Bradstreet valued Ray Robinson Enterprises, Inc.,
at $300,000.

With that kind of money behind me, I was a soft touch
for anybody with a good story.

I had made myself a reputation in boxing as a tough guy
with a buck. But your reputation is what people think you
are, your character is what you *really* are. Whenever I was
due a dollar in boxing, I didn't want to be made to take a
half-dollar. But once I got that money, I couldn't be a
hoarder from other people. I'd been born poor. I learned
early what it was to need help. But the way I believed, if
God had blessed me with a talent to make real big money,
then he entrusted me with a responsibility to care for those
without a talent. And when anybody convinced me they

needed some cash to see them through, I was inclined to give it to them, right out of my pocket.

"Never saw a man like you," my valet, Ben Killings, once told me. "You never come home at night with *any* money."

Around my café I'd be passing out fives and tens all night. It got so that Edna Mae wouldn't let me take any money with me unless I needed it for something specific. There were nights when I'd go through $500 in handouts when I had it on me. Years later I was told that some cats used to stop outside my café and say, "Let's go in and hit the champ for a fin," and they would succeed in getting it because I believed that they needed it for their baby, as they said. Most of the time their baby was twenty-two.

And in the afternoons, when I'd be in my birch-paneled office next door to my café, I was helpless. Almost every day, two or three little old ladies in old faded dresses used to come in and show me a dispossess notice because there was no way for them to pay the rent, and I'd open up the safe and hand out $25, sometimes $50 to get the landlord off their backs. Damn, I was a soft touch for a little old lady, especially the one who used to come every three months.

"Mister Robinson?" she said one day.

"Hello, there," I said, recognizing her. "What is it this time?"

"Same ol' thing," she said.

"Another dispossess notice?" I said. "It seems like you get one every three months."

"Yes sir, every three months, with three months due. I need a hundred and fifty to square it again."

"All right," I said, "but this is the last time."

"Oh yes, Mister Robinson, this is the last time."

It would be, until three months later, but I didn't mind. I had the money, and she didn't. She needed a roof over her head just as I did, and she had no way to make any money, but for me there was always a way. In the years I was boxing, any time I needed money, all I had to do was sign for a fight. Instant cash. When I went on the stage as a dancer, the money continued to come in.

"I ain't ever going to end up broke like Joe Louis did," I remember bragging shortly before my retirement from boxing. "I got my businesses, and my real estate, and my stocks. I got all my taxes paid up. No way for me to end up broke. Absolutely no way."

I had bragged too soon.

During my travels as a dancer, I had entrusted the direction of my business affairs to my business manager. He was the real-estate man who had handled the purchase of my buildings on Seventh Avenue, as well as my home and Mom's home. I thought so highly of him that when little Ray was baptized, he was the godfather. But after hurrying home from Europe following that frantic cable, I realized in glancing through my ledgers that somewhere, somehow, $250,000 had disappeared. I was threatened with foreclosures on my mortgages. My taxes were unpaid. My stock portfolio was virtually worthless.

"I've got no choice now," I told Edna Mae. "I've got to fight again. It's the only way I can make enough money to bail myself out."

My value as a dancer had slipped. Maybe I had made more money in my debut than Fred Astaire or Gene Kelly, but I wasn't making it now. Not that I couldn't keep dancing. Joe Glaser, my agent, told me that he could book me for at least $25,000 a year, but that wasn't enough.

"I need big money, Joe," I told him as we rode in his Rolls Royce, "a few big purses."

"I'll help you get them," he said. "I'll be your business

manager in boxing, too. And don't worry about the fore-closures on your property. I'll take over the mortgages."

Another friend was Ernie Braca.

"I'll help you get started again," he told me at his favorite table in Gallagher's restaurant. "But don't be impatient. You've got to go to the sticks. Get your name on the wire services but stay off TV until you're really ready for a big one."

At thirty-three, I wasn't concerned about my age, or my layoff, but I wanted to be assured. I checked with Dr. Nardiello.

"Don't rush it, Ray," he said. "Give yourself time to re-gain your timing. Your weight is fine, but that's a dancer's body now, not a fighter's. I'm sure you've still got your punch —a fighter never loses that—but your legs are what enables you to throw that punch."

Glaser, Braca, and Dr. Nardiello were among the few people who knew about my financial troubles.

My ego wouldn't let me make it public. After bragging about how I was going to end up differently than Joe Louis, than all the other fighters who had gone bust, I couldn't swallow my pride and admit it. At the news conference in my café announcing my comeback, I didn't have to wait long for the question about why I was returning to the ring.

"Do you need the money?" somebody asked me.

"Man," I said, putting on my best smile, "doesn't everybody need money, a little walking-around money?"

In the far corner, Joe Glaser smiled, too.

When I went up to Greenwood Lake it was like old times. George and Wiley were with me. So was June Clark, but Pee Wee Beale had died the previous year. After a few weeks, I went to Hamilton, Ontario, and coasted through a six-round exhibition with Gene Burton. Shortly after that, I agreed to begin my comeback against Joe Rindone in the Detroit Olympia on January 5, 1955.

I had fought Rindone in 1950 and had stopped him in the sixth round.

"Then you knocked out Olson, remember?" George said. "It's going to work that way again, Robinson, only you'll need a couple more tune-ups before you're ready for the title, before you're ready for the big money."

George was enthusiastic. He knew that if I was in the big money, so was he.

But the big money was the last thing in my mind when I jiggled through the aisles toward the Olympia ring. I had enjoyed returning to training camp and I had enjoyed the ritual in the dressing room. Pulling on the high white cotton socks. Slipping into my black leather boxing shoes. Putting on a jockstrap and over it a leather protective cup that I had had in the Golden Gloves, and sliding into my white trunks with the silver religious medal pinned inside. Having my hands bandaged, first with gauze and then with adhesive tape, and then having the gloves laced on me. But now, in my old blue satin robe with a short white terrycloth robe under it and with a white towel hooded around my head, I was beginning to doubt myself as I hopped up the wooden steps into the ring.

Suppose they're right, I was thinking, *suppose it's true that you can't come back.*

And in my corner, in that old moment of truth, when the announcer pointed toward me and blared, ". . . and in this corner, from New York City, the former world middleweight and welterweight champion, starting a comeback in this bout . . ."

All around me, the people were on their feet, looking up and applauding.

"Sugar Ray Robinson," the announcer said, waving for more applause.

In the years before, my confidence at the moment of my introduction had been supreme. Mentally, there was no way for me to lose. But this time I was never so nervous. I didn't know if the Sugar Ray Robinson the announcer had mentioned was the Sugar Ray Robinson of those other years. Across the ring was the man who was going to help me find out. Joe Rindone was out of Roxbury, Massachusetts, and he had been around. He looked it. He had a squashed nose and a hairy chest. He was the ugliest guy I ever fought. I always disliked guys with hairy chests—I didn't like getting into a clinch with them. But when the bell rang, he wasn't giving me as much trouble as I was giving myself. I couldn't put any punches together. My timing was terrible. But halfway through the sixth round, I nailed him with a left hook and right hand.

". . . three . . . four . . . five . . . ," the referee was shouting.

Rindone was trying to get his legs to work, but they wouldn't. The referee counted him out, but I never heard eight, nine, or ten. The crowd was making too much noise. I had drawn almost 12,000 people, the largest boxing crowd in Detroit in four years. I was as excited as the spectators were. I knew I hadn't done much, but when I flattened Rindone, I was as startled as I had been the night in Watertown, New York, when I flattened the tough Canadian kid. Seeing Rindone counted out, I thought, *Man, I still got it.* Joe Glaser thought the same thing. It wasn't but a few seconds after the knockout that he was in the ring with me.

"I'm the boss now," he was shouting in his hoarse voice. "I'm going to guide you to the title."

The title. The magic word. The word I wanted to hear.

When I did, I believed that I had looked better than I really had. In the dressing room, I told the sportswriters that I was satisfied, but that my combinations hadn't been sharp. I didn't want to sound too cocky. But in my mind, all I could visualize was Rindone going down and staying down, and I was thinking, *I still got it*. After the sportswriters departed, Ernie Braca stared at me.

"Who are you kidding?" he snapped.

"What are you talking about?" I said.

"You were *satisfied?*" he barked.

"Yeah," I said. "I won, didn't I, and I knocked the guy out, didn't I?"

"You used to finish a guy like that in the first round," Ernie growled.

"Robinson knocked him out in six in 1950," George said. "Same round."

"Rindone can afford to be five years older," Ernie said, still glaring at me, "but you can't. You were terrible. You got a lot of work to do."

"Not that much," I snarled.

Spinning on his heels, Ernie marched away. I snatched a towel and headed for the shower. When I came out, Truman Gibson, who put on the Wednesday night TV fights for the IBC in Chicago, and Joe Glaser were waiting for me.

"You looked good," Truman said.

"Not everybody seems to think so," I said.

"What?" said Joe.

"Never mind," I said. "What's on your mind?"

"Can you be ready in two weeks?" Truman said.

"For who?"

"Tiger Jones in Chicago. He's lost five in a row and we want to put you back on TV where you belong."

"For how much?"

"At least ten, maybe more. You'll get four from TV, plus

thirty-five per cent of the live gate. Good walking-around money."

"Good for now," I said.

"After you beat Jones," he said, "we'll get Gavilan for Miami Beach, a real good payday. Olson would be next."

"I don't know," Glaser said. "I think you're rushing yourself, Ray."

"You'll have a national television audience," Gibson said. "After tonight, everybody will want to see you again."

Truman Gibson had appealed to my ego.

"I'd like to be on TV again," I said.

I thought of how Ernie Braca had suggested that I stay off TV until I was really ready, but after the way Ernie had insulted me a few minutes earlier, I wasn't about to take his advice.

"Okay," I said, "I'll take Tiger Jones."

"Two weeks from tonight," Truman said. "January nineteenth, in Chicago."

"My town," I said, grinning.

More than ever, it was like old times. I was going back to the Chicago Stadium where I had stopped Jake LaMotta, where I had flattened Rocky Graziano, where I had never lost. When I arrived at the Bismarck Hotel, the bellboy hadn't put down all the bags when the phone started ringing. One of the first calls was from Harold (Killer) Johnson. In his younger days, he had played basketball with the Harlem Globe Trotters and been famous for a long set shot, the "kill" shot, as it was called then. I had known him for years and often visited his club on the South Side, the Archway Lounge.

"The victory party," he proclaimed over the phone, "will start at midnight after you dispose of the Tiger."

He had me laughing, as always. But in the gym, things weren't so funny. My timing was still off. My combinations weren't clicking. My hands weren't doing what my mind was telling them. But the betting odds had me the favorite at three to one. That made me feel good. So did the fact that Jones had lost five in a rew. His record made some people believe he had been imported to make me look good.

The rumor was that the Illinois Commission had plainclothesmen trailing him, to see if he was talking to gamblers.

Some rumor. In the first round, he bloodied my nose with a left hook. In the second, another left cut me over the right eye. Something else happened in that round. I let go a left hook, what I thought was a real good left hook. It caught Jones on the jaw. But nothing happened. Nothing.

When I hit Joe Rindone with that punch, he had gone down. So had maybe fifty other guys through the years. But not Ralph (Tiger) Jones. All he did was blink and let go a right hand to my midsection. Nobody had hit me like that on the dance stage.

Through the first six rounds, I wasn't doing much. It was obvious.

"Robinson," George said to me in the corner before the seventh round, "you're gonna have to knock him out to win."

I didn't answer. I already knew that. I also knew that I couldn't do it.

When the cards of the officials were announced, it was humiliating. Illinois uses the ten-point must system, meaning that the referee and the two judges must award ten points to the winner of a round, or ten points to each fighter if the round is even. One of the judges didn't give me even one round. He had seven for Jones, and three even, giving Jones 100 points on his card. The referee gave him 99, and the other judge gave him 98. I had almost pitched a no-hitter. I couldn't get back to the dressing room fast enough, but as it turned out, that was more embarrassing than the ring.

All the sportswriters wanted to know if I was going to retire again, if I realized that "they don't come back." I tried to tell them that I wanted to keep going, that I hadn't realized that Jones was too tough an opponent at this stage of my comeback, that I still wanted to have a few more fights.

When they stopped scribbling what I was saying, they looked at me as if they were embarrassed to be there.

When I looked out beyond them, I saw the same embarrassed look on the faces of all the people who were supposed to be with me—Joe Glaser, Ernie Braca, George Gainford, Harry Wiley. After the sportswriters filed out as if they were leaving a funeral, George helped me out of my bathrobe and he shook his head.

"Robinson," he said, "you never should've tried it."

"That's right, Ray," Wiley said. "Joe Louis couldn't do it. Nobody can do it. You were away too long."

"I made a mistake encouraging you," Glaser said.

"I warned you, Ray," Braca said, sympathetically. "I warned you in Detroit, but you wouldn't listen."

"Damn you guys," I flared. "I'm not through. You don't understand what it's like to be a fighter. Gainford, Wiley, you were never fighters. You've just been *around* fighters. None of you guys know what it's like to train for a fight, and overtrain, like I did. That's all I was, overtrained. I went stale. I had a bad night, that's all. Ain't I entitled to a bad night?"

Nobody answered. In silence, I took a shower and got dressed. Outside, Edna Mae was waiting for me. We went to the Bismarck, where I could be alone, where I could think, where it was quiet. It was quiet in the Archway Lounge, too.

On the train to New York, I stayed in my compartment

with Edna Mae. The other guys were playing cards, something I always loved to do, but not this time. I stared through the thick window at the farmlands covered with snow and the dirt-smudged slums the tracks always go through in the cities, but I never really saw them. At night, tossing in my berth, it was worse. I'd slide up the shade and whenever I'd see the autos, with their headlights on, waiting behind the black-and-white gates at the crossings, I'd think of how the photographers used to pop their flashbulbs in my eyes when I was the champion. Shortly before dawn, I made a mistake. I turned on the dim light next to my berth. When I looked out the window, there was a reflection of my face in the glass—my face with a big scab above the right eye.

The next morning, a photo of the same face was in Arthur Daley's column in *The New York Times.* Alongside it was the headline, "Is This Really a Comeback?" and below, he had written, in part:

> Once upon a time Sugar Ray Robinson was a thing of beauty in the ring. That's rather incongruous verbiage to be using in describing a prizefighter. But Sugar Ray was no ordinary prizefighter. He was an artist at his trade, a master craftsman. He could outbox the boxers and outpunch the punchers. He had blinding speed of hands, feet and brain. Watching him work was sheer delight.
>
> Tigers such as Tiger Jones could be eaten before breakfast by the Sugar Ray we once knew. He could down 'em with one disdainful gulp. However, this no longer is the Robinson of old. It's the old Robinson . . .
>
> Sugar Ray supposedly is on the comeback trail. Whether he realizes it or not, he's marching up a dead-end street. And with each step of the way he's crunching underfoot and shattering into fragments the precious memories of a once incomparable workman. He's had it. The past is gone beyond recapture. Robinson should quit immediately.

Sugar Ray is one of the few men in this fistic generation who can be properly bracketed with the almost legendary figures of the past. When a Tiger Jones can lick him, it proves his comeback is hopeless. He should quit while there still are illusions left.

All the other columnists took a shot at me but the one who hurt me the most was Jimmy Cannon. He wrote:

This is one I don't like to do . . . but I promised Ray Robinson I'd do it and so here it is. It may seem cruel but I don't intend it to be that way. There is no language spoken on the face of the earth in which you can be kind when you tell a man he is old and should stop pretending he is young.

He asked me to do it. Times change and so do men and he has a right to tell me I'm wrong. But if I didn't do it, exactly this way, trying not to be fancy about it and just getting it down, I'd be welshing. If he hadn't urged me to do it, this wouldn't be a difficult piece. Because Robinson anticipated it and asked me to protect him from himself, I feel I'm mixed up in it. . . .

Anyway, there was always fear in Robinson that it would happen this way. It was the fear of being ridiculed that haunted him the day at Pompton Lakes, N.J., before the second Randy Turpin fight that made him tell me it would be a friendly act if I became brutally honest when I thought he was fighting beyond his time. There isn't a pug he ever fought who could put fear in Robinson because he was a great fighter and being flashily secure was also part of the talent. It was going bad that frightened him and gracelessly taking lickings from guys like Tiger Jones who beat him up this week.

Of course, he'll resent this but I'm keeping the bargain. None in any field can take it. Old fighters, who go beyond the limits of their age, resent it when you tell them they're through. It never sounds reasonable.

The people quit on them and so do the promoters. The money is smaller and they bore people or they just fade into the oblivion of the losers . . . get Joe Louis to tell you about it. There's no place to go and so they stop and they think they did it themselves.

What made Robinson great will also hurt him now. Don't let the clothes or the big cars or the attention he demanded from barbers fool you. He is a fighter who goes as far as he can and he will stand up under it because that's the way he is. He'll last if he can and try to make a fight and that's no good at his age. He's been hoofing and the life of a night club performer is soft and what he had is gone.

The pride isn't. The gameness isn't. The insolent faith in himself is still there. It has to be or he would have said the hell with it after what Jones did to him . . . but the pride and the gameness and that insolent faith get in his way. He could show you why if it was someone else, but this is Ray Robinson and he turns away from the truth. . . .

He was marvelous, but he isn't any more. That's no disgrace, either. The years did it to him and not Tiger Jones but the records don't include such information. He must know how bad he was with Jones because there were nights when he was perfect. He knows and so do I and he's kidding no one.

It's up to Robinson, I've done what I said I would.

He had no right to put it in his paper that way. Our agreement had been private, not public. I'm friendly with him now but he hurt me with that column. I soon discovered that being hurt by my friends was something I would have to endure. Shortly after that, George Gainford dropped in to see me at my office. He was restless, as if he didn't know what to say.

"Robinson," he finally spouted after a few minutes, "I came to tell you that I'm not going to work with you no more. For your own good."

"*My* own good?"

"You don't need me no more, Robinson," he said, sounding as if he had rehearsed a speech. "You ought to quit, Robinson. You know that. Tiger Jones showed you that. You keep fighting, you gonna get hurt by some wild kid with a good punch. You listen to me, Robinson. You'll see, you gonna get hurt. When you do, I don't want it on my conscience that I was encouraging you to keep fighting."

"Go ahead, George," I snapped. "I still got Wiley."

"No, you don't," he replied. "Wiley told me that everything I said goes for him, too."

Before I knew what to say, George put on his hat and slowly closed the door behind him.

After nearly twenty years, George had walked out on me.

Run after George, I thought. *Talk him into staying with me, and talk Wiley into coming back.*

And then I realized what was going on.

Gainford and Wiley weren't walking out on me. They were walking out on my money. All these years, they had lived off me, lived high, lived like millionaires, but now they thought that there wasn't going to be any more money. They were deserting the sinking ship.

And right there, I vowed that the ship wasn't going to sink. I vowed to prove that I wasn't through, to pursue my comeback, to show Gainford and Wiley, to show everybody.

20

My Bag of Tricks

Several years earlier, I had established a training camp in an old house up near Greenwood Lake, a couple miles from where I had gone to work with Joe Louis when I turned pro. I called my place "Cabin in the Sky" because it was high in the woods of the Ramapo Mountains and the clouds would float by, almost as if you were in the sky with them. The day that I drove up there, with Edna Mae and June Clark, I realized it was the perfect place for me now. I needed to be away from everybody. I needed to be as near to God as I could get, because He had to guide me, and up in my cabin, with that sky around me, it was almost as if I could talk to Him.

I didn't need George or Wiley, or Joe Glaser or Ernie Braca. I needed people who were with me, like Edna Mae and June, not people who were against me, and I believed God was with me—at least He always had been.

In the morning, I'd get up early, with the mist hanging in the mountains, and do my roadwork in the cold, with my gray hooded sweatshirt on and with my big brown heavy shoes. Not far away was a small country churchyard and I'd always finish my roadwork there, kneeling in the churchyard and praying for guidance.

"Take your hood off when you kneel," June Clark said to me one morning.

"God doesn't want me to catch cold," I said. "He understands those things."

Not long after that, Sam Silverman phoned me. Subway Sam from Boston. He operated the Callahan Athletic Club. He was the only member, but Callahan was a good name to have on your office door if you were trying to sell tickets to the Irishmen in Boston.

"How about Georgie Small in the Baaastin Gaaahdin?" he said in his broad-*a* accent.

The money wasn't much, but I couldn't argue about that. As much as I needed the money, I needed the fight even more. It was scheduled for March 5, and one day a couple of weeks before that, George phoned Edna Mae one day and told her that he wanted to work with me again. But when Edna Mae mentioned it to me at dinner, my ego flared.

"I don't want to have anything to do with George or Wiley," I snapped. "Tell 'em to stay away from me."

I had Edna Mae and I had June Clark, who was the closest guy to me throughout my career. But the next day, George arrived at my camp, as Edna Mae had told me he would do.

"Robinson," he announced, "I see you got a fight and, well, I'm sorry I said what I did, but I'll work with you."

"The hell you will," I said. "Get the hell out and stay out. I don't need you. I never did, and I don't now."

He didn't expect that treatment, but he knew me well enough to realize that I wasn't fooling. The next day Wiley arrived with the same story. I gave it to him the same way, maybe worse. Telling them off made me feel better, but not much. For the first time in my life, I needed sleeping pills and Edna Mae was concerned.

"Who is going to be in your corner?" she asked me one night after dinner.

"Nobody," I said. "I don't want nobody in there with me for a reason. I want everybody to know that Gainford and Wiley have deserted me."

"You can't do that," she said.

"Yes, I can. When they walked out on me, they hurt me in my heart. I'm not angry at them as much as I'm hurt. Don't nobody like me for *me*? Don't these guys believe in me? The only reason they asked to come back now is because they're a little short, they can use whatever money they get."

"Honey," she said, "think about it another way."

"There isn't another way, there's just one way."

"Honey, no matter how you feel about them, remember that they know you better than anybody else. You're not going to be in that corner by yourself anyway. You know the Commission there wouldn't allow that, so don't talk foolish. If you get some new people for your corner, they won't know you, and you're trying to resume a career, not start one. Take them back. Please. I would feel safer if they were in your corner, and I think you would, once they're there."

The more I thought about it, the more I realized that her theory was correct.

My ego wouldn't let me tell Gainford and Wiley directly, but I got the word back to my café that I might change my mind. The next day, they arrived together. They were all apologies. They insisted that they had been thinking of my welfare, but now that I was going to have a fight anyway, they wanted to be with me. I didn't make a fuss over them, but I accepted them. Deep down, the hurt was still inside me, and from then on, they were just people who worked for me.

After I arrived in Boston, another problem developed. I came down with a virus.

Sam Silverman didn't want to call off the fight. He kept

telling me, "You'll be okay in time." Sam had some ticket money in the till, and he didn't want to give it back unless he had to. Along about that time, George came to me.

"I am informed," he said, in his best mysterious voice, "that they are trying to get Small to take a dive."

In boxing, *they* is a familiar and a favorite word. It might mean almost anybody. It might also mean a hoax.

"No good," I said. "Nobody ever took a dive for me before. And nobody's going to start now. Besides, I don't trust anybody. There's nothing Georgie Small would rather do than get a win over me. And with this virus, he just might."

The day before the fight, I still had the virus, but Sam didn't want to say anything to the newspapermen.

"Come to the weigh-in tomorrow," he said, "and we'll see how you feel. We can always call it off tomorrow."

At the weigh-in, my temperature was down to normal, but I still was too weak to fight.

"Maybe you'll feel better after a good steak," Sam said, refusing to give up. "The people want to see you."

"Sam," I said, "you don't have to go in that ring—I do. And the way I feel, I'm not going in there tonight."

Sam surrendered a few hours before I was scheduled to go on. But when the story got on the wire services, it sounded as if it was all my fault. Silverman was quoted as saying he was going to try to have me suspended. That was just a way for him to clear himself with the people who bought tickets. Across the country, some of the sports columnists wrote that Runout Ray was back in form. After the Jones fight, it was good to be back in any kind of form. But the form that counted was my form in the ring.

When my virus cleared up, I arranged to go against Johnny Lombardo in Cincinnati on March 29. Not many people remember Lombardo, who was out of Mount Carmel, Pennsylvania, but I'll never forget him.

During the early rounds, he had me in trouble. Not enough to put me on the floor. He couldn't hit that hard. But he messed up my timing. I couldn't get off. I knew I had to come on to win. And I did—but not by much. One of the judges thought Lombardo outpointed me. The other judge and the referee had me in front, giving me a split decision over Johnny Lombardo. Big deal.

Joe Glaser and Ernie Braca were there, and so was little Vic Marsillo, the guy who had handled Charlie Fusari and who was a good friend of Braca's. This time there was no scene in the dressing room. They waited until I got in my room at the Netherlands Plaza Hotel. Sitting in a corner were Gainford and Wiley, but they weren't saying a word. Joe Glaser was doing all the talking.

"Ray," he said softly, like a doctor telling me I had a rare disease, "I've been your friend, and I always will be."

I was sitting on the bed, looking at the floor. I knew I had looked bad. I had no excuse this time. I hadn't overtrained. I had just been bad. And this time I had to listen to what they said.

"Ray," Joe went on, "I'll get you back in show business. I'll take care of you."

"Joe's right, Ray," Braca said. "Stop before some kid busts you up. If that Lombardo could fight, he would've killed you."

"Robinson," I heard Gainford say, quietly, "what God giveth, God taketh away."

I didn't dare look at them. As I sat there, my eyes were filling with tears. And then, suddenly, there was another voice.

"What's the matter with you guys?" Vic Marsillo barked. "How can you guys forget so soon?"

Marsillo had always reminded me of Lou Costello, the

fat little comedian of the Abbott and Costello team. But right now, he sounded more like Edward G. Robinson.

"Ray," he snapped, "there's nothing wrong with you that a few fights can't cure."

All around the room, the other guys were staring at him. They hadn't expected him to disagree with them.

"You stick with me, Ray," he said, "you stick with the Little Colonel here, see."

It was like a movie. The little tough guy telling off the big shots. I thought it was great, because he was saying what I wanted to hear. He was showing faith in me.

"Take your time, Ray," he barked. "Pick your spots. It's not gonna happen overnight. But you can do it, Ray."

When he was through, none of my other advisers knew what to say. Soon they drifted out of the room, leaving me and Edna Mae alone. Edna Mae had been there through all the talk, but she hadn't said a word. When they left, she didn't say anything except, "Go to sleep, honey."

That night I needed two sleeping pills.

Marsillo's speech got me a reprieve. Braca arranged a match with Ted Olla in Milwaukee for April 14, only two weeks away. I knew I had to look better against Olla, a lot better. I returned to Greenwood Lake and resumed working hard, maybe too hard.

"I can't get that thing," I moaned one day.

By that thing, I meant my rhythm. I wasn't putting any punches together, I was flubbing on the speed bag. After the workout, Edna Mae asked me to take a walk with her.

"What's on your mind?" I asked her.

"Honey," she said, "can I say something about your boxing? About your workout?"

"Sure, you can."

"Well," she said, "it just seems to me that—"

"That what?"

"That you don't look like you used to. You look like you're trying to knock out everybody. You're so anxious to fight again, you just want to show everybody how great you once were by knocking out all your opponents. But that's not how you were great. You're not using the bag of tricks that made you great. That was your gift, the tricks were what God blessed you with, the tricks, the science, you don't use that anymore. You don't look like *the* Ray Robinson anymore."

I had stopped walking, and I was staring at her.

"You got it," I said. "You got what was wrong. All these guys around me, all these boxing guys, they don't observe that. But my wife does. My wife sees what I'm doing wrong."

The next day, I began by working on my left jab, as I had in the Salem-Crescent gym. I worked on all my punches, one by one. I checked my footwork. I checked everything. By the time I got on the train to go to Milwaukee, I felt prepared. The train arrived in Chicago early in the morning, then it swung up along Lake Michigan toward Milwaukee. Edna Mae and I were having breakfast in the dining car when the steward led a priest in a brown cassock to one of the empty seats at our table. He introduced himself as Father Jovian Lang, a Franciscan. In our conversation over breakfast, I discovered that he was going to Milwaukee for a library convention.

"May I phone you, Father?" I asked. "I'd like to talk to you about something."

He agreed, and that made me feel good. He seemed like a real guy, somebody easy to talk to. The night before the fight, he came to see me. It was as if God had sent this man to help me. I told him about my comeback, how I had lost to Tiger Jones, how I had looked bad against Johnny Lombardo. I told him that, with so many people against me, I wondered if I was doing the right thing.

"Don't stop now," Father Lang said.

"I was hoping you'd say that, Father," I said.

"I think God has selected you to do all this."

"But why?"

"We don't know why. It's not important to know why at this point. But if God has given you ten talents, He expects you to do ten times as much work. To sacrifice ten times as much so that you might set an example for others."

"I think I understand, Father," I said.

The night of the fight, Father Lang gave me a priest's blessing in my hotel room. I needed it. Not only to guide me in the fight but to help me through the intrigue. Shortly after I arrived in Milwaukee, I discovered that my man, Ernie Braca, also had an interest in Ted Olla, my opponent. Not only that, I had heard that Olla had been approached about letting me look good for ten rounds. Olla, to his credit, refused. The way I heard it, he said, "Hell, *I* can knock Robinson out."

Not quite. Not Ted Olla.

In the third round, I knocked *him* out. For the first time, I had that thing. I was able to put some punches together. And thanks to Father Lang, I had some confidence. It must have showed, because Joe Louis was there and when he came into the dressing room later, he shook my hand.

"He's arrived," he told Joe Glaser. "Go ahead with him."

After that, George and Wiley tried to make me believe that they always had confidence in me. Three weeks later, I outpointed a rugged journeyman, Garth Panter, over ten rounds in Detroit. The date was important, May 4, the day after my thirty-fourth birthday. That night some of my old Detroit friends had a party for me, and naturally my pop was there. I had a good time, because I knew I had looked good, but nobody had as good a time as Pop. With me fighting again, and winning, he had somebody to be proud of.

"You know where Junior gets his punch?" he said.

"I have no idea," George answered, baiting him.

"From me," Pop said. "When I was working my farm in Georgia, before I came to Detroit, I had a big ol' mule I used to ride around. One day we were out in the fields and that mule didn't want to go back to the barn. Didn't want to budge. I balled my fist and hit him between the eyes. And that mule went to his knees. When he got up, he knew who was the boss. He trotted right back to the barn. And that's where Junior gets his punch from."

He had everybody laughing with that one, even me, because I had never heard that story before.

It was a good party. Glaser and Braca and George and Wiley, and the Little Colonel, Vic Marsillo, we were all one big happy family again.

After we got back to New York, we had a big decision to make on my next opponent. I had reached the point where the IBC wanted to give me a shot at Bobo Olson's middle-weight title. But first, I had to earn it with a good win over a contender. We settled on Rocky Castellani, who was ranked as the number-one contender. He was a rangy, hard-hitting guy out of Erie, Pennsylvania, who had lost a fifteen-round decision to Olson in a title bout the year before. He wanted another shot at Olson, and he thought he could take me. So we got Olson to agree that the winner would get a title shot. The match was made for July 22 in San Francisco. One morning when I was doing roadwork out there along the beach, Olson jogged by, going the other way.

"Hi, Carl," I called.

He waved and said, "Hiya, Ray," but when he was out of earshot, Gainford laughed.

"Why did you call him Carl?" George said.

"That's his name," I said. "Carl Olson."

"I know," George replied, "but when a man is the champ, you're supposed to call him Champ."

"He's not the champ. He just happens to have *my* title."

That was big talk for somebody who was a three-to-one underdog to Castellani. During the early rounds, I worked him over in the midsection but in the sixth, I got careless. With a hard hitter that's a mistake. He caught me with three quick punches—a right to the jaw, a left hook, and one of those clubbing right hands that feels as if you've been whacked with a baseball bat. I went down in a heap. I heard the referee counting ". . . four . . . five . . ." and he seemed to be counting quickly.

In those split seconds, all my problems seemed to go through my mind.

Was it worth it to get up? Would he knock me out? Was this the wild kid with a good punch that George had warned me about? Except for the Maxim thing, I had never been knocked out, and was this awkward slugger, this club fighter, was he going to be the first man to really knock me out?

The hell he was, I told myself.

At eight I grabbed one of the ropes and flung myself up in time. Castellani rushed me.

Use your bag of tricks, I thought.

With one glove on the top rope to support myself, I flicked the other glove in Castellani's face as I slid from side to side. It confused him for a few seconds. That was all I needed for my head to clear. I took it slow in the seventh, conserving my energy. In the eighth I knew I had to gamble. I needed the last three rounds. I got them and salvaged a split decision.

I had earned a shot at Olson for *my* title. The world was moving for me again.

When I went to Chicago to sign for the Olson match, Ernie Braca accompanied me. On the train coming home, we were in the dining car when the steward requested if two women might sit in the two empty chairs at our table.

"It depends how pretty they are," Ernie winked.

They qualified. They were from San Francisco, a pair of Nob Hill socialites and good conversationalists. When they realized who I was, they told me that they had seen me against Castellani. After coffee, one of them suggested that I drop in to visit them at the Hotel Pierre in New York. When they left, I turned to Ernie.

"Did you notice anything?" I asked.

"No, what?" he replied, looking up.

"They invited *me*," I said, "not us."

I wasn't as popular with the odds-makers. They had me a four-to-one underdog against Olson. The sportswriters didn't think much of my chances. After the Castellani fight, Frank Graham had written in the *Journal-American* that years ago Mike Jacobs should have permitted me to fight for the lightweight title because it "would have been possible for Ray to read in the book that he was the lightweight, the welterweight and the middleweight champion . . . and it would be nice for him to look back on it when Bobo finishes him off."

In the days before the Olson fight, he wrote that I "had a good workout . . . but the gym at Greenwood Lake is a long way from the ring in the Chicago Stadium—a way that cannot be measured in miles alone."

True enough. I had measured it in dollars and desire. I was desperate for money. My end would approach $50,000. In order to assure another big payday, I had to win. If I lost, I was through, a has-been who had come close but had missed. In order to protect themselves, the IBC had forced me to sign an exclusive contract. If I won, I had to fight for them or with their blessing. Unlike the earlier years, I had no choice, no bargaining power. It was take it or leave it, and this time I had to take it.

I had to take it from my entourage, too. George and Wiley, Joe Glaser and Ernie Braca, all the people who once had told me to quit—now they were raving about me. Hypocrites. But what really annoyed me was the IBC's attitude. They treated me like a challenger.

Before my other title fights in Chicago with LaMotta and Graziano, the IBC publicity man there, Ben Bentley, always was assigned to my camp. His job was handling the interviews with the sportswriters and the radio-TV people. But this time he was working in Olson's camp. He had deserted me.

"Why isn't Ben with me?" I asked Truman Gibson.

"Olson likes him," Gibson said, "and he asked for him."

"I like him, too, and I'm asking for him now."

"You're not the champion, Ray," he said, "Olson is, and he has his choice."

"You want Olson to win, don't you?" I snarled.

He walked away without answering me. His attitude was typical of all the IBC people. But that only increased my desire. My confidence was solid already. I had never had too much trouble with Olson. I had knocked him out in the twelfth round in 1950. I had earned a fifteen-round decision in 1951. This time my plan was to go for a quick knockout.

After the weigh-in, instead of returning to the hotel, I holed up at Killer Johnson's house.

"I want to be by myself," I told Drew Brown, a new man with me. "Keep everybody out of here."

Drew Brown went by a nickname, Boudini, and he had been with me for a few months. He liked to run in the morning with me, and he liked to pray in the churchyard with me, and he seemed to like me for me. At least he hadn't turned on me as the others had. After the way George and Wiley and Ernie Braca and Joe Glaser had given up on me, I was withdrawing more and more into myself, unable to trust anybody. Now, in the hours before the opportunity to regain my title, I realized I had to win, that a loss would end my comeback because none of the promoters would take me seriously anymore.

"Here's your steak," Edna Mae called, knocking on the door.

Edna Mae had prepared my meal, like she always did the days I fought. In boxing you learn not to trust strangers with your food when you're going into the ring a few hours later. I'd heard stories about food being tampered with from the time I was around Jack Blackburn in Joe Louis's camp.

Not that there's anything fancy about a fighter's meal. The best food is the simple food.

In my early years, I always had poached eggs the afternoon of a fight but I had learned that a steak was more nutritious. I usually ate with people around me, laughing and telling jokes or playing cards, but not this time. I ate alone and when Boudini came in to take the dishes away, I stretched out on the bed and tried to take a nap. It was no use. In my mind Olson's round face was bobbing and weaving in front of me.

"Nothin' to worry about, Robinson," George had told me. "You took Olson before, and you always look great in Chicago."

I always had until I lost to Tiger Jones, but I did like to fight in Chicago. For one thing, I liked the gloves. Different commissions have contracts with different equipment manufacturers. We always used Frager gloves in Chicago. They were my favorites, because the thumb was part of the mitt. With these gloves, you couldn't be thumbed. Suddenly, the

longest hours had ended and we were in the car on the way
to the Stadium, and then in the dressing room, and in the
ring. When the bell rang, Olson came out strong. But I was
on time from the beginning. I dominated the first round. In
the second he was digging a few good punches into my belly
when I let go a left hook that stunned him.

His eyes were dazed, and when his gloves dropped, I realized I had a chance to finish him.

The crowd realized it too and their roar exploded around
me. I was so excited, my arms were trembling with emotion.
I was about to regain *my* title and in those split seconds, my
mind worked the way it had been taught to work. Many
years earlier, in that rowboat on Greenwood Lake, Jack
Blackburn had told me how to finish a man.

"Don't lose your head, Chappie," he had said. "When a
man's in trouble, that's the time to hold your head. That
man will still be there. Haste makes waste."

I respected his advice because he had tutored Joe Louis,
and Joe was the best finisher ever. If he got a man in trouble, forget it. And if a cat even stumbled accidentally, Joe
finished him. After my lesson from Jack Blackburn, I had
developed into a good finisher and now, when I needed it
most, at the age of thirty-four and with Bobo Olson wobbling in front of me, his advice was controlling my mind,
and through it, my muscles.

Without rushing, I ripped a right uppercut at Olson and
followed with a left hook.

And suddenly, he was on his back. At eight he made a
move to get up, but he rolled over and he was counted out.

Hopping through the ropes, George and Wiley and June
Clark lifted me onto their shoulders and paraded me around.

Ben Bentley, who did the public-address announcing in
Chicago, jumped into the ring and grabbed the microphone.

"Ladies and gentlemen," he proclaimed, holding my right

arm aloft, "the winner by a knockout at two minutes and fifty-two seconds of the second round, the world middleweight champion for the third time . . ."

In the roar of 12,411 spectators, I remembered how he had done the publicity in Olson's camp.

"Ain't you holding up the wrong man's hand?" I snarled at him. "Ain't you got the wrong winner?"

In my corner, George and Wiley were dancing, and down below, Joe Glaser and Ernie Braca were waving their arms and shouting and slapping the shoulders of everybody they knew.

You bastards, I thought. *You bastards told me I was through. You told me to quit.*

Emotionally, I collapsed. I was sobbing so much that my body shook. I felt the tears rolling down my face. They were tears of happiness but also tears of anger. They were tears of pride but also tears of revenge. Wrapping a towel around my face, George led me out of the ring. I let him do it, even though I had really wanted to walk out of that ring alone, the same way I had made my comeback.

At the Archway Lounge that night, Killer Johnson had his party.

"We've been saving the food," he laughed, "since Tiger Jones."

My joy at regaining my title hadn't even been dimmed by the Internal Revenue Service. Their agents had put a lien on my earnings for $81,000 in unpaid taxes.

My tax troubles had begun, but I didn't care. I was the champ again.

21

Turmoil and Taxes

When we boarded the Twentieth Century Limited for New York, I took out a new pack of cards and snapped the cellophane on it.

"Well, the boss is going to play this time," Wiley said, laughing. "Nice to have you back, boss. Missed you last time."

The last time had been the lonely trip following my loss to Tiger Jones. This time I didn't want to hide. I wanted to take my bows where everybody could see me—everybody who had warned me that "they never come back," everybody who wanted my autograph, everybody who wanted to shake my hand, like the conductor.

"You were great," he said after taking our tickets.

"Well, thank you, ol' buddy," I said. "By the way, what time do we stop at 125th Street in the morning?"

"We don't stop there," he said, "we go right through into Grand Central Terminal."

"It would save us a lot of time," June Clark said, "if we could stop there. Our office is right near there. Couldn't you check it out?"

"I'll find out," he said.

Sometime later he returned to tell me that the engineer had agreed to make a fast stop at the 125th Street platform.

When the conductor departed, George was puzzled. He hadn't heard me ask the conductor.

"This train don't stop at 125th Street," George said.

"It will tomorrow," June said. "It will for the champ."

The next day, the customers were three deep at the bar in my café. The sweet sounds had returned—the customers calling me "Champ" and the bartenders jingling the cash register. Taped to the mirror behind the bar was one of Jimmy Cannon's columns in the New York *Post*. He had described my comeback as "the greatest in the history of sports," and he no longer was advising me to retire. In the *Journal-American*, Frank Graham had written that I "was a most remarkable man, and most unpredictable." I was anticipating another Neil Award as the Fighter of the Year for 1955. Several days later, when the Boxing Writers' Association had its vote, George phoned me.

"You'll never believe it, Robinson," he said.

"Why not, was it unanimous?" I asked, quite seriously.

"No," he said, "Basilio got it instead."

Carmen Basilio was the welterweight champion, but more important, he was an IBC fighter, one of Jim Norris's favorites. Some of the IBC people had lobbied for Basilio, on the basis that he had never won the Neil Award and that I had. But nobody had ever made a comeback like mine. To me, the Neil Award was important, and on the phone that afternoon with George I wept.

"Forget it, Robinson," he said, "you'll win it in '56."

I haven't forgotten it to this day, and I never will. I feel I deserved that award. Not getting it was my biggest hurt in boxing. And when I began to train for my rematch with Bobo Olson, I was determined to show everybody that my knockout over him hadn't been a fluke. The return bout was scheduled for Los Angeles, in old Wrigley Field, on May 18. After a few weeks at Greenwood Lake, I set up a training camp in a cabin out on the edge of the California desert, near San Jacinto, some fifty miles southeast of Los Angeles. One night about two weeks before the fight, George took me aside.

"You're too sharp, Robinson, you been working too hard," he said. "You better go to bed with Edna Mae tonight."

I knew what he meant. One of the big sacrifices in being a champion is sex. If you're a fighter, you need your energy. You can't leave it with a woman, even if she's your wife. This sacrifice had created a problem with Edna Mae. She often complained, "When you're the wife of a fighter, your love life suffers." And she had a legitimate gripe. Before a big fight, I would abstain from sex for about six weeks. I needed six good weeks to build myself into condition. But every so often George would realize that I was too sharp, too soon. When a fighter hits a peak in training, it's hard to hold him at that peak for more than a few days. He usually declines. But if he's near a peak early, a good trainer drops him below that peak and then brings him up to it again in time for the fight.

That's what George was doing for me now, just as Jack Blackburn had told me years before. To make it official, George mentioned it to Edna Mae.

"You know best, George, you know best," I told him. "If you tell me to go to bed with Edna Mae, I'll do it."

"How come this is the only time I know best, Robinson?" he said. "How come you will listen to me about this?"

I had to laugh at that, but sex is an important psychological factor in training for a fight. In abstaining from it, you're not only stronger but you *think* you're stronger. You're meaner because your nervous system is on edge. And when you walk into the center of the ring for the referee's instructions and stare at your opponent, you dislike him more than ever because he's the symbol of all your sacrifices. But for a weak one, a sneaker, as trainers call them, sex works the other way. When he goes up into the ring, he's got a guilty conscience. He doubts his stamina. He believes that his opponent is better conditioned than he is. Mentally, he's beaten before the bell rings.

But when sex is prescribed during training, it's more enjoyable than usual. The next day, you're really ready for the grind again.

By the time of the Olson match, I was at my peak. When my opportunity developed in the fourth round, I finished him. But in the box office, the IRS agents had grabbed almost $90,000 out of my $105,000 purse. I needed another title bout.

A few months later the IBC matched me with Gene Fullmer, a stocky little Mormon from West Jordan, Utah, and the number-one challenger. We were scheduled for December 12 at the Garden, but I developed a virus. The new date was January 2, 1957, but I was having trouble sleeping.

"How about some sleeping pills?" I asked Dr. Nardiello.

"No," he said. "I don't want you to get used to them, but I'll give you a few tranquilizers. By bedtime, you'll be so relaxed that you'll go right to sleep."

I was so relaxed, I went to sleep in there with Fullmer. The tranquilizers had lulled me. That night I was in the ring but *Ray Robinson* wasn't. Fullmer's style bothered me too. He had a barroom brawler's style, which I hadn't expected because Mormons don't drink. In my stupor, I even let him get me against the ropes, something I seldom did. When your back is on the ropes, it feels like it's being touched with lighted matches—rope burns, they're called. One of the ropes even broke, and I almost fell out of the ring. It wasn't my night. Fullmer got the fifteen-round decision, but at least I got $140,000 and the IRS agents let me keep it.

I finally had some walking-around money but I was

walking around as an ex-champion. Fullmer had my title.

The return was set for Chicago on May 1, but I was having trouble training. I was so tired I wasn't able to run much in the morning. I'd get up early and go down to the park near Lake Michigan but after I'd run a mile or two, I'd poop out.

"Robinson, what the hell is the matter with you?" George said to me after a bad workout.

"I don't know," I said, "but I'm having trouble concentrating. Maybe it's all mental."

I prayed with Father Lang, the Franciscan priest who had guided me spiritually before the Olla and Olson fights in my comeback. As a challenger, I was on another comeback and for one of the few times in my career, I watched films of my opponent. I had done it for Randy Turpin the second time, but usually I didn't bother with films, even for guys I hadn't seen before. I preferred to learn about somebody when he was in the ring with me, not from when he was in the ring with somebody else. But for the return with Fullmer, movies were necessary. I needed to study his style. I needed to know all I could about him. Suddenly, watching the films one day, I saw what I had been hoping to find. He liked to throw a right hand to the body and when he did, his jaw was open for my left hook.

"Operation Left Hook," the Garden publicity man, Murray Goodman, called it.

Through three rounds I waited, watching his hands as he bulled at me. In the fourth he was moving at me again, his head low, his tiny eyes squinting with sweat. I feinted a left hook, leaving my midsection open. You've got to let a fish see the bait before it'll bite, and Fullmer bit. He let go his right hand, exposing his jaw.

His jaw looked as big as any of the jaws on the Mount Rushmore monuments.

Snapping a left hook with all my strength, I nailed him as he moved toward me, adding to the impact. His head snapped back and he went down as if I had hit him with an ax. At eight, he attempted to get up but his legs wouldn't work for him.

"Operation Left Hook!" I heard Murray Goodman shouting.

Suddenly, dramatically, I was the champion again. I had won my title for the fourth time with the most perfect punch of my career. Never before had Fullmer been knocked out. He was on his feet now, blinking his eyes and looking around, asking his handlers what had happened, and all around me the noise of the crowd was making my kind of music.

In my dressing room later, I was explaining to the sportswriters, "The punch was—"

"Was beautiful," Fullmer said from behind the cluster of writers. "I just came in to congratulate you, Ray."

"That's right," his manager, Marv Jensen, said, "and I want to add my congratulations. It was a great punch, a perfect punch."

"Well, thank you," I said. "It's really nice of you guys to come in here like this."

It not only was nice, it was unheard of. In other sports, it's quite common for an opponent to enter a rival's dressing room. In the World Series, the losing manager almost always goes to the winning team's dressing room and congratulates the manager. It happens in football and basketball, too. In boxing, once you're out of the ring, that's usually the last you see of your opponent. Gene Fullmer and Marv Jensen were different. Win or lose, they were gentlemen. But in boxing, that can be a mistake. While they were being gentlemen, the IBC had been scheming to deprive them of a third title bout.

The night before, Jim Norris had visited me at the Conrad Hilton Hotel.

"If you beat Fullmer," Norris said, "we've got something big for you—Basilio outdoors."

Norris was maneuvering his boy, Carmen Basilio, who had lost the welterweight title in 1956 in a fifteen-round decision with Johnny Saxton. In a rematch, Basilio knocked him out in nine. In a third match, Basilio knocked him out in two. Norris wanted to put Basilio in with me—the welterweight champion against the middleweight champion.

"Two champions for my title," I said, "that should be worth a lot of money."

"It will be," Norris assured me, "and the commissioner really wants the fight."

"But doesn't Fullmer have an agreement for a third fight if I beat him tomorrow night?"

"Leave that to us," Norris said. "The commissioner and I will work it out with Fullmer."

Norris obviously had discussed the details with Julius Helfand, the chairman of the New York State Athletic Commission. Not that it mattered much to me. I knew that I'd make more money with Basilio. And after I knocked out Fullmer, I really put it to Norris.

"Jim," I said, "I want forty-five per cent of the live gate."

"I don't see how we can do that, Ray," he said. "After all, Basilio is a champion too."

"In this fight he's a challenger. I'm the champion."

I got the 45 per cent, but to protect the IBC treasury, Norris suggested that my money be deferred over a period of four years. That couldn't be put into the standard contract filed with the commission, so an additional contract was drawn up. It also included a clause that a television commitment, either for home TV or theater TV, could not be made without my written consent as well as the IBC's. Marty Machat, a theatrical lawyer I had come to know, had drawn up the contract. Several days later, Norris asked me to visit him at the Garden in his second-floor office with the big dusty windows overlooking Eighth Avenue.

"We've got a great theater-TV deal," he began.

"That's terrific," I answered. "I'm listening."

"Nate Halpern's company, Theater Network Television, has guaranteed the availability of three hundred and seventy-five thousand seats in various theaters and arenas around the country."

"What's so great about that?"

"It's the biggest theater-TV deal ever for a fight," Norris said.

"It's the biggest nothing to me."

"What are you talking about, Ray?"

"Jim, this deal can be bettered."

"I don't see how," Norris said, "but I'll ask Halpern to take a survey and line up as many locations as possible. Fair enough?"

"Fair enough," I said.

Theater-TV was in its infancy. The first theater-TV network for boxing had been organized six years earlier, in 1951, for the Joe Louis-Lee Savold fight in Madison Square Garden. Another had been used for the first Rocky Marciano-Jersey Joe Walcott heavyweight title fight in 1952. Neither had been much of a success. But the idea intrigued me because it represented so much potential income. Several days later, the situation intrigued me even more. My attorney, Marty Machat, received a letter from Norris explaining that Halpern's survey had resulted in a *lower* total of available seats. The number was down to 250,000.

"Marty," I said, "Halpern can't be the only one capable of setting up theater-TV. If he can do it, somebody else can."

As a lawyer who represented several entertainers, Marty knew many show-business people. In searching for someone to organize a rival theater-TV network, he discovered Irving Kahn. Small and chubby, Kahn operated a firm known as TelePrompTer; his machines enabled TV people to read a script off an enlarged tape rather than memorize it. Kahn had never operated theater-TV, but he knew how it was done and he knew how to obtain the proper equipment. Marty arranged for Kahn to see me at my Greenwood Lake camp.

"Mister Kahn," I asked him that day, "are you willing to pay for this fight, I mean really pay?"

"That's why I'm here," he said. "I can guarantee you half a million spectators—not seats, spectators. I want to put this fight on theater-TV and I'm sure we can get together on the money if you tell me your price."

"I want two hundred and fifty thousand for myself, a hundred and twenty-five for Basilio, and the Garden has to make money, too."

"Those numbers sound reasonable," he said, "and I'm sure I'll be able to satisfy the Garden."

"Then as far as I'm concerned, we have a deal. My contract with the Garden calls for the best TV deal, and your deal is better than Halpern's. I'll call Norris and arrange a meeting to present your offer."

I phoned Norris and, without telling him about Kahn's offer, asked to see him on Monday. He agreed. Kahn departed. Later that day, Harry Markson phoned me.

"Mister Norris isn't feeling well," he explained. "He has to see his doctor Monday, but he'll be here Tuesday morning."

On Tuesday I arrived with Kahn, his lawyers, and Marty Machat and George Gainford. Waiting with Norris was Ned Irish, the executive vice-president of Madison Square Garden. I outlined Kahn's offer and explained that while Nate Halpern was guaranteeing the availability of seats, Kahn was guaranteeing customers.

"It's not how many seats you got," George Gainford interrupted, "it's how many asses you got in them seats."

His irrefutable logic would become known in boxing as Gainford's Law, but Norris and Irish were not impressed.

"It's a nice deal," Norris said, "but it's too late. Ned Irish signed a contract yesterday with Halpern."

Yesterday was when Norris had to see his doctor instead of me. Somehow I didn't consider it a coincidence.

"You had no right to do that," I roared. "It's in our contract that my written consent is necessary regarding the disposition of the ancillary rights."

"The what?" Norris said.

"The ancillary rights," explained Marty Machat, "involve all the rights subservient to the actual event itself."

"That's a nice legal phrase," Norris said, "but the point is that we've already signed a contract with Nate Halpern."

"Never mind, Jim," I said, "there's no problem."

He glanced at me, wondering what I had in mind.

"Since you've already signed the contract," I said, "*you* fight Basilio, and have Ned Irish work in your corner."

I stormed out into the hall. Marty and George joined me. Moments later, I was told there was a phone call for me from Julius Helfand, the chairman of the State Athletic Commission.

"Ray," a voice said, "Commissioner Helfand."

"You find out things real fast, Commissioner."

"The only thing I'm interested in, Ray, is having a fight on September twenty-third. I'm not concerned about your squabbles with Jim Norris, but I want you to promise me that you'll be in the ring with Basilio at the Stadium."

"The only thing I'm interested in, Commissioner, is the IBC living up to the other contract."

"What other contract?" he said. "We only have one contract on file here, the standard form."

"No, you don't, Commissioner. On the top of the standard form is typed, THIS IS PART II OF THE ORIGINAL DOCUMENT. The original document, Commissioner, has the clause about my written consent being necessary for the TV rights."

"Ray," he said, "we'll have a hearing on this, but I want you to go through with this fight."

"There'll be a fight, Commissioner, as long as you go through with upholding that contract."

At the hearing the following Monday, Helfand decreed that if I didn't show up on September 23, I would be suspended and my title would be taken away. I agreed to appear, but the squabble over the TV situation had not been settled.

"I'll be there," I told Helfand, "but if I see, or even am told of, a television camera or radio in Yankee Stadium, I will not be responsible for my actions. I will walk out of the ring."

My ultimatum had not solved the theater-TV deal, a source of important money for me. In order to get it settled, I had to negotiate with Norris. After the commission meeting, I stopped at his office. He pointed to a sandwich wrapped in wax paper on his desk.

"Take it, Ray," he said. "Corned beef on a poppyseed roll. Delicious."

Jim always had to have his corned-beef sandwiches on poppyseed rolls. Mushky McGee, an assistant everything at the IBC, had delivered them from a nearby delicatessen. Any other sandwich might have appealed to me, but corned beef was too greasy.

"No, thanks, Jim," I said. "You like them. You have it."

After we began our discussions, Jim started to cough as if he were going to vomit. We rushed him into the men's room, where he vomited and collapsed.

"Call an ambulance!" somebody yelled.

"It looks like a heart attack," somebody else said.

"Keep him warm," another shouted.

He looked awful. All the color had drained out of his face. He always had a tan, but suddenly he was gray. Kneeling there, I suddenly realized that the IBC people around me would assume that I had aggravated him into a heart attack.

"Jim," I whispered, massaging his heart, "everything's going to be all right. I'll do anything you say."

Within minutes, the ambulance, its siren wailing, was outside. Moments later, the hospital attendants had him on a stretcher. On the way into the ambulance, I stayed alongside the stretcher.

"You'll be all right, Jim," I said. "Everything will be all right. Anything you say, Jim. I'll do anything you say."

I meant it. I wasn't going to continue arguing with a man having a heart attack. His illness was first diagnosed as food poisoning. The corned beef had been sprayed accidentally with insect repellent in the delicatessen kitchen. His lawyer, Seymour Friedman, and Ned Irish also suffered food poisoning from similar sandwiches. After a more thorough examination, Norris was discovered to have had heart damage. He was in the hospital seven weeks, but he never blamed our negotiations for it.

"Why do you put up with Robinson? You don't need him," Norris once was asked by Harry Markson.

"I know," Norris replied, surely recalling his long stay in the hospital, "but he's such a *good* fighter."

With Norris in the hospital, the theater-TV problem was

resolved at another meeting at the commission. Halpern offered to guarantee me $255,000, which was $5000 more than Kahn's figure. Marty Machat and I stepped outside the hearing room to discuss it with Kahn.

"Irving," asked Marty, "will you raise your offer?"

"No," he replied, "I don't want to get into a bidding contest. I made a generous offer and I think you should stand by me."

"I'd like to," I said, "but we're involved in a principle of the best deal, and Halpern's offer is now the best deal."

"Do me a favor, then," Kahn said. "See if you can get me a few locations to handle on Halpern's network for this fight."

"You're a sharp man," I said. "You want experience?"

"The next time," Kahn said, "maybe we'll do business."

Halpern agreed to let Kahn operate locations in four of the smaller cities. The squabble was over. I hadn't been able to concentrate on preparing for Basilio. Other distractions developed. Marty Machat, in checking my contracts, had suggested that I reorganize my advisers. Two years earlier I had added my man Killer Johnson to the payroll. He was one of the managers "of record," along with George and Ernie Braca. Also on the payroll was Joe Glaser.

"Do you realize how you're being cut up?" Marty said.

"I got a lot of people," I said, "but I need a lot."

"As a group, they're making more than you are," he said. "You've got George and Killer splitting thirty-three and a third per cent. You've got Braca getting ten per cent, and Glaser getting ten per cent. That adds up to fifty-three and a third per cent, more than half of your money. Add the money you give Wiley and June Clark and everybody else around you, and there's not much left for Ray Robinson. My advice is to get rid of a few."

"I need everybody," I argued.

"Not everybody," he said. "George and Killer, they *do* something for you, they help you, and so do the other people around the camp, but Braca and Glaser don't do anything for you. All they're doing is waiting for you to pay them."

The more I thought about it, the more that number 53⅓ annoyed me. I told Braca and Glaser I didn't need them anymore.

Not long after that, and shortly before the Basilio fight, I was served with legal papers. Braca was suing me for $169,084.60 for breach of contract and Glaser was suing me for about $80,000, the mortgage he had obtained on my business buildings in 1954.

Several months later, we settled with Braca for about $18,000 and Glaser later foreclosed.

Maybe the turmoil affected my performance, maybe not. I thought I won. So did the referee, Al Berl, who gave me nine rounds. So did the people in the crowd of 38,072 who booed the votes for Basilio by the two judges, Artie Aidala and Bill Recht. But once again, I was an *ex*-champion. I was disgusted.

"I don't know if I'll ever fight again," I said in my dressing room. "There's too much intrigue."

At ringside, the IBC people had been *too* happy about Basilio's victory. I had sliced him over the left eye in two places. He needed two stitches in each cut, but instead of having them taken in his dressing room, he bothered to go downtown to St. Clare's Hospital where Norris was still convalescing. His boy Basilio visited him the next day, with *my* title.

To make it worse, the Internal Revenue Service had my money.

After the bell had rung for the first round, an IRS agent had served a notice of levy ordering the IBC to hold *all* my money, both from live gate and the ancillary rights. I owed the government about $80,000 in taxes from the previous year, in disallowed expenses. The government wanted to get square. The situation also afforded an opportunity for the IRS to withhold my 1957 taxes, but the government didn't know about deferred income. My money was to be spread over four years: 40 per cent that year, 20 per cent in 1958, 20 per cent in 1959, and the final 20 per cent in 1960.

When my earnings were official, they added up to more than half a million dollars: $228,666.71 from the live gate, plus my guarantee of $255,000 from the theater-TV, plus about $30,000 from the radio and movie rights.

As soon as the IRS discovered the payment plan, their agents claimed it was illegal. They argued that since I had earned all the money in 1957, I had to pay taxes on it all. They were so upset that they invoked a rare section of the Internal Revenue Code which enables them to terminate a taxpayer's year. They computed my tax on my total earnings for the year, including the two Fullmer fights.

"Robinson," George said, shaking his head, "you need more lawyers than sparring partners."

Marty Machat arranged to have a tax lawyer, Howard Rumpf, handle my negotiations with the IRS director in New York City. After a few sessions, the district director agreed to release $100,000 in order for me to pay the people around me. My case went to the national office in Washington. Another tax lawyer, Bob Raum, accompanied us to our hearing in the huge gray Treasury Building. We walked into a big room with a long conference table. We sat on one side and, a few minutes later, half a dozen of the government's tax people strolled in and sat on the other side.

"Now, y'all," said the government man in charge, "what can we do for y'all?"

That's all I need, I thought, *a Southerner ruling on a Ne-*

22

My Belief

I had earned more than half a million dollars but I hadn't collected a penny of it.

"And the word," a friend of mine told me a few days before the return with Basilio, "is that the IRS agents are going to pounce on your purse again."

The return was scheduled for March 28, 1958, a Tuesday less than three days away.

My man Irving Kahn of TelePrompTer was handling the theater-TV arrangements. The negotiations with Jim Norris had been smooth. Basilio was the champion, but my contract for the first fight had stipulated that if Basilio won, I was to get the same share in the return as he did, 30 per cent of everything. All was quiet, or so Norris and Truman Gibson thought. But in my room in the Conrad Hilton that Saturday afternoon, I was scheming to prevent the IRS from attaching my money. I phoned Gibson.

"Truman," I said, "I want my two-hundred-thousand-dollar guarantee by tomorrow. In cash."

"Don't be ridiculous, Ray," he said. "Even if I had the authority to give it to you, I couldn't get it. The banks are closed on Saturday and Sunday, you know that."

"Not your bank," I said.

"What do you mean, not *my* bank?" he said.

"The bank Norris owns."

Norris and his business partner, Arthur Wirtz, controlled one of the Chicago banks.

"You tell Norris," I said firmly, "to have somebody open up the bank by tomorrow and have that money delivered here."

"I can't do that," he groaned. "I can't ask Jim to do that. Maybe on Monday, when the bank is open, but not today."

"Truman, don't 'no' me. Either open up the bank or I'll call off the fight. You know me, Truman, I don't pretend."

Several minutes later, he phoned me back.

"I'll bring the money tomorrow," he said, "but you make your own arrangements to put it down in the hotel safe."

"I knew you could do it, Truman. I'm proud of you."

I had my money, but I also had something else, a virus. I had tried to keep it quiet, but there's no way to keep something like that an absolute secret. I discovered that the word was out on Monday night when Frank Sinatra visited me. Over the years, Frank had seen several of my fights. He had made a special trip from Las Vegas for this fight and my man Frank always liked to place a bet, a knowledgeable bet.

"How do you feel?" he asked.

"I feel pretty good," I lied.

"Out in Vegas, all the smart money is betting Basilio. He's eight to five and on my way over here, somebody told me that they had it from a good source that you couldn't win, and I asked him if his source was Sugar Ray because that's the only source I'm interested in. How do you feel? Is anything the matter with you?"

"Frank, I feel fine," I lied.

"Out in Vegas there's a rumor that you've got a virus."

"Smart money ain't so smart," I lied again. "I'm okay."

"Are you going to win?" he asked.

"Frank," I said, "every fight I go into, I *think* that I'm going to win. It doesn't mean that I *am* going to win it, but I *think* I'm going to win it. I don't mind if you bet Basilio. You're my friend and I'd like to see you win your bet, and maybe you ought to bet with the smart money."

"But the smart money isn't going to be in the ring," he said. "*You* are."

"Let me tell you something, Frank," I said, honestly. "I'm going in there and get that title, and I don't care what anybody says, or what the smart money thinks."

"That's all I wanted to hear, Ray," he said.

I didn't tell Frank that everybody around me had been pleading with me to postpone the fight. The virus had lingered in me for about a week. Dr. Nardiello was with me, and so were Dr. John Holloman and Dr. Robert Bennett. Each of them advised me to request a postponement. Ordinarily, I would have agreed. Over the years, I had asked for delays for a lot of reasons. Ever since the loss to Jake LaMotta in 1943 I had made sure that I was in perfect condition, but somehow it was different this time. On the night before the fight, I attempted to explain it to Father Lang, my Franciscan priest.

"If you're not well," he said, "you're endangering your health."

"Father," I said, "I just feel like I've *got* to go through with this fight. This is my belief. You know me. I'd usually call off a fight if I sneezed. But you also know how I believe that if God is with me, I don't care what the situation is, and if He's not with me, it wouldn't make any difference what my physical condition is. This time, I'm sure that God is with me. That is my *belief*."

"Ray," he said, "I admire you. I'm a priest, but I've never put my belief to that test."

"I believe," I said, "that God will carry me through this fight. Somehow, someway, He'll carry me through."

"I've never been put to a test between God and common sense," he said. "I don't know if I'm that strong."

"Father," I said, "God will give me more strength than the virus will take away."

The doctors of the Illinois Athletic Commission were not as easy to convince. The weigh-in was scheduled for noon in the ring at the Chicago Stadium. In my dressing room, I was stripping down to my shorts when a couple of commission doctors arrived to give me the routine physical. One of them slid a thermometer under my tongue. When it was removed, he studied it and glanced up quickly.

"You've got a hundred-and-three temperature," he said, "you can't fight with that."

"You must have made a mistake, Doc," I said. "I'm in great shape, Doc."

"I'm sorry," he said, "we can't permit you to fight with that fever."

Outside, I could hear the public-address system blaring, "Ray Robinson, will you please step into the ring."

"C'mon, Doc," I said, "they're waiting for me. I got to go and weigh in."

"You're staying here," he said, "until we tell Lou Radzienda about this."

Lou Radzienda was the chairman of the commission, an old buddy of mine for years in the gyms around Chicago. He huddled with the doctors for several minutes. He kept nodding his head.

"Ray," he said, finally coming over to me, "there's no way that . . ."

"Please, Lou," I said, leading him into a corner for more privacy, "don't call off this fight."

"The doctor's report goes into the minutes of the commission meetings," he explained to me.

"Lou, please, do me a favor, ol' buddy."

"You don't understand," he said. "Suppose something happens to you. Do you realize what we'd be exposing the state to, what you'd be exposing me to if something happens?"

"Nothing's going to happen," I argued.

"You're ill. Anything can happen."

"Give me until five o'clock to get my temperature down. I'll have Doc Nardiello check me then and he'll phone you. He's a New York Commission doctor. He's official. Lou, you got to do me this favor. Five o'clock, Lou."

On the public-address system, I was being paged again, with urgency.

"C'mon, Lou, I got to weigh in. Five o'clock, Lou, five o'clock."

"All right," he said, "but if you're not better, the fight's off."

That afternoon the odds on Basilio went to two to one. If the gamblers had been able to confirm the virus, he might've been favored at five to one, maybe more. I was in bed at the Conrad Hilton. Shortly before five, Dr. Nardiello took my temperature.

"It's down a little, a hundred and one," he said.

"Doc, I'm all right, believe me that I am. You've been with me all these years, you've got to go along with me."

"I shouldn't be doing it," he said.

He picked up the phone and dialed the commission office where Lou Radzienda was waiting for the call.

"He'll be all right," Doc lied for me.

To make sure, he gave me two injections. Penicillin for the virus, B-12 for strength. In the fourth round that night I got through with a right hand that sliced the skin over Basilio's left eye. By the sixth, that eye had closed. As the rounds went by, it puffed up like a big black bulb. Basilio was half blind, as if he were "walking across Times Square

against the traffic with a hand clapped over his good eye,"
as Bob Considine wrote in the *Journal-American*. "Basilio
had to get in close and feel for his man, like a fighter in a
dark closet. He had to sense where to aim, what to throw. It
was a fight between a mole and a hawk."

The mole had stamina. The hawk was exhausted. The
virus was weakening me more and more.

Basilio was unable to fight his fight. When the fifteenth
round began, I knew I had piled up enough points to win.
In the final seconds, as the crowd of 17,976 began to roar, I
was convinced that God had been with me. Not only had He
guided me through fifteen rounds, but somehow He had
shut Basilio's eye. At the bell, I plopped onto my stool.

For the first time in my career, I was too exhausted to
stand in triumph, but I had won my title for the fifth time.

I stumbled to my dressing room with my arms draped
around George and Wiley. I toppled onto the rubbing table.
Outside, fists were pounding against the big metal door,
and in my daze I noticed a policeman leaning down toward
me.

"The press," he said, "the press wants to come in."

"Later," I gasped. "Tell 'em I'll see 'em later."

As it developed, later would be more than two hours later
in my bed at the Conrad Hilton. I had half-fainted in the
dressing room. When I was conscious enough to leave,
George and Wiley carried me again. At the hotel, I was so
exhausted, I didn't realize that I went up to my room in
an elevator. I hadn't ridden in an elevator in more than
twenty years, ever since my bad experience in the Empire
State Building, but I wasn't aware of what was going on as I
returned to the hotel. I was beat, but not beaten. And as
the champion again, I was a celebrity. I always knew when
I was a celebrity, because when I was, other celebrities came
to see *me*. Like that night, two of my visitors were Walter

Winchell and one of my favorite Chicago people, night-club columnist Irv Kupcinet.

"You were marvelous, Sugar Ray," barked Winchell. "More marvelous than ever."

My belief had carried me through fifteen rounds and now Jim Norris wanted a third fight with Basilio. I demanded 45 per cent, but Basilio was asking for 30 per cent, an unreasonable amount for a challenger.

Our negotiations with Norris dragged into 1959, then Norris suddenly no longer ruled boxing. On January 12, the United States Supreme Court upheld a 1957 decision by Judge Sylvester J. Ryan in the Southern District of New York that the IBC was in violation of the Sherman Antitrust Act. In short, Judge Ryan's decision involved "divestiture, dissolution, and divorcement" of the IBC. I wasn't sorry. I had despised the exclusive contracts the IBC always demanded.

Norris and his partner, Arthur Wirtz, sold their interests in Madison Square Garden to the Graham-Paige Corporation for nearly four million dollars.

The new owners appointed Harry Markson the managing director of the newly named Madison Square Garden Boxing Club. Teddy Brenner, who had built a reputation in the smaller clubs around New York, was the new matchmaker. The first big match that Brenner wanted to make was between Basilio and me.

"We'll guarantee you three hundred and fifty thousand," he told me one afternoon in my Harlem office.

"Not enough," I said. "In fact, Teddy, you got to go a lot higher than that."

The next day, Ned Irish came to see me and went to $450,000. It still wasn't enough. I had been negotiating with Irving Kahn, my man at TelePrompTer, and he had mentioned that if he organized the promotion, my end would

be a guaranteed $750,000—three-quarters of a million. I
had to go for that. But the new owners weren't about to
quit. Admiral John Bergen, the chairman of the board, came
to see me himself. The admiral was a salty little guy who
looked like an admiral even in a gray flannel suit. I liked
him right away.

"Ray," he said, without any nonsense, "we'll guarantee
you more money than the Garden ever guaranteed anybody."

That was very nice, but he hadn't mentioned any numbers, so I just sat there and waited for him to be specific.

"Five hundred and fifty thousand dollars," he said, "and
in addition, you get fifty per cent of the net gate over four
hundred thousand, and also fifty per cent of the theater-
TV net over four hundred thousand."

"And our conservative estimate of net gate," interrupted
Markson, "is eight hundred and fifty thousand."

"And another thing, Ray," the admiral said, "we know
you're talking with Irving Kahn, but remember this—the
Garden is an established organization, a solid company. I
may be new, but Harry Markson has been around for years,
so has Ned Irish, and you'll be dealing with a solid company.
When you come in the day after the fight, you'll get your
check."

"I didn't once," I said, thinking of the first Basilio fight.

"That wasn't the Garden's fault, Ray, you know that,"
Markson said. "That was the Treasury Department. You always got your money every other time. Like the admiral
says, we're a solid company."

"Would you say Western Union is a solid company?"
I asked.

The admiral didn't seem to know what I was referring to.

"Admiral," I said, "Western Union owns something like
nineteen per cent of the stock in TelePrompTer, Irving

Kahn's company, and he says that Western Union has backed his guarantee to me of three-quarters of a million."

The admiral knew he was beaten, but he showed me some class.

"Ray," he said, his little jaw jutting out, "you are a businessman, but unlike other businessmen, you don't sell a product such as an automobile or a television set. You sell *yourself* and if you can get seven hundred and fifty thousand for putting yourself in a ring for another promoter, then you have to take it. From our projections we simply can't go any higher. I'm sorry, but good luck."

He really was new around boxing. No other American promoter had ever talked that nice to me.

Not everybody was being nice. I hadn't defended my title since the second Basilio fight, more than a year earlier. General Melvin Krulewitch, the new chairman of the New York State Athletic Commission, was threatening to take away my title. So were the men who headed the National Boxing Association.

It wasn't fair. I was prepared to fight, but Basilio was being used by Jim Norris.

I arranged for Johnny Attell to promote a third match with Basilio in Philadelphia. His guarantee for Basilio was $225,000, supplied by Irving Kahn, but Basilio wouldn't accept it. Obviously, he had been told by Norris to ignore anything that involved me. When the New York Commission ordered a hearing on whether to vacate the middleweight championship, I showed them a certified check for $225,000, Basilio's share. I also displayed documents that had been approved by the Pennsylvania Commission.

"I can't make another fighter fight," I said to General Krulewitch.

After that the New York Commission backed off, but the NBA continued to harass me. I had other problems. My sister Marie was pregnant, after more than twenty years of marriage, but she was having trouble carrying the baby. In her fifth month, she lost it. She was in the Medical Center, in a big room that looked out on the George Washington Bridge and across to the Palisades in New Jersey. She was going to have an exploratory operation to discover what had gone wrong and Mom was there with her. When I got up to go, Mom walked out into the hall with me.

"Ray," she said, "I think the doctor is going to give us some bad news."

"What do you mean, Mom?" I said. "Losing the baby was our bad news."

Without saying anything else, she turned and went back to the room. After the operation, I cornered her doctor to learn what he had discovered.

"Ray," he said, "your sister has cancer."

"How about the operation?" I said. "Couldn't you cut it out in the operation?"

"We sewed her back up," he said.

"But couldn't you have done something?" I said. "You're a doctor, aren't you?"

"It's too far gone," he said.

"How long is she going to live?" I asked.

"Four months, maybe five."

Four months, maybe five. Just like that. My sister Marie was going to die. My sister who had been like a mom to me, like a big brother, like a cheerleader. *Junior*, I could hear her saying when we were hungry kids, *you take my meat, I got to watch my weight.* I could see her coming out of the house to protect me when some older kid was chasing me. I could hear her shouting, *C'mon, Junior,* her voice above the thousands of voices at my fights. Now she was going to die. But my belief in God wouldn't let me be convinced. On my way downtown each morning, I had always stopped at a little church not far from my office. Now I really had something to pray for.

As the weeks passed, her condition got worse. She was in with other cancer patients. She knew what she had.

In my prayers I had told God that if it was His will that she die, He must help us hold our belief in Him and help us prepare to lose someone so dear to us. One day in church I was praying, staring up at the big crucifix, and maybe I imagined it, I don't know, maybe I dreamed it, but a voice spoke to me.

"Be still and know that I am God," the voice said, "for your sister shall be saved."

I took that to mean that Marie was going to get well. In the weeks that followed, she kept getting weaker and weaker but I refused to believe that she was going to die, because the voice from the crucifix had told me differently. Without telling her about the crucifix, my faith in her recovery was so strong that she gained spiritual strength from it. In her last hours, I was sure something would happen to cure her. She was in bed at Mom's house and Pop had come in from Detroit to see her.

"Junior," she whispered that last day, "I'm so sick, I'm so tired."

"Honey," I assured her, "everything will be okay now, you'll see."

In my belief, I thought everything would be all right. On my way out of the room, Mom grabbed me and told me that she might not live the night. I told her, for the first time, about the crucifix and about how the voice promised me that Marie would be saved.

"You misinterpreted it," Mom said. "Saved means that her soul will be saved, not her life."

My misinterpretation had confused me to the extent that I didn't care whether I lived or died. I knew all about saving a soul, but in my concern I had never thought of it that way. I had wanted Marie to live, to get well, to be saved from death, and in my concern that's all I was aware of. Now that Marie was about to die, now that Mom had spoken of the saving of her soul, now I realized it, but I couldn't sit around that house waiting for her to die. I had to *do* something so I got in my car. I was driving, but my mind was back in that bedroom with Marie, my Marie, and—wham! I had smashed my car into the rear end of another car stopped for a red light.

I wanted to pay the other driver out of my pocket for his damage, anything to avoid a discussion. He insisted on exchanging licenses and insurance cards. It took more than half an hour. I drove back to Mom's house. When I arrived, one of Marie's friends was in the doorway, crying.

"She just died," she told me. "She just smiled and closed her eyes."

I had believed so deeply. I had expected the doctor to tell me that Marie would be *saved*, that she would be healthy again, but now she was dead.

In the months to come, much of my world would die with her.

23

Millie

When the National Boxing Association vacated
its middleweight championship on May 4, 1959,
I didn't think it was fair, but I continued to
reign in New York and Massachusetts. More important, I
was coveting Archie Moore's kingdom among the light-
heavyweights.

"You can take him, Robinson," George had assured me,
"You're only thirty-eight, he's forty-two."

"No, he's forty-five," I said. "I checked that out. His
mother gives his birthday as December 13, 1913. I got to
believe his mother ahead of him. She ought to know when
he was born. You ever know a baby who knew what year it
was on the day he was born? That makes him forty-five."

"Going on forty-six," George laughed.

It had been a long time since George had enjoyed a payday, and a long time for me. The money figured to be sensational. Archie Moore had been the light-heavyweight champion since 1952. Several months earlier, he had knocked out
Yvon Durelle in Montreal. He was a hot property. At this
age, and with his quips and his goatee, he sold tickets.

For once, Jim Norris agreed with me.

Although the Supreme Court ruling had dissolved the
IBC, it permitted Norris to promote independently. He had

organized a new firm, National Boxing Enterprises, with headquarters in Chicago. He was desperate to put on a big match to show everybody that he was still in business. The big match was Archie and me.

I received a phone call one day in New York from a man who introduced himself as Matty Fox.

"I own a pay-TV company, I can make you a lot of money," he said. "Let's have dinner on my yacht."

The next evening, Marty Machat and I arrived at a pier on the East River and boarded a long white yacht. Matty Fox was a small, round man with big ideas. His pay-TV firm, Skiatron, was going to revolutionize the television industry. He was going to install coin-slots on home TV sets.

"And for a fight with you and Archie Moore," he said, "we could make millions by charging a dollar in millions of homes."

He told me how he had discussed his plan for baseball with both Walter O'Malley, the owner of the Los Angeles Dodgers, and with Horace Stoneham, the owner of the San Francisco Giants, and how someday this would be the big thing in sports.

"And to get it started," he said, "I'll guarantee you and Moore a million dollars to split between you."

Here was a man talking real money, but after we walked down the gangplank and got into my car, Marty cautioned me.

"Don't jump for everything this guy says," he told me. "I checked on this guy."

"You checked on him?" I said. "I checked that boat. That's all the checking I need."

"Ray," he said, "he doesn't *own* that boat, he hasn't *paid* for it. He's leased it, and he owes plenty. The same with his penthouse. I'm not saying he won't pay for it someday, but don't let that yacht make you think he's a big man. So far he's only talking big."

"Yeah, Marty, but a million dollars—"

"If you want to talk to Archie about it, go ahead, but remember, the money is not a sure thing, and I think it's best to let me work out the deal with Jack Kearns. We're making progress and Norris will go high. He really wants the fight."

"Well, I ought to tell Archie anyway."

"Do it your way," Marty said, annoyed.

The next day, Archie and his wife Joan were due in town. I phoned them and invited them to my house in Riverdale for dinner. Edna Mae prepared a feast—shrimp creole, filet mignon, and apple cobbler.

"Just the thing to put weight on," Archie laughed.

"That," I said, smiling, "was what I had in mind."

Archie always put on weight easily, and in order to make the 175-pound limit, he used what he called an aborigine diet he once discovered in Australia. After dinner Joan and Edna Mae drifted into the living room. Archie and I went upstairs to the private steam room I had installed.

"I can have it fired up in ten minutes," I said, "and you'll melt that dinner off."

"No, no, Ray," he said, rubbing his goatee, "we are to talk business, are we not?"

I outlined the offer: half a million for each of us from the Skiatron man, Matty Fox.

"Let us not rush, Ray," he said in his formal way. "Let there be no indiscriminate moves."

He wanted to know more about the Skiatron firm. I explained the possible bonanza of pay-television. This appealed to him. He proposed a plan in which we might be able to save on taxes.

"Why," he asked, "don't we each take two hundred and fifty thousand and the rest in stock in Skiatron?"

"That's not the deal he offered," I explained. "He offered us a million to split."

"But it's worth a request," he said. "Get those dollar signs out of your eyes, Ray. Listen to Archie Moore, the elder statesman of boxing. Think of the money you will save on taxes."

"You can save just as much with deferred income," I mentioned. "You can defer the payments over years."

"Interesting," he said, rubbing his goatee again. "Indeed, the proposition is interesting, but somehow it smells of Camembert. Nevertheless, I will consider it. But now we must be on our way."

Downstairs, on stage to the last moment, he bowed to me.

"It would be well, Raymond, for you to consider my request, and I will consider yours," he said. "Again, my compliments to Edna Mae. Her cuisine was superb."

Reaching for his wife's arm, he said, "Come, my dear Joan, our taxi is here."

The next day, Archie took a plane to Montreal. The promoter there, Eddie Quinn, guaranteed him $250,000 for another title defense against Yvon Durelle, and that ended our deal. He finished Durelle in three. Easy money, but I've never forgiven Archie.

When the fight with Archie vanished, I was desperate to defend my New York-Massachusetts middleweight title.

During my negotiations with Archie, Fullmer and Basilio had signed for a match to determine the new NBA middleweight champion. Fullmer stopped him in the fourteenth round, but Fullmer wasn't interested in fighting me. Neither was Basilio, who was talking about retiring. They were the only two that I knew I might draw some big money with, but one day George blustered into my office.

"Robinson, we got a match," he announced. "Paul Pender in the Boston Garden."

"Paul who?" I said, quite seriously, thinking that George had to be kidding.

"Paul Pender, the New England middleweight champ," he said. "He's won nine in a row and Sam Silverman will guarantee you seventy thousand."

"For that money, I'd fight Paul Revere in Boston."

Pender was a tall, skinny Irishman of twenty-nine, who had worked as a fireman in Brookline, over the city line from Boston. He started boxing professionally in 1949 and did well, but after he was knocked out in 1952 by Jimmy Beau, he retired. He was out of boxing for more than two years, then he made a casual comeback. Two fights in 1954, three in 1955, including a loss to Fullmer. By the time we got into the ring at the Boston Garden on January 20, 1960, he had put together ten consecutive victories

To my surprise, he made it eleven. To the surprise of the referee, too. Joe Zapustas scored eight rounds for me, only four for Pender, with three even. The judges voted for Pender. One of them somehow gave him eleven rounds for flicking his jab at me and running away. I had to admire Pender's ability to run. For the first time I was in with a man who had better legs than I had, but he used them to run instead of fight.

"Robbery!" roared George in the dressing room. "It's worse than the Brinks robbery."

"Forget it, George," I told him. "I've won a lot of split decisions over the years."

I meant it. Throughout my career, I had never griped about officials. I wasn't going to start now, even if a home-

town decision had stolen my title. The rematch was set for
June 10, again in the Boston Garden. Again the referee,
Jimmy McCarron this time, voted for me. Again the judges
voted for Pender. Again, in the dressing room, George hollered "robbery."

For the first time I had lost twice to the same opponent,
and twice in a row.

I had lost my marriage, too. Edna Mae and I had agreed
to disagree. We had enjoyed some beautiful times, but we
had battled through some bad times. She never liked the
idea that *I* was the celebrity in our marriage, not her. I never
got used to her show-biz habit of letting guys kiss her, guys
I didn't know. And our families had created friction. Mom
didn't like her at all, Edna Mae being a showgirl and being older and being married before. They never got along.
And her Aunt Blanche was always intruding, as she did the
night I walked out. I was downstairs near the door of our
big house in Riverdale, and I was telling Edna Mae that I
was leaving her.

"Let him go," Aunt Blanche called from upstairs. "He
won't be gone two weeks."

I went, and I didn't come back, but I would've gone
anyway. Edna Mae and I had lost our feeling for each other.
In our beautiful times, she had cared for me like a mother.
But that care had disappeared, in small things, like the fat
on my meat. I always liked the fat trimmed off, and she had
always done that for me, but one night at dinner, my roast
beef had a slab of fat on it.

Maybe that was being too hard on her, but that's the
way I am. With my mate I'm very selfish. I'm right behind
God.

Looking back, it wasn't her fault and it wasn't mine. We
never had a solid marriage. Before the breakup, she was
going her way and I was going mine.

Over the years I had maintained my friendship with Millie Bruce, the girl I had met in Los Angeles when I was in show business. I had sent her presents from Paris, before my comeback. I had seen her again in Los Angeles, but all she talked about was her boy friend. Every so often I had put in a long-distance call to her. I was able to talk to this girl, something I sometimes had trouble doing with Edna Mae. More important, I respected Millie.

"Now don't forget," I always told her, more courteous than serious, "if you ever get to New York, call me. Don't forget."

One evening in the summer of 1960 I was in my café when the bartender held up the phone for me.

"I'm at the Park Sheraton," Millie announced.

"Great," I said, "I'll come down and help you unpack."

"Oh, we've been here four days," she said.

"Four days! Why did you wait four days to call me?"

"We've been going to parties."

"Who's *we*," I asked, figuring her boy friend was with her.

"The girls in the club," she said.

"The girls," I said. "That's nice."

"My charity club in Los Angeles, the Rinky Dinks," she said. "We're having a meeting with our New York chapter."

"Is your meeting over?"

"It will be in about two hours."

"I'll be down then."

She was waiting, but she wasn't alone. She introduced her roommate on the trip, Anne Marlborough.

"You still don't trust me," I laughed.

"Not with that shirt you have on," she said, staring at my net shirt.

"That's to keep my body cool," I said.

"See that it stays that way," she said.

I drove them uptown in my flamingo convertible to a club,

The Spot. I wanted to make an impression so I arranged with Curly Hammer, who had taught me how to play the drums, to let me sit in on the drums for a few numbers. I got Millie and Anne back to the hotel around midnight.

"I'll call you later," I said.

"Later?" she said. "I'm going to bed."

"Just to say good night," I said.

I phoned about one, and we talked until about five. She told me that she was going to be busy the next night, but we made a date to go to Jones Beach in the morning the following day. I was up to do my roadwork, and I phoned her about six o'clock.

"Hello," she grunted.

"Get your bathing suit on, baby, we're going to get the first spot on the beach."

"I just got in from a party," she said.

"I'll call you later," I said, annoyed.

I phoned about ten and woke her up again. This time she asked to put it off until the next day.

"But my sister Evelyn fixed fried chicken," I said.

I heard her talking to Anne Marlborough, and then she told me, "We'll be ready about one."

"You better be," I said.

She was, but in my car on the way to Jones Beach, she dozed off. The surf really woke her up. That night Millie, Anne, Evelyn, and I had dinner together in the Park Sheraton. Around midnight, I phoned her again, and we talked until four. In the morning, I had several dozen yellow roses delivered to her room. I phoned that afternoon.

"Do you have a date with anybody else tonight?" I asked.

"Yes," she said, sleepily, "but I'm going to break it."

"Terrific," I said. "I'll pick you up about six and we'll drive up—"

"No, Ray," she said, "I'm breaking it to get some sleep."

"That's a good idea," I said, scheming. "You break it and go to sleep."

That evening, I phoned again.

"Baby," I said, knowing that she had broken her other date, "please take a ride with me, alone. It's important."

"All right," she said, reluctantly, "but get me home by midnight."

I drove up the Henry Hudson Parkway, past the George Washington Bridge, and parked overlooking the river. For the first time we were alone. I leaned over to kiss her. But when she struggled, I got annoyed. In my frustration, I smacked her.

Suddenly, *slap*, she swatted me across the face.

"I'm not one of your women, Ray Robinson," she snapped. "I'm not even your girl. Don't you try to force a kiss on me, and don't you ever hit me again. You drive me back to the hotel right now, you understand."

I understood, all right. I understood that this broad was different.

On the drive downtown, I began to tell her about my problems with Edna Mae, and with my career, and with Marie's death. By the time we got to the Park Sheraton, we were friends again, but I didn't try to kiss her. I didn't even make a date for the next night, but in the morning, I had yellow roses delivered to her room, and when I phoned her she didn't sound angry. We went out to dinner that night and later, I kissed her, gently, and she responded.

"From now on," I said, holding her, "you're not going out on any of the club dates, you're going out with me."

"But I have to go back to Los Angeles the day after tomorrow," she said. "My vacation is over. If I took another week, I wouldn't get paid for it."

"I'll pay you for it," I said. "You stay here another week."

Our romance had begun, but soon it was time for her to return to Los Angeles. In the TWA terminal at Idlewild Airport, she looked into my eyes.

"What should I do about my boy friend when I get back home?" she asked. "I was just about engaged to that man."

"You go out with him like nothing happened here," I suggested, "and if you still love him, marry him."

As soon as she disappeared inside that airliner, I was sorry I had told her that. I had to figure a way for me to get to Los Angeles to see her, to give her guy some competition, to remind her of our romance. Not long after, I was negotiating with Gene Fullmer for a shot at his NBA middleweight title. As the challenger, my end would be 20 per cent of everything. Not what I had been used to, but not bad. The site was a problem, but one day George mentioned Los Angeles.

"Take it," I said.

In the weeks before the fight, I lived in a big log cabin out in the desert near San Jacinto. I phoned Millie and invited her and Leola King, her girl friend from San Francisco, to join my entourage for the week end. Edna Mae wasn't there, but Mom was, along with George and Wiley, June Clark, Honey Brewer, and my voice teacher, Jaharal Hall. When Millie and Leola arrived, I showed them around the cabin. Suddenly, Millie stopped and stared at a white blanket hanging over my bed.

"Oh, no, Ray," she said. "You can't mean it."

Woven on the blanket was this message: I am magnificent, lovable, sensational, wonderful, the best, perfect, handsome, sparkling, beautiful, marvelous.

"It was there when I rented this place," I explained, smiling, "but I'm not about to take it down."

My room had three big beds in it. That night both Millie

and Leola slept in my room. With me in training, they were safer than they would have been in a monastery. But about four o'clock that morning, Millie shook me awake.

"Ray," she whispered, "somebody is in the bushes."

"It's probably some little animal," I grunted. "They're out there all the time."

"Oh, no, I'm sure it's him," she said, meaning her boy friend.

"You're sure it's him," I said, really awake now. "He wouldn't come out here at this hour."

"It wouldn't surprise me," she said.

"Go back to bed, baby, go to sleep."

Her guy had been angry when she told him about staying an extra week in New York. He had warned her not to see me again. In the morning I was napping after my roadwork and the others were having breakfast in the kitchen when my bedroom door slammed, waking me up. Leola was standing near it, staring at me as if she were a sentry.

"What's going on?" I asked, sleepily.

"Nothing," she said, "nothing at all."

Anytime a woman says that, something is happening. I got up and strolled out into the kitchen. Through a window, the dust from a beige Cadillac convertible clouded the road.

"Who was that?" I asked.

"Remember when I woke you up at four o'clock?" said Millie, trembling. "I told you somebody was outside."

"What's the matter, honey?" I said, comforting her. "What are you talking about? What's been going on?"

"That was my old boy friend who was here," she said.

"That was him driving down the road?"

"And that was him at four o'clock snooping around. I'm

sure it was," she said. "He had the nerve to come in and order me to go home with him, and oh, Ray, I was so frightened."

"Damn, why didn't you wake me up?"

"If I had, there would've been trouble," she said, "and I didn't want that. I didn't want to upset you."

"You upset me just talking about it."

"Your men protected me, George and Wiley and June and Honey, they stared him down. It's all over. Forget it, honey, please forget it."

"I'm never going to forget it," I said.

"Ray," she pleaded, "he's the one who made a fool of himself, not you. If you go after him, you'll look foolish. You will be doing exactly what he did. Stay here, honey, and train for your fight."

"Yeah," said George, "beat Fullmer's ass instead."

I did, but only the referee, Tommy Hart, thought I did. He had me ahead, 11-4, in the point system used in California. One judge had Fullmer ahead, 9-5. The other judge had it even. Anytime there's a draw, the champion retains his title. After my two losses to Pender, I had trained well for Fullmer and fought well. When the decision was announced, a thunder of boos erupted from the 13,465 customers in the new Sports Arena.

The people thought that I had won, but in boxing the people don't count. It's the men who mark the scorecards.

Fullmer had remembered the left hook I had nailed him with in Chicago, and that's all he seemed to be concerned about. Throughout the fifteen rounds, he had his right forearm high, protecting his jaw from my left hook. I was disgusted with the decision, but my 20 per cent came to nearly $50,000, enough to invite Millie to New York for a few weeks.

"I can't go," she said, "I've got my job."

"Then come to Chicago on the train with me," I said, "and fly back. You can do that on the week end."

"You think of things nobody else does," she said.

It made for a nice train ride.

24

The Woman in White

She was all in white—a silver-blue mink coat, white sweater, white silk pants, white slippers. And white skin.

Slender and elegant, in her mid-twenties, her long reddish brown hair swept on top of her head like a crown, she was sitting at a big round table in my café on New Year's Eve. Actually, it was about two hours into 1959. My café was swinging. I was strolling among the customers, shaking hands and wishing them a Happy New Year. She was in a group of about ten people, all whites. That wasn't unusual. My café had a mixed clientele. All the good Harlem spots did then.

"How do you do, Mister Robinson?" she said when I introduced myself at her table. "I've been chatting with your sister."

Evelyn was sitting at the next table, and they had noticed each other's clothes and hairdos. But what impressed me was that she wasn't wearing make-up. It takes a real face to get away with that, and her face was classic, like Elizabeth Taylor's or Vivien Leigh's. Whenever I looked back at that face, she was talking to Evelyn. When she left, I dismissed her from my mind. Another pretty customer.

About a week later, I was visiting Ann Slaydon, an acquaintance of Killer Johnson, in her East Side apartment. "Do you remember that white girl in the silver-blue coat who was in your café the other night?" she said. "She's coming here to see me in a few minutes."

"Yeah," I said, recalling her, "a pretty girl, with no make-up. Yeah, I remember her. Maybe I'll wait for her."

Ann told me her name. I'll call her Beverly. She was a divorcée for the second time. She had grown up in Miami Beach. She married her high-school sweetheart when she was seventeen. Three years later they were divorced. She moved to New York where she worked as a model. Her second marriage had been to a wealthy construction executive. After their divorce, she had toured Europe, dating some of the international playboys. But when she arrived at Ann's, she mumbled hello and disappeared into the kitchen. I followed her.

"What are you doing in here?" I asked.

"I haven't had dinner," she said, trimming the fat off a slice of roast beef.

"You don't like fat either?"

"No," she said, not looking up.

"You don't wear anything on your face, do you?"

"No," she said.

"Don't you say anything else?" I asked.

"I'm hungry," she said, chewing.

"Do you have to eat while I'm talking to you? Put your knife and fork down."

"I told you I'm hungry."

"Are you in love with anybody?" I said.

"Pardon me?" she said, looking up.

"Are you in love with anybody?" I repeated.

"No," she said, cutting her meat.

She ate a few more mouthfuls and then she glanced at me. For the first time I noticed her flashing violet eyes.

"I had a nice time at your club," she said.

"Yes," I said, "my sister told me all about you the next day."

"Your sister is lovely," she said.

"Put the knife and fork down," I said.

"I'm sorry, but I'm hungry."

"And you're not in love with anybody?"

"No."

"Do you go out with anybody?" I asked.

"I go out with a lot of men."

I was staring at her face.

"What are you looking at?" she snapped.

"You don't wear any stuff on your face," I said. "Not even lipstick."

"No," she said. "I told you that before."

"I like that. I think that's nice," I said, glancing at my watch. "I'm sorry, I've got to leave now, but I'd like to see you again. I'd like to be your friend."

"Yes, I've got a lot of friends."

"I'm sure you do," I said, "but everybody can always use one more friend. What's your phone number?"

She hesitated. She obviously didn't want to give it to me.

"T E, for Templeton," she said, rattling the numbers.

"That's a nice neighborhood," I said, knowing that a Templeton number was on the fashionable East Side.

"I'm just off Sutton Place," she said, not bragging.

"I'll call you," I said. "I'll call you pretty soon."

I called about an hour later, but there was no answer. I phoned her a few more times that evening. Each time there was no answer. Early the next morning, I phoned again. No answer. I tried about noon. This time she answered.

"Where were you all night?" I began.

"What?" she said, mystified. "Who is this?"

"Your new friend," I said.

"Oh, *you*," she said, explaining that she had stayed over-night at the place where the party was.

"That's not so good for your health."

"I beg your pardon, Mister Robinson."

"You should be home at a reasonable hour and get your sleep," I said. "You shouldn't stay out all night like that. You have to take better care of your health."

"Mister Robinson," she started to say.

"Sugar Ray," I said. "It's Sugar Ray."

"Your sister calls you 'Robinson,' so that's what I'll call you," she said. "Robinson, I'm sure you have my well-being at heart, but I wish you would mind your own business."

"Beverly," I said, using her name for the first time, "I'll call tonight to make sure you're home early."

That night, I sent her a candygram—a box of candy and a telegram wishing her good night. When I phoned, she was there. We talked half an hour. The next day I sent her a sing-ing telegram, a good-morning message, and I had red roses delivered to her. Every night and every morning she got a telegram. And red roses almost every day. Once I sent her a big stuffed toy tiger, "to watch over you," I told her. We spoke on the phone every day for maybe a month, but I hadn't seen her since the night in Ann Slaydon's house.

"Beverly," I said one morning on the phone, "why don't you come up to my café tonight?"

"I'd like that, Robinson," she said softly. "Is it all right if I bring some friends?"

"As long as you bring yourself," I said, "bring everybody in your apartment house."

At my café that evening, I was peering out the front win-dow when a long black Cadillac pulled up. Several people got out, and then I noticed a slim broad wearing a silver-blue mink coat, like the one Beverly had on the first two times I saw her. But this broad had her hair down around her shoulders. *That's not her,* I told myself, *she wears her hair on top of her head,* but when she strolled into my café, she was so dazzling, she stopped the clock from ticking. Even with her hair down, I said to myself, *If that ain't her, it ought to be.* It was.

I made a big fuss over her and her friends. I sat them at the best table and ordered their food for them. Fried chicken. My café had the best fried chicken in the world. When they finished their dinner, I had my band play their favorite songs. After that, I sang a song for them. I'd been taking vocal lessons. Richard Rodgers, the composer, had heard me sing and suggested lessons. That night I stood near Beverly's table and sang "Mister Success."

"And there he is," Beverly said, smiling at me when I had finished. "Mister Success himself."

With her hair around her shoulders, she was even more lovely. When it came time for her to go home, I offered to drive her downtown.

"I'd like that," she said. "I've heard about your pink car."

"It's flamingo, Beverly," I said. "Other people have pink cars."

Outside, I opened the door on her side of the front seat and she slid in. When I got behind the wheel, she was sitting as far away from me as she could. I drove through Central Park. She was looking out the window but, out of the corner of my eye, I noticed her peeking at me every so often.

"You've never had a Negro boy friend have you?" I said, breaking the silence.

"No," she said, "I never have. I've never been with any Negroes at all."

Emerging onto Central Park South, I turned left and she guided me the few more blocks to her apartment house.

She didn't invite me upstairs, and I didn't suggest it. I was playing it cool. I was fascinated by her. That was the word: fascination. Not infatuation. And not sex. Sitting there in the parked car outside her apartment, she seemed surprised that I wasn't making a move at her.

"Well," I said, "you need your sleep."

"Is that all you're going to say, Robinson?" she said. "Is that all you're going to say to me?"

"Beverly," I said, "What if you fall in love with me?"

"Robinson," she said, "you're not Negro, you're Black Satin."

After that, I took her out quite often. But except for my café, we didn't go to any night clubs or anyplace where we might be seen by any of the Broadway columnists. Instead, I took her bowling and to movies, and she seemed to like that because it was so different from the life she had known with those playboys. She didn't have to be dined and wined. She had fun on hot dogs. But wherever we went, I usually had Evelyn along so that people wouldn't be able to pinpoint her as my date. Jane and Evelyn got to be really fond of each other. Mom took a liking to her, and that surprised me.

"Son," she said to me once, "this child loves you."

"Mom," I said, "I like her, too, but you know that in my position I can't get that involved with her."

"I don't believe that way," she said.

"Mom, it's not as easy as saying it."

"But you know that God made people," she said, "and people is plural. We are all people. He made everybody. My mother's father was white. What difference does it make what color you are? You and Edna aren't happy, but you and this child are."

"But we have to live in this world," I said.

"She's a good girl. You'd be happy with her."

"That's not it, Mom. I've been blessed with being a symbol among people, and people look to me and I think that marrying this girl would cause me a lot of trouble. I just can't relax to it. I like her, but I'm very much afraid. I wish that it had never started. But since it has, I'm in between. I don't want to treat her bad."

"Son, always be nice to this girl—no matter what happens."

The more I thought about my situation with Beverly, the more mixed up I was. It got so that I couldn't sleep nights. My mind was cluttered not only with Beverly but also with my breakup with Edna Mae, with Marie's death. When I couldn't get to sleep, I'd phone Beverly, maybe at one or two in the morning.

"Put your clothes on," I would say, "we're going for a drive. Be ready in fifteen minutes."

When I pulled up in front of her apartment, she was always waiting in the lobby.

"You're the only man, Robinson," she once said, "who tells me to put my clothes *on*."

I fascinated her, too. Not my color. If you get to know somebody well enough, their color vanishes. What fascinated her was that I treated her differently than other men did. And I told her things. Even though she didn't wear make-up, I knew she had great vanity within her. When I told her about her vanity one night in the car, she was amazed that I had figured that out—no other man ever had. We had great conversations in the car. At night we'd ride all over—up into Westchester, out on Long Island, over to New Jersey. In these conversations, I won her heart. No other man had won her heart before. She had given her heart to a man, but if she got angry with him, she would take back her heart. With me, it was different, like the time in the car when she got annoyed about something, I don't remember what it was exactly.

"Oh, go to hell," she snapped at me.

I pulled the car over to the curb and reached across to the door handle on her side and opened the door.

"Out," I ordered.

"Robinson," she said, "what are you doing?"

"Out," I repeated.

"What is all this?"

"Get out and stay out," I said, "until you learn how to talk to people."

And out she got.

I hadn't really stranded her. We were in downtown Manhattan, not too far from her apartment house. I knew she could catch a cab without any trouble. But I had to show her that she couldn't talk to me the way she had talked to other men. I didn't know how she'd react, but after not phoning her for a couple days, when I did phone, she apologized and we made up. Now I was in deeper than ever. I invited her to go to Florida with me for a vacation. Evelyn was going, June Clark was going to handle all the arrangements. He got a nice room for Beverly in one of the white hotels. The rest of us stayed at the Sir John Hotel in Miami. During the day, Beverly would come over to our hotel and sit by the pool with us and live with us except for returning to her hotel at night.

"But I'm so lonesome there," she said. "Can't I stay here with you?"

"All right," I said, "you can move in with Evelyn—in her room."

But when she moved in, she noticed the tension immediately. In those days, especially in the South, it was unusual for a white person to be living at a Negro hotel, and whenever she was around the hotel, she noticed the other people whispering.

"I'm not going down and sit by that pool anymore," she told me the next day.

"Yes, you are," I growled. "You're going to do everything that I do, everything."

She did, but neither of us was happy doing it.

All day long, the tension was there. The other guests were staring at her, and at me. I had been stared at for twenty years, but this was a different stare. They were staring as if *both* Beverly and I were white. That night, in her room with Evelyn, the tension exploded. Beverly had been criticizing the way the other Negro guests acted toward her.

"You," I snarled, "with your nose in the air."

"Me!" she roared. "*Me* with my nose in the air. How about all these people here, how about their noses?"

"You think you're better, don't you?"

"You mean because I'm white?" she said.

"I don't know why."

With that, she flung her white beaded purse against the wall behind me. She had that kind of a temper. She had a reputation for throwing lamps, overturning tables, that sort of thing. And when her purse whacked into the wall, Evelyn quietly left the room but I sat on the bed and glared at her.

"You don't understand, Robinson," she growled, her face red with anger.

Striding toward me, she slapped me across the side of the face with her hand. I reached up and slapped her across the face. She slapped me back, and I slapped her again. Again she slapped me. Again I slapped her.

Suddenly, Evelyn was in the door.

"Hey, Neck," I said, using my old nickname for Evelyn, "tell your roommate that I'm tired, I'm going to sleep."

I got up and went to my room.

In the morning, I was scheduled for a TV interview by the pool. That evening, we were to attend a banquet over on the Beach. The following day, we planned to fly to Nassau in the Bahamas. But after the episode the previous night, June Clark didn't know what to do about Beverly.

"Should I get her a plane ticket?" he asked me as the TV guys were setting up near the pool.

"Certainly," I said. "She's going to Nassau with us. She'll get over the argument."

He went up to her room, which wasn't too far away, and I could hear him talking to her, and I could hear her even easier.

"I'm not going anywhere with Robinson," she was snarling. "I'm leaving and going to New York."

"Now, now," June was saying, "Mister Robinson is on television down by the pool and they want everybody to be quiet."

"Quiet!" she roared. "It'll be quiet after I leave."

Moments later, June returned to the pool. He was all flustered at the situation.

"What are we going to do with this girl?" he said.

"You'll see," I said calmly. "She'll come. She'll be at the banquet, and she'll go to Nassau with us. Don't bother asking her again. She'll be with us."

Apparently she could hear me, because her voice came booming out of her open door.

"I'm not going with you, Robinson," she yelled. "Not tonight. Not tomorrow. Not ever."

The TV people were ready to film the interview. The man with the microphone sat down next to me alongside the pool and he began to ask me questions.

"Well, yes," I was saying, "my next fight is going to be very important because—"

Beyond the cameramen I saw Beverly parading toward the lobby. Behind her was a bellboy with her bags.

"Hey, look there," June Clark yelled to me. "She's leaving the hotel."

"She'll be back," I assured him. "Don't you worry, she'll be back."

You never saw so much commotion. Next to me, the man holding the microphone didn't know what I was talking about. The cameraman didn't know what to do. Evelyn threw her hands up to her head. But my man, June Clark, trotted after Beverly.

Soon Beverly was shouting, "Nobody is going to be mean to me!"

June somehow sweet-talked her into returning to the room she shared with Evelyn. She sulked all afternoon. She was acting like a spoiled child, and I ignored her. Until then, whenever she needed anything, I always had hurried to her. This time I decided to leave her alone. Along about five o'clock Evelyn began to get dressed for the banquet.

"Are you coming with us?" Evelyn asked.

"I most certainly am not," she snapped.

About an hour later, Evelyn, June, myself, and a few other people had gathered in the lobby for the ride over to the Beach. Suddenly, she appeared in a gorgeous purple dress. And with her hair up, a danger signal. Whenever she was peeved at me, she wore her hair up because she knew I preferred her to wear it on her shoulders.

"Oh my," Evelyn said, seeing her, "you're here."

Off we went to the banquet over on the Beach.

We hadn't been there long when something happened to renew the tension. We were sitting together at a big round table, in the Eden Roc ballroom I think it was, when a waiter handed me a small slip of paper. It was a note from a woman at the next table. She had written her phone number on it. Beverly had seen me crumple the note into my pocket, as if trying to hide it.

"What's going on?" I heard her whisper to Evelyn.

"I imagine it's another one of those notes with a phone number on it," Evelyn said. "Women are always doing that."

"Women *what?*"

"This happens all the time to him," Evelyn said.

"I never heard of such a thing," she said.

Turning to me, she demanded to know what had been written on the piece of paper.

"Nothing," I assured her, "nothing at all."

That lit another fire under her temper, but by the morning she had cooled off enough to join us on the flight to Nassau.

As often happens to two people after an argument, we found ourselves attracted to each other more than ever. Our love affair really bloomed in a tiny pink hotel on the beach. It was like being in heaven. The surf of the turquoise-colored ocean sliding across the sand. The palm trees. The red and yellow flowers. The warm sun in the daytime and the big tropical moon at night. This time, Beverly didn't room with Evelyn. She roomed with me.

But after about ten days of idyllic communication in Nassau, I knew that we had to return to reality soon. I was as much in love as anybody can be, but I knew a marriage wouldn't work, at least I knew it wouldn't work for me.

Whenever I thought about it, I visualized big headlines, like SUGAR RAY MARRIES WHITE DIVORCEE.

After we returned to New York, she kept telling me how lonely she was without me. But we were in New York now, not in a little pink hotel in the Bahamas. One night she visited my café. We sat around for a few hours, then I drove her downtown. Neither of us was talking, and when I parked in front of her lobby, she was crying.

"What about us, Robinson?" she said.

"Beverly," I said, "what can I say?"

"You've got to tell me something," she said. "If I knew what to do, I'd do it. Every night I cry myself to sleep. I understand your problem. I don't want to hurt you. I love you so much I want to help you, not hurt you, but what about *me*, Robinson?"

"I don't know what to do. I've prayed to God: Why can't you be black? Why can't I be white?"

"We could go to Europe," she said. "We could live together over there. You know how much different it is over there."

"I couldn't do that," I said. "My whole life is here. America is my home, all my businesses are here. I enjoy it there, but I have to live here."

"The hell with that," she said. "If a woman loves a man and if that man loves her, she should have that man."

"Beverly," I said, "you know it ain't that easy. Not anymore. Maybe if I was still the champion, it would be different. That title means money, and money talks. I would be able to buy respect with money. But without the title, everybody would beat you down and they'd beat me down too."

"To me, you'll always be a champion," she said. "You're a king, and kings don't die."

"In boxing, they die," I explained. "As soon as you lose a title, you're a dead king."

"Oh, Robinson," she said, "I don't want to do anything to hurt you. If somebody was going to shoot you, I'd stand in front of you and let them shoot me first, you know that.

But other prominent Negro men have married white women. Sammy Davis. Harry Belafonte."

"They're not Sugar Ray Robinson," I said.

Snapping the car door open, she disappeared into her apartment building. In the months that followed, I began to see her less and less. She began dating a multimillionaire and returned to café society. One evening I strolled into the Harwyn, a lively East Side club in those days, to appear on Faye Emerson's TV show there.

Across the room Beverly was sitting with her date and another couple. I tried to avoid her glance, but whenever I peeked at her, she was staring at me.

After the interview, I hurried past her table and nodded, but kept going. Outside, I was about to get in my car when I heard a woman's high heels clicking across the sidewalk. Suddenly, from behind, she grabbed my arm.

"Oh, Robinson," she said, "this whole thing is absolutely horrible."

Her hair was down around her shoulders, the way I liked it, and she was wearing one of her gorgeous white dresses. Behind her, on the sidewalk, her friends were staring at her, and at me.

"Beverly, please go away," I said, "before I put you in my car and take you with me."

She let go of my arm. She turned and went back to her friends, and I drove away.

Several days later, I was training at Greenwood Lake when I walked into the gym for my afternoon workout and saw her sitting in the front row of the spectator seats. She was wearing a white beaver coat, a white picture hat, a white turtleneck sweater, and white boots. She was only a few feet from the ring ropes, and as I warmed up, she stared at me.

I worked one round, feeling her eyes on me. Without a word, I turned and disappeared into my dressing room.

"Tell the people," I explained to George, "that I don't feel well today. Tell them the workout is over."

I took my time getting dressed, hoping that she would not wait. But when I went outside, she was sitting in a white Cadillac, peering out at me from under her big white hat. I glanced at her but kept walking. Behind me, her car started up and she drove down the dirt road toward the main highway.

25

Two Pink Pills

Through the years, whenever I appeared on Ed
Sullivan's television show, I parked my flamingo Cadillac convertible outside the stage
door of his theater at Broadway and 53rd Street. After the
show, we usually would be leaving together and he would
glare at the car.

"If you'd drive a Lincoln," he had often told me, "they'll
give you a free one."

I always thanked him for his generous offer, but I preferred the Cadillac lines. By the time the 1961 models came
out, my preference was not the deciding factor. My bank
account was. My money from the first Basilio fight was
still being held by the Internal Revenue Service. The money
I had made from the two Pender fights and the Fullmer
fight in Los Angeles had maintained my standard of living,
but that was about all. Whatever was left over, I had put
into my café and my other enterprises. Without my title,
they were beginning to lose money again. I decided to ex-
plore what Ed Sullivan had told me about a Lincoln car.
Several days later, a new Lincoln Continental, with a perfect
flamingo paint job, was delivered outside my café. Instead
of a bill, the driver handed me a set of keys.

"Enjoy the car," he said.

Not long after that, I had Bob Williams drive it to California. I had signed for another fight with Fullmer, this time in Las Vegas, but I was using the same log cabin in San Jacinto where I had prepared for the Fullmer fight in Los Angeles. I wanted to be near Millie, and I wanted her to see my new car.

About a week before the fight, which was scheduled for March 4, 1961, I checked into the Dunes Hotel on the glittering neon Strip. I had never had a fight in Vegas, but I knew the way of life since I had been there in show business. I strolled into the coffee shop one evening about seven o'clock. The hostess showed me to a table.

"Pardon me, Mister Robinson," she said, holding her menus, "are you having breakfast, lunch, or dinner?"

She wasn't putting me on. Some people in Vegas sleep all day and work all night. It's a twenty-four-hour town. Time is nonexistent in the casinos. There are no clocks. That way the gamblers won't realize how long they've been at the dice table or the roulette wheel. The drapes are drawn so that no light gets in. There's no way of knowing whether the sun is out, or the moon.

Not that I bothered too much with the casinos. I was more interested in the entertainers on the Strip that week. Nat Cole, the King, was singing his ballads. Eleanor Powell was clicking across the stage in her dancing shoes. Al Hirt was blowing his trumpet. I caught them all. And when I was on stage, in the ring set up every afternoon in the Dunes night club, they caught *my* act.

I expected the way of life in Vegas, but I never expected the trouble that would surround me.

Several weeks earlier, the chairman of the Nevada boxing commission, Dr. Joseph C. Elia, an eye-ear-nose-and-throat doctor from Reno, had struggled to get me another match with Fullmer after witnessing our atrocious draw. He had

campaigned for me to get another title shot. He had arranged
for some of the Strip hotels to accomodate the Negro people
who would be there to root for me. And in our discussions,
he had promised me a square deal in Nevada.

"I guarantee you one thing," he said. "We won't import a
referee from another state. We'll use one of ours."

Shortly before I arrived at the Dunes, I got a phone call
from Dr. Elia in Reno. He had resigned from the commission.

"I've been overruled by the other commissioners," he
said. "In protest, I'm resigning because I can't deliver my
promises. I'm sorry, Ray. I did the best I could."

I was surrounded by enemies, starting with one of the
local promoters, Norman Rothschild.

Although the Madison Square Garden Boxing Club had
put together the match for television, Rothschild had been
brought in from Syracuse as a co-promoter. He had put on
several fights featuring Basilio in Syracuse. And any friend
of Basilio had to be an enemy of mine. The other co-promoter was a Vegas guy, Mel (Red) Greb, the only man in
town who didn't understand what a percentage meant. Ringside seats were priced at $40, but Greb had sold sixteen of
them at $1000 each. The extra $960 was set aside for charity,
a local boys' club.

"Red," I told him, "you're playing with my money."

"What are you talking about?" he said. "We're giving the
money to charity. I'll show you the check made out to it."

"What's the price printed on those tickets?"

"A thousand dollars," he said, flashing one.

"Red, if I'm in for twenty-five per cent of the gate, then I
deserve two hundred and fifty of the *printed* price. Give the
rest to charity if you want to, but don't fool around with my
percentage unless you ask me. I've got four thousand coming
to me from those sixteen tickets."

There were other problems, too.

The commission rulebook stipulated that the ring be twenty feet square. The size of the ring is important. The bigger the ring, the better for me. I depended on my bag of tricks, on my speed. The more room I had to move around in, the more I could use my speed. With someone like Fullmer, the smaller the ring, the better it was for him. Fullmer was slower than me, but stronger. In a smaller ring, it would be easier for him to corner me, to get me against the ropes. I was aware of the size of the rings in the major arenas all over the country. Of all of them, I liked the Madison Square Garden ring the best, because I had grown up in it. I always knew where I was in that ring. I knew the canvas too. There were no dead spots, and the padding was firm. Your feet wouldn't sink into it. You could glide across it. But this was the first time I had ever fought in Vegas and I wanted to check the ring.

"Go over to the Convention Center," I told George early in the week, "and measure the ring."

When he returned, he told me that the ring was only sixteen feet seven inches. To make it worse, the padding was soft, another advantage for Fullmer. I phoned the new commission chairman, Jimmy Gay.

"You told me it would be a twenty-foot ring," I said.

"The ropes must have been loose," he said. "Don't worry, Ray, when they're tightened, it'll be twenty."

Turning to George, I asked about the loose ropes.

"They weren't loose, Robinson," he said. "They were tight as a drum."

"Make sure to check it later in the week," I said.

Other problems developed. At the rules meeting at the commission office three days before the fight, I requested six-ounce gloves. I was shooting for one solid left hook like the one that had stiffened Fullmer in 1957. With six-ounce gloves, the impact would be sharper.

"Six-ouncers are all right with me," Fullmer said.

"I'm sorry, gentlemen," Gay said, "in this state, we use eight-ounce gloves."

"But if Fullmer agrees," I said, "let's use six."

"I'm not against six or eight," Fullmer said, "but if you talk about us being in agreement, we might agree that there shouldn't be a referee or judges."

"No ref and no judges is fine with me," I snapped.

"But that's not for us to agree on," Fullmer said, "it's for the commission to rule on."

"It will be eight-ounce gloves," Gay proclaimed.

"What about the color of the trunks?" I asked. "In my contract, I wear white."

"No, you don't," said Marv Jensen, Fullmer's manager.

"It's in my contract," I said. "Look in my contract."

"I don't care what your contract says," Jensen said. "The champion gets his choice, you know that. You were the champion so long, you think you still are. But you're not and Gene prefers to wear white trunks."

"I've got two pairs of white trunks," interrupted Rothschild. "You can both wear white."

"No way," yelled one of the television people attending the meeting. "Nobody will be able to identify them."

I glanced at Fullmer's white Mormon face. He was trying not to laugh, but it broke me up.

It was my only laugh of the week. The next day Admiral Bergen and Harry Markson arrived from New York. They informed me that the television sponsor demanded the fight be shown in South America on a twenty-four-hour delay.

"No good," I said. "That would kill the value of the movie rights down there."

"Ray, we've got to do this," Markson said, "or we'll substitute another fight."

"You do that, Harry," I said. "You go right ahead and do that. In fact, I'll do it for you. As of right now, consider me out of the fight."

"Now, Ray," the admiral said.

"Forget it, Admiral," I said. "Before I came here, one of the commissioners told me that I'd have no trouble in his state, but the only thing I've had is trouble. He begged me to fight Fullmer here, he thought it would be good for Nevada, but it hasn't been good for me."

Shortly after they departed, my phone rang. Governor Grant Sawyer was calling from Carson City.

"Ray," he said, "I'm coming down tomorrow to try and straighten everything out for this fight."

He was to arrive on Friday evening, the night before the fight. That afternoon I had sent George to recheck the size of the ring.

"It's still sixteen seven with tight ropes," he said, "and the padding's still soft. And, Robinson, I hear that Carter is in town."

Frank Carter was a California referee, from San Francisco. His presence meant that he had been imported to work the fight. His arrival was serious. I had used the gloves and trunks and the television situation in South America as weapons to annoy my enemies, but the size of the ring and the identity of the referee were serious matters. At my age, they might make a big difference in the outcome. I phoned Jack Cuddy of United Press International, who had come out from New York to cover the fight.

"The fight's off, Jack," I told him. "Put it on the wire. I'm calling the fight off."

My reason was the size of the ring. The referee was a factor, too, but I had no proof of that. But all week Norman

Rothschild had stalled me on the ring. By the time the governor arrived in my suite, Cuddy's story was the big news in Vegas.

"What's going on, Ray?" the governor demanded.

"I won't fight in this size ring and if Carter is the referee," I told him.

"Where can we get another ring now?" he asked.

"Truck one in from someplace, Governor. Truck one in that's twenty feet square, like it says in the commission rulebook."

"If I get one, will you fight tomorrow night?"

"How about the referee, how about that Carter?"

"I can't make any promises on the referee. I'm not a boxing man, but there's no reason why we shouldn't have a twenty-foot ring in here by tomorrow."

"All right," I said, "get the ring and I'm in."

By the next afternoon, a new ring had been trucked in from Long Beach, California. When it was set up, I dispatched George to measure it.

"Twenty feet on the nose," he told me. "I used the carpenter's steel tape."

The moment I stepped into the ring that night, I suspected that George had been wrong. All my life I had been measuring rings mentally, and as I scanned this one, I knew that it wasn't twenty feet.

"Are you sure it's twenty?" I asked him.

"Measured it myself, Robinson, with a steel tape. A steel tape can't be wrong."

"It doesn't look twenty to me," I said.

"Forget the ring, forget the ring."

Across from me Fullmer was jogging in his long black robe, jogging with *my* title. When the bell rang, he came at me in a crouch, his round face a blank, his right arm shielding him from my left hook. In the final moments of the third round, he nailed me with a good right hand. I went back against the ropes and held on. I heard the bell, but it had rung weakly, and in his anxiety, Fullmer kept pummeling me. He hadn't heard the bell. Neither had the referee, Frank Carter. Fullmer bulled me along the ropes before Carter realized that the bell had rung.

Another time, I didn't hear the bell at the start of a round and when I stood up, waiting for it, Fullmer was all over me.

I knew he was winning rounds. He had to be. Whenever we clinched, the spectators shouted and yelled for Carter to break us. In the late rounds, I had to shoot for a knockout. During the final round, he walked into my left hook the same way he had in Chicago four years before, but this time it only staggered him.

If only he had made that mistake earlier, when I was stronger. If only the referee had been different. If only the ring hadn't seemed so small.

As soon as the unanimous decision was announced, I ducked through the ropes and through the aisle to my dressing room. I had seen the blood on the towels from where Fullmer had cut me over the eyes and pounded my nose. I wanted to see what my face was like.

"Give me a mirror," I said to George.

"You're all right, Robinson," he said. "You looked worse after you beat Turpin."

"I looked ten years younger, too."

The wounds weren't too bad. I was more scarred mentally. Not from the loss, but from the aggravation throughout the week. Some time later, I discovered that the ring had not been twenty feet after all. Al Buck of the New York *Post* had measured it himself.

"It was seventeen feet," he told me.

"Then why did George say twenty?"

"Because the tape was at the twenty-foot mark, but three feet had been sheared out of the tape, and the two ends had been soldered together to fool George on purpose. When the tape was stretched out, it looked like twenty feet, but it was only seventeen."

"Only in Las Vegas," I said.

I had $84,013 coming to me, but the commission had the nerve to hold it up while it considered possible discipline against me for my threat to call off the fight. Governor Sawyer talked the commissioners out of that. It would be my last title fight. It never occurred to me that way at the time, but it occurred to others.

Several months later, I arrived at Wiley's Gym one afternoon to train. I headed through the gloomy locker room toward my tiny private room with the small green carpet on it.

"Sorry," said the man in charge that day, "but Mister Wiley said if you don't pay, you don't train."

Don't pay? All these years, I had worked at Wiley's Gym as his guest, and he always had told me that I'd never pay a dime as long as I wanted to work there. All these years, I had taken Wiley with me all over, and now . . .

"You made a mistake," I told the man.

"That's what Mister Wiley said," he assured me.

"Then he made a mistake," I snapped.

The next day, Wiley straightened it out.

At the time, I was training for a fight in the Garden with Denny Moyer, a kid from Oregon. I got a decision, but when the crowd booed, Markson and Brenner thought it would make a good rematch. They set it for February 17, 1962.

The night of the fight, I was in my mother's house, taking a nap, when someone shook me awake. It was George.

"C'mon, Robinson," he said, "time to go. We got to get going to the Garden now, Robinson, let's go."

"It's only five-thirty," I said, glancing at the alarm clock. "What's the rush? We've got lots of time."

"Now, Robinson," he said, "they're always squawking that we get there late, so tonight we're going to be early."

"I don't want to sit around for three hours in the dressing room."

"When you get down there, you can rest," he said. "C'mon now, Robinson, you got to get up and we got to get going."

"All right," I said, annoyed but not wanting to start a real argument. "I'm awake now, anyway."

When we arrived at the Garden, it was empty. Some of the workmen were inside, and some of the special cops, but other than that it was empty. No spectators, the doors hadn't even been opened yet. None of the preliminary fighters were even there.

"What is this, George?" I said. "What am I doing here this early?"

"Well," he said, "at least nobody can say that you're late this time."

Reverend William Johnson, a little red-headed minister, was with us. He was sitting with me on the gray wooden bench in the dreary gray dressing room with the glaring ceiling light. After we were there a few minutes, George disappeared outside. About five minutes later, he returned and a few minutes after that, a doctor I recognized strolled in.

"Sugar Ray," he said, holding two pink pills in the palm of his right hand, "these will help you."

"Help me?" I said. "I never needed no pills before to help me. What do I need with these pills?"

"They're in case you get cut," the doctor said. "They help congeal the blood. They're good for you. I just gave a couple to Moyer."

I popped them in my mouth and took a sip of orange juice.

When it was time to go into the ring, I had been in the Garden almost four hours. After the second round, I was convinced that I had left my fight in the dressing room. I bloodied Moyer's nose in the first round, and I was working on him when I began to feel warm and drowsy just before the bell ended the second round.

"I don't know what's the matter with me, George," I said in the corner, "I can't raise my arms."

"What are you talking about, Robinson?" he said. "You looked great the first two rounds, great."

The next eight, I was terrible. I had all I could do to stay on my feet through the final bell.

"From the third round on," Jesse Abramson wrote in the *Herald Tribune*, "Robinson was a target for a vigorous youth who had no respect for the ex-champion. It became Robinson's chief concern to last the ten-round route. He did it on his vast experience, on dancing legs, on pride, by back-pedaling constantly, by disengaging from every brief exchange and running to new positions where Moyer had to pursue him. Robinson's head snapped back, he wobbled from all sorts of punches—hooks to the head, rights to the ribs, even jabs. He saved himself from a knockdown by clutching Moyer as he sagged in the ninth. He was troubled badly in the tenth and barely lasted to the bell."

I lost the decision, unanimously. My first loss in a non-title fight since Tiger Jones.

I couldn't understand it. I was almost forty-one, but I had outpointed Moyer three months earlier. He hadn't improved that much. He was doing the same things, but I wasn't doing anything. I sat at the kitchen table in Mom's house later that night with Reverend Johnson and we tried to figure what went wrong in the fight.

"May I ask a question?" he said.

"Sure you can. What's on your mind?"

"Those pink pills," he said.

Until that moment, I hadn't thought about the two pills. After I had swallowed them, I had dismissed them from my mind. But now I focused on them.

"The doctor said that Moyer had taken the pills too," I said. "Wiley will know."

Wiley was always my man in my opponent's dressing room. Under the commission rules, you're permitted to have one of your handlers watching the other fighter have his hands taped, watching everything that goes on in his room. I dialed Wiley's phone number.

"Wiley," I said, "did a doctor come in and give Moyer any pink pills before the fight?"

"Are you crazy, Ray?" he said. "You know no doctor is allowed to give a fighter any pills."

"But did any doctor try to give him any before the fight tonight? Did he take anything?"

"Ray," he said, "I was watching him every minute and he didn't take no pills at all."

I was convinced that I had been doped. Other people in boxing were convinced that I was through. Several days later, when I went down to the Garden to see Harry Markson about my next fight, he told me to sit down in the big leather chair across from his desk. Then he carefully locked his door.

"Ray," he said, "I'm afraid we can't use you here anymore."

"Are you serious, Harry?" I snorted. "I'm going to win the title again."

"Not the way you fought the other night."

"That was a bad night," I said. "Ain't I entitled to a bad

night? I had a bad night against Tiger Jones in my come-back, but I came on to win the title."

"Ray, I'm sorry," he said, "but I couldn't let the Garden be responsible—"

I didn't let him finish. I got up and put on my coat and he unlocked the door. I walked out without another word. I walked through the gloomy hallway to the big glass windows overlooking the Garden lobby, the lobby I had filled about twenty-five times on the nights I was fighting in the Garden.

And now, Harry Markson *couldn't let the Garden be responsible*.

In the months to come, the world would close in on me even more. I took a fight in L.A., to see Millie, but Phil Moyer, Denny's brother, got the decision. I took a fight in London with Terry Downes. He got the decision. Not long after that, Edna Mae obtained a Mexican divorce. Millie was with me, in Europe, and we got engaged in Vienna. I knew she loved me, because there wasn't anything else for her to love. My flamingo Continental had been sold. My café had been closed. The symbols of my success had disappeared. Only *me* was left.

Or so we both thought until the envelope from the Treasury Department arrived on May 15, 1963.

Inside it was a check for $123,935.85, a refund from my 1962 tax report. Ever since the Internal Revenue Service had held my $313,449.82 from the first Basilio fight, I had used it as a credit against my income taxes. When I filed my 1962 report, the IRS still owed me $123,935.85. Instead of maintaining it as credit, I requested a refund.

To my surprise, I got it.

"It must have been a mistake," my tax lawyer, Bob Raum, told me when I phoned him. "You better hold it a few days."

"I just cashed it," I said.

I had needed the money desperately to pay some debts but I needed a significant victory even more. I thought I might get it in a match with Joey Giardello in Philadelphia, but he got the decision. In the fall, I went to Paris where Charlie Michaelis booked me. In five fights, I didn't lose. Two of my victories were over Armand Vanucci.

"I never heard of Vanucci," Lew Burston said to me on my return. "Is he any good?"

"He's very big in Paris," I said. "He's a guard for the Mona Lisa at the Louvre."

I hadn't impressed myself in those fights, but at forty-two, my mirror told me that I was in good shape. One more whirl, I convinced myself. One more whirl at my title. But before that, I would tutor a new heavyweight champion.

26

Cassius Clay

In the early weeks of 1964, Cassius Clay was bragging that he was "the greatest," that he was going to dethrone Sonny Liston as the world heavyweight champion in their title bout February 25 at Miami Beach.

Not many people took Cassius seriously, but I did. His big talk was an act, but his ability wasn't.

I had been following his career ever since the summer day in 1960 when I drove up in front of my café and a lean, muscular, handsome teen-ager walked over and shyly stared at me.

"Mister Robinson?" he said quietly.

"Yes, ol' buddy, what can I do for you?"

"Mister Robinson, you don't know me but I'm on my way over to Rome."

"That's a nice place."

"I'm going there for the Olympics," he said. "I'm on the United States Olympic boxing team. I'm going to win an Olympic gold medal."

"Good luck," I said.

"My name is Cassius Marcellus Clay," he said.

"Cassius what?"

"Cassius Marcellus Clay, the Second," he said. "I'm from Louisville, Kentucky. I'm the Golden Gloves champ and the AAU champ. You're my idol, Mister Robinson, you're the greatest fighter."

"Well, thank you," I said.

"And when I turn pro after the Olympics," he said, "I want you to be my manager."

"That's very thoughtful of you," I said, "but—"

"You're the greatest fighter and if you're my manager, you'll teach me all your tricks. That's why I had to see you before I went to Rome, to get it all set. I've been waiting here three hours."

"Three hours, just to see me?"

"That's right, Mister Robinson, I want you to be my manager."

"But that's impossible."

"Not now," he said. "After the Olympics, when I'm able to turn pro."

"No, you don't understand."

"Understand what?" he said.

"That I can't manage you. I'm still a fighter myself. That's a full-time thing. I couldn't possibly be fighting myself, and managing you at the same time."

"Oh," he said, sadly.

"I'm sure you're a good fighter," I said, trying to cheer him up, "but as long as I'm a fighter myself, I wouldn't be able to manage you properly."

"I understand now," he said.

"Good luck in Rome," I said.

"Thank you, Mister Robinson," he said, "but maybe if you do retire, maybe you'll be my manager then. Mister Robinson, if you retire, you'll have the time to be my manager then. If you forget, I'll remind you."

"You do that," I said, turning away.

"Thank you, Mister Robinson," he continued, his big eyes still staring at me. "Thank you, anyway."

"Okay," I said. "I've got things to do."

Inside my café, I turned to look at him again. He was on the sidewalk, staring back. I waved and he walked away. Over the years, I had been stopped by some awful pests, but at least this kid was a polite pest.

"If that kid can fight like he can talk," I said to somebody at the bar, "he'll be something."

He soon proved that he could. He won his Olympic gold medal in the light-heavyweight class at Rome. When he turned pro, he kept on winning. He kept in touch with me. He would phone every so often and tell me about his fights and his next opponents, about how he had copied my style.

"You are the king, the master, my idol," he would say, quite seriously.

By now, his mouth was making more headlines than his fists. He was predicting the round that he would knock out his opponent in, and he was making good on the boast. He was reciting poetry. He was calling himself "the greatest."

By the spring of 1963, he had talked himself into a main event with a heavyweight contender, Doug Jones, at the Garden. The newspapers in New York were on strike at the time, but that meant he had more time for TV. Once he was on TV reciting poetry with some beatniks at a Greenwich Village coffee house. That was too much. That was no way to train for a fight. The next day I told him that at Wiley's Gym.

"Well, what should I do?" he asked me.

"What you need," I said, "is somebody to watch over you, somebody to keep you happy and relaxed. I knew a man like that, Drew Brown, he likes to be called Boudini. He was in my camp a few years ago. I'll send him up to see you. You'll like him. He'll help you."

"Sugar Ray," he said, "if this man helped *you*, he's got to help me."

He hit it off right away with Boudini. He liked to laugh and Boudini did things that made him laugh. When he was training for Liston, he and Boudini had an act they'd put on for the writers and photographers.

Boudini would yell, "Float like a butterfly, sting like a bee." Then they'd both shout, "Rumble, young man, rumble," and Clay would break up laughing. Boudini had him relaxed and happy, as a fighter should be, but Boudini knew when to be serious. One day my phone rang at six in the morning. It was Boudini.

"Ray," he said, "you've got to talk to Cassius."

"What's the matter?" I said. "What's gone wrong?"

"He ain't doing his roadwork. Just now, he ran two blocks and came home. Yesterday he did the same thing, he ran a couple hundred yards and quit, said he don't need it. He thinks he's in shape, but he ain't. He ain't running at all."

"I'll talk to him," I promised.

When I phoned Cassius, I didn't want to sound as if I knew anything, so I talked about things in general at first, then I maneuvered to the point.

"How's your training going?" I said.

"Good," he said. "Boudini's my man, just like he was your man."

"How's your roadwork?"

"I'm doin' what I've always done."

"Is that enough?"

"Always has been."

"But this time," I reminded him, "you might have to go fifteen rounds. You've got to be prepared to go fifteen rounds. Proper roadwork is the only way you can get ready to go fifteen rounds. How many miles are you running each day?"

"I never run much," he said.

"I used to start off with a couple miles—running, jogging, sometimes running backwards. The last few weeks before the fight, I'd increase it to three miles, and then to four, and eventually to five miles."

"Five miles a day!"

"No other way to do it, man," I said, "no other way."

"*You* ran all that?"

"For every big fight," I said.

"Man," he said, all shook up.

"Cassius," I said, "if you believe in me, you'll make sure you do those miles in the morning. But don't do it for me, man, do it for yourself. You're the one who's going in with Liston."

The next morning, Boudini told me later, Clay was like a kid with a new toy. All he wanted to do was run.

After that, Cassius phoned me every day, sometimes twice a day, and told me how he was training. Angelo Dundee was supervising his workouts and advising him, and Angelo is a sharp boxing man. But sometimes a fighter likes to discuss his training with somebody besides his trainer. When Cassius wanted advice, he phoned me.

"And now I got a big question for you," he said one day on the phone. "How should I fight Liston?"

"The same way I fought Jake LaMotta," I said. "The matador and the bull. You can't match strength with Liston, just like I couldn't match strength with LaMotta. He was the bull, but I was the matador and I outsmarted him. You can beat Liston the same way. I'll send you the film of my La-Motta fight and you study it."

"Better than that," he said, "you bring it. You must be here for the fight. You must be with me."

I was between fights, so I agreed. On the flight to Miami, I realized that he had slicked me into becoming sort of his manager after all. He had me advising him on his training and his tactics, as he had asked me to do that day outside my café in 1960. Instead of resenting the way he had charmed me, I was enjoying it. But when I arrived at the pink stucco home he had rented in the Negro neighborhood of Miami, the scene was unlike anything I'd ever seen for a fighter a few days before the biggest thing in his life.

Noise, man. Wall-to-wall noise.

His sparring partners, including his brother, Rudolph Valentino Clay, were there, and that was good. But some young girls were there, too—"foxes," Cassius called them. And some middle-aged men—Black Muslims, I later discovered. All I knew was that there was too much commotion, and too much temptation.

"Cassius," I told him when I got him alone, "you've got to clear out these people."

"What for?" he said. "All these foxes keep me goin'. They give me more incentive."

"Man, they'll give you nothin' but trouble. Save your incentive for after the fight."

I wasn't sure that he'd go along with me, but he did. The house quieted down. He got more rest. He had more time to think about how he was going to fight Liston, how he was "going to bait the Bear," as he called him. He liked to taunt Liston. One day he had stopped at the hotel where Liston was training to shout and yell at him. The day of the fight, I had a talk with him before we left for the weigh-in.

"When you see Liston," I said, "play it cool. Don't go mouthing off, man. The fight is *tonight.*"

"Don't worry," he assured me, "everything's gonna be all right. The Bear already is in my trap."

The moment he saw Liston, he forgot his promise. He started to shout and yell about how he was "the greatest," about how he was going to beat Liston like he was his daddy. The more he shouted, the wilder he got. His eyes looked as if they were going to jump out of his head. I was trying to calm him down, so were Boudini and Angelo Dundee, but nobody had any influence over him. He was like a maniac. The commission chairman fined him $2500. One of the commission doctors pronounced him "on the verge of hysteria." In the midst of the excitement Bill Faversham, one of the Louisville millionaires who had bankrolled Clay, took me aside.

"Ray," he said, "please do me a favor."

"I'll try, Mister Faversham," I said. "What is it?"

"Stay with Cassius the rest of the day."

"You don't want me for that, you want a padded cell."

"Ray, he'll listen to you."

"He didn't here," I replied. "I warned him not to make a scene here."

"But he doesn't listen to *us* at all."

"All right," I said, "I'll try to calm him down when we get back to the house."

"You're our only hope, Ray," he said.

The strangest thing was, when we got in the car to return to the house, Cassius had cooled off completely. I couldn't believe it. When I finally had him alone in the house, I sat down across from where he was resting in his bed.

"Now, listen, Cassius," I began.

"I'm all right, man," he said. "Calm and collected."

"That's not the point," I said.

"Then what is?" he said quietly.

"If you're not going to listen to me, Cassius, then you don't need me here with you. I'm trying to be your friend, trying to give you advice. But if you're not going to take it, I'm not going to bother to give it. Everything you're going through today, waiting for a title fight, I went through dozens of times. Now either you listen to me or I leave."

"Sugar Ray," he said slowly. "Sugar Ray, the greatest. I must listen to you."

"All right, then," I said. "When you go in that ring tonight, no nonsense."

"Okay, no nonsense," he said. "But that Bear turns me on. He thinks he's so tough. And he can't beat me. No way."

"That's just it," I said.

"Just what?" he wondered.

"You've got to prove that he can't beat you in the *ring*, man, no place else. That's where you've got to make a fool out of him. All this talking don't win you the fight. Nobody at the weigh-in raised your hand and pronounced you the new champion because you outtalked Liston. You got to beat him in the ring. That's the only place it counts. In the *ring*."

"Sugar Ray," he said, looking up, "you know what the business is all about."

The rest of the afternoon and in the early hours of the evening he was perfectly relaxed. He dozed off for a nap. He watched TV and when he saw his antics at the weigh-in, he laughed so hard he shook. But that night in the dressing room, I had another scare. Willie Reddish, who trained Liston, came in to check the taping on Clay's hands. Reddish teased Clay about the wild weigh-in.

"Man," Cassius said, "I'll whip you right here, and I'll whip your Bear in the ring."

Reddish, who had once been a heavyweight, went into his stance and flicked a couple playful jabs. Clay hopped off the rubbing table and made a big bluff out of going after Willie. He didn't get far. Angelo grabbed him. So did Boudini. And so did I.

"Sit down and stay there," I said.

When I saw the little smile in the corner of Clay's face, I realized he was fooling with Reddish, but I don't think Reddish realized that. When Reddish returned to Liston's dressing room, I'm told he shook his head and said, "That kid is crazy." Crazy like a fox, because when the fight started, Clay made a mess of Liston. He stuck his jab in Liston's face whenever he wanted to, and he had him bloodied up long before Liston stayed on his stool when the bell rang for the seventh round. I don't know if Liston had a sore shoulder, as he claimed, but I know he had a sore face.

The moment Clay realized that he had won, he started leaping around the ring.

"Eat your words!" he shouted at the sportswriters at ringside. "Eat your words!" Virtually all of the sportswriters had rated Clay a braggart instead of a boxer.

When he spotted me in the ringside seats, he yelled, "The matador and the bull!"

Now that Clay was the champion, I had a decision to make. Several days before the fight, he had mentioned that he wanted me to join him as an adviser on strategy and theater-TV plans. Meanwhile, I had discovered his association with the Black Muslims. The day after the Liston fight, he announced his conversion. He had been tutored by Malcolm X, then the chief aide to Elijah Muhammad. Malcolm X was a brilliant man, a true orator. But he wasn't my style.

"Cassius," I told him, thankful for the excuse. "I'm still a fighter. I just can't get involved with you full-time now."

He accepted that, and I hustled back to New York. He changed his name to Cassius X, and he later changed it to Muhammad Ali. He would phone me every so often, but I went to Europe again. During my trip, he required hernia surgery that delayed his November return with Liston. In February 1965, when he was still recuperating, I was in Kingston, Jamaica. When there's snow in New York, it's always nice to arrange a fight somewhere in the Caribbean. When the promoter there heard me discussing my friendship with Clay, he had an idea.

"Call the champ in Miami," the promoter said, "and invite him down to work in your corner as a second."

It was a good stunt. Clay had never been to Jamaica. As colorful as he was, he had to add to the crowd, and therefore to my percentage. When I phoned him, I told him I'd give him $1000. He was on the next plane, along with his first wife, Sonji, and Boudini. When he strutted down the ramp, he was waving and yelling.

"The greatest second has arrived," he was shouting, "for Sugar Ray—the king, the master, my idol."

He always used the same line. The way he dramatized it, I always had to laugh at it. He was a funny kid. I mean funny comical. He could be funny weird, though. One of the Muslim tenets is that pork is an evil meat. At dinner that night, Sonji and Millie were quietly discussing the menu.

"The stuffed pork is delicious here," Millie suggested.

"I'd love to have that," Sonji whispered, "but he won't let me."

"He what?"

"He orders everything for me. You watch. He'll never order pork. Muslims don't eat pork."

"But you're not a Muslim," Millie said.

"No, but I'm married to one," she said.

When the waiter returned, Clay ordered his meal, and Sonji's meal, without even asking what she'd like to have. I forget what they had, but I know it wasn't the stuffed pork. After dinner, the four of us sat on the terrace near the swimming pool. It was a beautiful tropical evening. Warm, but with a slight breeze blowing through the palm trees near the beach. The sky a deep blue, and cloudless. Suddenly, a shooting star soared across it. Seeing it, Clay jumped to his feet and ran around to the other side of the pool.

"What's going on?" Millie blurted.

"The white man!" Clay roared. "The white man is destroying the world!"

"Don't be ridiculous," she said.

He was serious. The next day, Millie was in the swimming pool when Sonji strolled by, fully dressed.

"Get your bathing suit," Millie said.

"I don't dare," she said. "He won't let me expose my legs to anybody."

"Expose your legs?" Millie said. "In a decent bathing suit?"

"He wants me to wear those long Muslim dresses," she said. "I'm not even supposed to wear slacks. If our doorbell rings, and we're having Muslim guests, he makes me put on one of those Muslim dresses."

At the fight that night, Sonji was sitting with Millie near my corner when he embarrassed her again.

He was up in the ring with me, helping me slide my bathrobe over my gloves, when I saw his eyes flash. He stared at Sonji and hollered, "You pull your dress down. Pull it down, you hear?" When I turned to look, I couldn't understand what he was shouting about. Man, that was a couple years before the miniskirt arrived. If her skirt showed anything, it was her knees. If that.

I finished Jimmy Beecham in two and we were at a reception when Clay made another scene.

Sonji was telling Millie, "I'm in hell, I'm living in hell. Believe me, hell couldn't be no worse than living with this man." Sonji had a glass in her hand. As she was talking to Millie, she looked up to see Clay standing over her.

"What are you drinking?" he snapped.

"Wine," she said. "Is that bad too?"

He slapped the glass out of her hand and took her away. The next morning they departed. The night before, when we were sitting around the swimming pool after the shooting star episode, he had asked me to convert to the Muslims.

"The white man is destroying the world," he was saying.

"Don't talk foolish," I said. "You don't make any sense."

"Allah," he said. "Allah is the only one who can save us all. And his prophet is Elijah Muhammad, the leader of the nation of Islam. The last time I saw Elijah Muhammad, in Chicago, he told me to tell you that if you would embrace the Muslim faith, he'd collect seven hundred thousand dollars for you."

"For me—seven hundred thousand dollars?"

"There are seven hundred thousand of us Muslims," he said, "and Elijah told me that each one would gladly contribute a dollar if you joined us and announced that you have embraced the Muslim faith. The great Sugar Ray Robinson, a Muslim."

"I think Mr. Muhammad might be a good man but I believe in God, and for seven hundred *million,* I wouldn't change my belief. Cassius, a religion is something you've got to believe in. You believe in yours and I respect your right to believe what you want. To me, any sort of belief in God is good—Catholic, Protestant, Jewish, Muslim. But from a little kid, I've believed in Christianity and in the Bible, life with Jesus Christ. All the Christian religions preach love for your fellow man."

He didn't seem to know what to say.

I continued, "You know your slogan—'The white man is a devil, the white devils.' That's not right. You can't live in this world hating people. You can't live without the white man, or the black man, or the red man, or the yellow man. People should be against hate, not with it."

"All right," he said, "but if you ever change your mind—"

"I won't change my mind," I said. "You tell Mr. Muham-

mad thanks for the offer, but I don't wish to change the way
I am, a Christian believer in God."

And that ended the conversation near the swimming pool.

Although I disagreed with his Muslim faith, and I disap-
proved of his treatment of Sonji, who divorced him soon
after that, somehow I liked him. Most of the time, Cassius
Clay is one of the most likable people that I've ever known.
I hoped that our differences wouldn't ruin our friendship.
They didn't. We continued to phone each other quite
often. He made a big fuss over me when he trained in New
York for his fight with Zora Folley, his last title defense before he refused to enter the United States Army in 1967.

"Sugar Ray," his voice boomed over the phone one night,
"you have to work in my corner."

"You have all the good corner men you need," I told him.
"You don't want me there, too."

"I worked in your corner in Kingston, Jamaica," he said.
"Now you have to work in mine."

To him, it was like a debt. He offered me $1000, the same
amount he had earned in Kingston. At that time, I really
needed that grand, and he probably realized that.

"All right," I said. "I'll come down to the Garden tomorrow
and we'll talk about it."

In the dull gray basement of the Garden, a ring had been
set up for Cassius to work in. As I arrived, he was inside the
ropes, shadowboxing. When he took a breather, he spotted
me.

"The king, the master, my idol!" he shouted.

About three hundred people were there, watching the
workout. When he pointed at me, their heads spun.

"Sugar Ray Robinson," he announced. "The greatest—"
In a stage whisper, he added, "except for me," and everybody laughed. His voice boomed again. "Here he comes,

the king, the master, my idol! Sugar Ray Robinson! He will be in my corner, advising me of his secrets, when I oppose Zora Folley."

I didn't work in his corner, but he didn't need me. His fast hands and his fast feet were enough. Folley went in the fourth. Cassius is the fastest heavyweight I've ever seen, and his speed would enable him to conquer most of the slow-moving heavyweight champions, like Rocky Marciano. Cassius would be too fast and too fancy for Rocky, but his speed wouldn't help him against Joe Louis. Before the second Billy Conn fight, Joe said, "He can run, but he can't hide." It would be the same with Cassius against the ropes. Louis would break both Clay's arms. Before he was champion, Cassius was knocked down by Henry Cooper and Sonny Banks. If they could knock him down, Joe Louis would knock him out. I never saw any of the heavyweight champions before Joe Louis, but Jersey Joe Walcott, with his shuffling sideways style, would have given Cassius trouble.

As it turned out, I did give Cassius some advice but he spurned it.

The night before his fight with Folley, my phone rang at about eleven o'clock. Cassius sounded more serious than I had ever heard him.

"Sugar Ray," he said, "can you come down to see me? Please, I have got to see you tonight—now."

He was staying at Loew's Midtown Motor Inn, across Eighth Avenue from the old Garden. When I knocked on his door, he opened it himself. He was the only one in the room. He handed me a wad of bills.

"Here's your thousand," he said.

"But there's no way I can be in your corner," I said. "I don't have a license as a second."

"Man, you *wanted* to," he said. "That's good enough."

"What's going on, Cassius?" I said, not thinking that he

preferred to be called Muhammad Ali. "Why did you call me here at this hour?" And then it hit me. "I mean, Muhammad."

"Never mind the Muhammad," he said. "You don't have to call me that."

"Well, what's on your mind?" I said. "You got a fight tomorrow. You should have been asleep two hours ago."

"It's the Army," he said.

"What about the Army?" I asked.

"They want me—soon."

"I know that," I said. "I read about it in the paper last week."

"But I can't go," he said.

"You've got to go," I said.

"No," he said, "Elijah Muhammad told me that I can't go."

"What do you mean, you *can't* go?" I said, really annoyed.

Sitting there on the bed, his eyes on the floor, he didn't know how to answer me.

"That's what he told me."

"I don't care what Muhammad told you," I continued, "but I do care about you. If you don't go in the Army, you'll go to jail. When that happens, they'll take your title away. When you come out of jail, you won't be permitted to fight. Do you realize that you're forfeiting your entire career?"

"Well," he stumbled, "Muhammad told me."

"But if you go to jail, none of those other Muslim leaders are going to jail with you. I know you respect your religion, but at the same time, you must live by the law of the land—wherever you live, you must live by the law."

"But I'm afraid, Ray, I'm real afraid."

"Afraid of what?" I said. "Afraid of the Muslims if you don't do what they told you?"

He didn't answer me.

"Now, look, Cassius," I said, "I told you what I think. That's all I can do for you. I'm your friend and I'm always going to advise you with what I think is right."

"Thanks," he said quietly. "Thanks for coming."

He stood up and we shook hands. It would be the last time I would see him to talk to when he was the heavyweight champion. Not long after he knocked out Zora Folley, he refused to be drafted into the Army. That same day, his title was vacated by the New York State Athletic Commission and the World Boxing Association. It wasn't fair. The title was his property right. He had fought for it, and the only way he should lose it is in the ring. The least the New York Commission and the WBA could've done was wait until his conviction was affirmed.

That night we talked in his room, I looked into his handsome face as I left. His eyes were glistening with tears—tears of torment, tears of indecision.

The more I thought about it, the more I sympathized with him. Two years earlier, those tears had been in my eyes.

27

À Tout à l'Heure

One day in the spring of 1965, I parked my gray Buick station wagon outside my office on Seventh Avenue and hurried across the sidewalk.

"You're rich again, Sugar," a passerby shouted. "I read about all that money you got from the government."

"Yeah, man," I said, wearing a blue suit that was five years old, "everything's gonna be swinging again, man."

I was lying. Several days earlier, on April 6, the United States Tax Court had ruled that I was entitled to the $313,-449.82 that the Internal Revenue Service had held from my first Basilio fight. I was *entitled* to it, but there wasn't any money for me to get. Over the years, I had used that money as a credit on my income taxes. In 1963, when I cashed the refund check for about $123,000, that was the end of it. I was lucky the Tax Court ruled for me. If the decision had gone the other way, I would have been in almost as bad shape on my taxes as Joe Louis had been.

My case had been bound in a big black book, two inches thick, by George Delson, the tax adviser who argued it for me.

When the Tax Court ruled in my favor, I autographed the

book, "To my pal George, who won the toughest fight I ever had."

I never got a dime out of that ruling, but after it made the papers, everybody assumed I was in big money again. My ego wouldn't let me tell them differently. Instead, the only money I had was what was left of the couple thousand I had earned when Cassius was my second in Jamaica. The tears of torment and indecision were in my eyes.

"Try it with me once more," I pleaded with George, "one last time."

He went with me to Portland, Maine, and Pittsfield, Massachusetts. The money wasn't much, maybe $700, but it kept me going on my last whirl to another title shot.

"You've got the feel of the ring, Robinson," he kept telling me, "and when your chance comes, you'll be ready."

I had turned forty-four. If my chance came, I had to be ready. I arranged a trip to Honolulu, for a fight with Stan Harrington. On the way, I had another one scheduled in the Tijuana, Mexico, bull ring with a Mexican mailman, Memo Ayon. The dust from the dirt streets is in the air in Tijuana. As I sweated, I felt the grime forming on me.

"Wipe my arms," I told George between rounds. "Wipe my chest and back—get this dirt off me."

I was more worried about the dust on me than the fight. I wasn't having any trouble with the mailman. But when the decision was announced, Ayon had won. It had to be the worst verdict of my career. Millie was with me, and we drove to Los Angeles that night. She had a second-floor apartment over where her Uncle Wright and Aunt Babe lived. Uncle Wright Fillmore had been the head instructing waiter on the Southern Pacific Railroad, and he made better sense than most preachers. In my times in Los Angeles, I had enjoyed sitting in his back yard, under his lemon tree and his fig tree, munching on walnuts as he talked.

"One thing about Millie," he had told me a few days earlier, "if it comes your part in life to drink skimmed milk, she'll drink it, and if you have milk with some cream in it, she'll drink that, too—and she'll never let on there's a difference between 'em."

As we drove up the freeway toward Los Angeles, his words drifted through my mind. Millie had been around me for most of the last three years. Through those years, I had never had the money that I once had, but somehow I was much happier. Despite my frustration, she had created an inner peace within me, an inner peace that I would need for the rest of my life.

"We're not going home," I told her.

"Why not?" she asked. "Where are we going?"

"Las Vegas."

"What for?"

"To get married," I said. "We'll get married and come right back."

I drove to the Los Angeles International Airport. We got on the next flight to Las Vegas. At McCarren Field there, we got into a cab.

"Take us to the marriage license bureau downtown," I said, "and then we want to go to one of the wedding chapels."

After we obtained our license, the cab driver took us to a wedding chapel near The Sands hotel. Inside, it was like a miniature church. I didn't think it was that pretty, but Millie was saying, "Oh, it's lovely, Ray, it's lovely."

I had my sunglasses on, and I was using my real name, Walker Smith. I didn't want any publicity.

"You look familiar," the justice of the peace said to me. "I'm sure I've seen you before."

"You ain't seen me in *here* before," I said. "My bride and I just happened to be passing by."

We were married on May 25, 1965, with the cab driver, Benjamin Franklin, as our witness. He drove us back to the airport and we hopped on a return flight to Los Angeles. The next day, we took a jet to Honolulu for my fight with Stan Harrington. He busted me up over the eye, with a butt, and he got the decision. I was a bloody bridegroom.

When we returned to New York, we moved into one of the bedrooms in Mom's home. It wouldn't work out over a long stretch, but we would be traveling most of the time so it would be silly to rent an apartment. I went down to Washington, D.C., and won a ten-round decision.

"Say," I asked George after the fight, "what was that cat's name?"

"Young Joe Walcott," he replied, "no relation to Jersey Joe."

In the next couple of months, I arranged two more bouts with Walcott and won the decision each time. Meanwhile, I had lost to Ferd Hernandez in Vegas, in the night club of the Hacienda Hotel, and to Stan Harrington again in Honolulu. But if I could put a couple of victories together, my name might carry me into a title bout. Don Elbaum, who promoted in Pennsylvania and Ohio, had the same idea. He set me up with Peter Schmidt in Johnstown, Pennsylvania.

"If you look good against Schmidt," Elbaum said, "it might lead to something big, Archer in Pittsburgh."

Joey Archer was a leading challenger, a flat-nosed Irishman from the Bronx, a good boxer but no punch. With a win over Archer, I'd be in line for a title shot. When I arrived in Johnstown, I thought it was the grayest place I've ever been in. All those steel mills, gray. The smoke, gray. The river, gray. The sky, gray. Even the leaves on the trees looked gray. But not to Elbaum. He'd been waiting all his life to promote a card with me on it. He was a little round-faced guy with curly black hair and sunglasses. That night he threw a press party in a local night club, the Golden Key, and he had his sunglasses on.

"Twenty-five years in professional boxing," Elbaum said in his speech, "and to honor Ray, we have a present for him."

Opening a box on the table, Elbaum pulled out a set of boxing gloves and held them up to show the audience.

"These gloves," he announced, "are the very same gloves that Ray wore in Madison Square Garden the night he knocked out Joe Echevarria in 1940 in his professional debut —twenty-five years ago almost to the day. It wasn't easy, but we got them and Ray," he said, turning to me, "it's a little surprise from us to you."

Next to me, I noticed Millie weeping. I felt like crying, too. What a nice thing he had done.

"Hey, Champ," a photographer called, "put on the gloves. You and the gloves, a great shot."

"No, no," Elbaum snapped, snatching the gloves, "I think Ray is a little tired after his trip."

Hiding the gloves behind him, Elbaum waved the photographer away and resumed his speech.

"That's it, everybody," he said. "Thanks for coming and remember—the fight is Friday."

I couldn't understand what was going on. I'd never seen a promoter discourage a sure picture in the next day's newspaper, particularly a picture with such human-interest quality. But when I glanced at the gloves again, I realized why. Both of them were right-handed.

"Some surprise," I said to him, winking.

"Well," he shrugged, "nobody's perfect."

His timing wasn't too perfect, either, even though he had Willie Pep on the card. Willie had retired in 1959 but now he was on a comeback that nobody took seriously. Willie needed some money. Promoting a card with me and Willie on it had always been Elbaum's dream. "The Two Great-

est Fighters of All Time" was the blurb on his show cards all
over Johnstown. Fifteen years earlier, when Willie and me
were world champions, we would've sold out Yellowstone
Park. We might have sold out the Cambria War Memorial
Arena in Johnstown in 1965 except that Elbaum put us in
there on a Friday night in October. On a Friday night in
October, the biggest thing in Johnstown, maybe the only
thing, is high-school football.

"Maybe it'll rain," Elbaum kept saying.

It didn't. The arena, modern and clean, holds 5000 people, but there weren't more than 1000 in it when I walked
through the empty aisles and hopped up the steps to the
ring. At the weigh-in that morning Schmidt had said to me,
"I can't tell you what a thrill it is to meet you." He sounded
as if he meant it, but he must've had a bigger thrill when he
hit me in the mouth with a right hand in the fifth round.

From behind me, I heard George shouting, "Careful, Robinson, careful!"

In the eighth round, I put Schmidt down. In the ninth,
I did it again. I wasn't worried about the decision. I was
more concerned with the Pittsburgh promoter, Archie Litman, who was there to scout me for the Archer fight.

In my dressing room, Litman, a husky, pleasant guy,
walked over.

"You still want Archer?" he said.

"You name the date," I replied, "and I'll be there."

"November tenth," he said.

"Don't forget," said Elbaum, "I'm putting you in Steu-
benville on the twentieth of this month with Rudolph Bent.
You won't have any trouble with him."

"And you won't have any people," I said.

"We will in Pittsburgh," Litman said. "Enough to guarantee you ten thousand."

"Ol' buddy," I said, "I'll be there."

The money was secondary. My end of the Johnstown fight was $790. In Steubenville, Ohio, another gray river town not far from Pittsburgh, I got about $500. The next night, Joe Giardello lost the middleweight title to Dick Tiger. I figured I would have had less trouble with Tiger than I would have with Joey. Tiger was a straight-ahead plodder, perfect for me. The matador and the bull all over again. When I arrived in Pittsburgh for the Archer fight, all the sportswriters had the same question: Why was I fighting?

"To win the title again," I'd say. "The beautiful end of a beautiful story."

None of them took me seriously. They wrote down what I had said. They had to. I knew it was a good quote. But then there always was a pause in the conversation, as if they were giving themselves time to feel sorry for me. I'd heard people say that I was fighting from memory, and I knew some of them were feeling sorry for me. But damn it, I wasn't feeling sorry for me. I was feeling great, but I had to put up with that attitude from everybody.

One evening a couple nights before the fight, I was in my room at the Carlton House, playing cards with Millie and George and his wife, Hazel, when the phone rang.

George answered it, and his eyebrows shot up and he looked at me.

"Joe Glaser," I heard George say. "It's been a long time, Joe."

When I took the phone, Joe's scratchy voice was saying to me, "Ray, promise me now, if you don't win this fight, you'll quit. Promise me, Ray. I'm coming out to see the fight, but you've got to promise me that if you lose, you'll quit. I'll find some things for you to do—night clubs, television. Promise me, Ray."

"All right, Joe," I said, "I promise."

I didn't have to promise him. I knew that if I didn't

get past Archer, it wouldn't make sense to go back to Tijuana or Johnstown or any of the other towns where I could
always get a few hundred dollars. When I put down the
phone, I did something I must've done a hundred times that
week. I made a fist with my left hand and pounded it into
the palm of my right hand.

"I wish you'd stop that, Robinson," George said, "you're
gonna hurt your hand."

George was looking out for me, but he knew what I was
thinking. One more left hook. One more left hook like the
one that took out Gene Fullmer. Archer was supposed to
have a tough chin. He had only been down once in his career. But nobody had a tougher chin than Gene Fullmer,
and I took him out with my left hook. Another thing, Archer
had no punch. He hadn't knocked down anybody in five
years. When we were in the ring, under the bright lights at
the shiny new Civic Arena, and the referee called us out for
the instructions, I stared at Archer's square chin, measuring
it for one more left hook.

Shortly after the bell, I threw the hook, but Archer swung
his head and it missed by several inches. Not only that,
Archer stuck a jab in my face. He knew the moves.

In the second round, I jolted him with a good combination. In the third, I threw the hook again and caught him
with it. But nothing happened. He blinked, but that was all.
In the fourth, I feinted him with a left, but my legs got tan-
gled. He swung a big right hand that plunked me on top of
the head. Not on the jaw, on top of the head. My feet were
so mixed up, I was off balance. The next thing I knew, I was
on the seat of my white satin trunks.

Ain't this awful, I was thinking, *how am I ever going to
tell anybody that he didn't knock me down, that I did?*

I took a nine count. When you're down, what difference
does the count make. Kneeling there, I realized that it had

been the most embarrassing thing that had ever happened to me. After that, I never really did much. I could hear Millie shouting for me, "Get him, Ray, get him, honey," but I couldn't respond.

At the final bell, I just wanted to get out of that ring. Disappear. Vanish. But that was impossible. I knew I had to stay there and wait for the announcement and I always had stayed there when I knew the announcer was going to tell me that I had won. While I was standing in my corner, several dozen people gathered in the aisle below me and stood there, applauding and looking up at me. Man, that gave me a feeling.

After the decision was announced, I was turning to climb through the ropes when I saw Millie.

"That's all right, honey," she said, looking up at me with tears in her eyes. "You didn't get hurt."

She meant physically. Inside, I was in agony. I wished I could disappear. But when I got to my dressing room, a strange thing happened. All the sportswriters were around me instead of over in Archer's dressing room. Television cameras were there, too. After a few minutes, Archer came over to go on TV with me. Imagine the winner coming to the loser. He told me, "Ray, you were the greatest middleweight I ever saw." He made me feel better. Everybody was trying to cheer me up, but some of them tried too hard.

"The Ray Robinson of old," I remember somebody said to me, "you looked like the Ray Robinson of old."

Man, be serious, I thought. I hadn't been the Ray Robinson of old. I had been an old Ray Robinson.

Over against a wall, George was holding court for some sportswriters. I heard him boasting, "Well, we have an offer for a return bout with Archer, but we wouldn't have it here, not with these officials."

Damn it, George, I thought, *none of those officials put me on my ass.*

The embarrassment was awful. The next day papers all over the country would print wire-service stories telling how I had been knocked down by Joey Archer. After the writers drifted out of the dressing room, I couldn't get back to the hotel fast enough.

Up in the room, I was getting undressed to get into bed when there was a knock on the door.

George answered it, and I could hear a strange male voice outside saying, "I've got a few hot dogs for Mister Robinson. He'll remember. Tell him I'm the hot-dog man from the place on the corner."

The day before, Millie had stopped for a hot dog in his place. She raved about it, and I told him that I'd be in to have one after the fight. He had promised to bring a few to my room.

"Here they are, Mister Robinson," the hot-dog man was saying now. "I even heated the buns. I'm sorry you lost."

"Well, thank you," I said, not knowing what else to say. "This is very nice of you. I really appreciate this."

I did, but he was gone before I could say anything else. Millie took them out of the bag while I finished undressing and when I got into bed, with the pillow propped behind me, she handed me one of the hot dogs.

"Look at you," George said, laughing. "All you need is a plate of beans and you're back at Bickford's."

Back at Bickford's, where we used to eat after returning to Harlem from one of the bootleg fights. George must have thought he was still arranging things for me.

"That return with Archer," he added, "you ought to consider that, Robinson. That could draw big again."

Good old George, always trying for another payday. But instead of getting angry, I shooed him out of the room. I wanted to talk to Millie, more than I'd ever wanted to talk to her before.

"Honey," I said when we were alone, "I'm not going to have any more fights."

"Oh, Ray," she said, and she was crying with her head nestled in my neck, "I'm so happy you decided. I didn't want you to fight anymore, but it had to be your decision."

"And I promise," I said, "no comeback."

With my money from the Archer fight, I could afford to rent an apartment on Riverside Drive. I didn't want Millie to be living in Mom's house, where the same friction that affected my marriage to Edna Mae might develop. In our new apartment a few days later, the phone rang. It was John Condon, the boxing publicity man at the Garden.

"Ray," he said, "can you come down to see me tomorrow? I've got an idea for something special that I think you'll like to do."

I always respected John, one of the most honest men I ever knew around boxing. The next day, when I arrived in his office that looked out on Eighth Avenue, he closed his door and motioned for me to sit down.

"Ray," he said, "after all you've done for the Garden, the Garden should do something for you."

Man, I thought, *a few years earlier the Garden would have liked to shoot me, that's what.*

"Ray," he continued, "now that you've retired, you should have an official farewell. Let the people see you again, and let you say good-by to them from the ring. It would be a great thing for you, and a great thing for boxing. There isn't enough sentiment in boxing. When a fighter retires, he's forgotten. But you shouldn't be allowed to retire without a ceremony."

"What kind of a ceremony?"

"We've got a welterweight title fight coming up on December tenth, Emile Griffith against Manuel Gonzalez. For maybe half an hour before that fight, we'll darken the Garden. What I'd like to do is bring in the five guys you won the middleweight title from, let them say a few words, maybe have somebody give you an award, and, as a climax, have you make your farewell speech. But there's one thing, Ray."

"What's that?"

"If you do this, you can't ever fight again. You can't announce a comeback next week, or next month, or next year. If you do, it would look like we pulled a hoax on everybody."

"Don't worry, John, I'm through. I wouldn't do anything to spoil this."

When the R.K.O.-General television people heard about the plans, they thought it was a great idea. They were going to televise the Griffith-Gonzalez fight, and they wanted to open the show with my farewell. They made one mistake. They forgot they had to deal with me.

"I'm sorry," I told one of the TV executives at a meeting at the Garden, "but you'll have to pay me."

"Well," the TV man said, "we weren't planning to do that. After all, we thought you'd want it on television."

"If I want it on," I replied, "I want to get paid for it, too. You're showing commercials, ain't you?"

"Well, yes," the TV man said, "but it seemed to us that you would consider it good for boxing if it was on."

"I want it good for Sugar Ray, too," I said.

Behind his desk, Harry Markson, who had sat in on many of my battles in the same office with Jim Norris, smiled and said, "Nothing has changed, has it, Ray?"

"Not when it comes to money," I said.

The way it worked out, the farewell ceremonies began at

nine-thirty in order to be sure they would be over by the ten o'clock television time. Too bad it wasn't on TV, it would have been good for boxing. I wore a hip-length, white terry-cloth robe with SUGAR RAY in thin pink letters on the back. When Johnny Addie, the ring announcer, bellowed, "The greatest fighter in the history of boxing!" that was my cue-line to hop up the wooden steps into the ring. All around me, the old Garden was dark except for the spotlight on the ring. Basilio was there, and Fullmer, and Bobo Olson, and Randy Turpin. LaMotta was there, too, but the State Athletic Commission wouldn't permit him to be introduced in the ring because he had confessed to fixing his fight with Billy Fox. During the ceremonies, Vincent Impellitteri, my mayor, presented me with a big gold trophy inscribed to "The World's Greatest Fighter." Suddenly, I had to make my speech.

"I don't know whether to be happy or sad," I remember saying, looking up at the shadowed faces in the balcony, "but it fills me full. I'm not a crybaby, but it just gets to me. I know it's not good-by, but it is farewell. *À tout à l'heure.*"

One of my favorite French phrases, meaning, "I'll see you later," seemed just the right touch to finish with. It must have been, because suddenly the applause was all around me, a different applause than I had ever heard as a fighter. Entering the ring, or after a victory, the cheers had always come in a burst. But this applause had some dignity to it, and some sadness. Next to me, Gordon MacRae began to sing, "Should auld acquaintance be forgot . . ." and that, I realized, had to be my exit line.

Slipping through the maroon ropes, I stood on the narrow apron, held the top rope and stared at it.

On my way down the wooden steps, I realized that the people were on their feet all around me, giving me a standing ovation. As I paraded through the aisle, a familiar scratchy voice growled at me from the front row.

"You big ham," Joe Glaser said.

Winking at him, and waving to the 12,146 spectators, I strode toward the 50th Street exit and disappeared down the stairs into the gloomy corridor—for the last time in a bathrobe.

About two hours later, I was the guest of honor at a midnight banquet for me in the upstairs room at Mamma Leone's.

Mayor Lindsay was there, and so was my mayor, Vincent Impellitteri. Basilio, Fullmer, Turpin, Olson, and La-Motta were there, so was Cassius Clay. After a few short speeches, everybody sat around for a couple of hours. Man, I wanted to talk all night, I wanted to keep that night going forever, but soon the waiters in their red jackets began scooping up the dirty dishes.

"I think," Millie said, nudging me, "that we're supposed to leave."

Outside, in the winter chill of 48th Street, a few people stood with us while the parking-lot attendant got our car.

"You'll always be our champion," one of them called as I drove away with Millie. "You'll always be our champion."

Behind us, on the sidewalk, they were waving to us but as my station wagon moved along 48th Street, we were alone. It was like the end of the movie about Joe Louis's life, when he's been knocked out by Marciano and he's walking through the street by himself, except that I wasn't alone. I had Millie. Thank God that I had Millie.

Twenty minutes later, I carried the big trophy inscribed to "The World's Greatest Fighter" into my new apartment.

I had to put it on the floor. The only table in the apartment was a beige metal card table, with thin legs, in the middle of the bare wooden floor in the living room. We had our meals on it. The only other piece of furniture in the apartment was an old scratched wooden bed.

For the first time in his life, "The World's Greatest Fighter" really knew what it was to need.

28

Only Big Ones

As a kid, I hadn't needed money. Mom somehow fed us and clothed us and kept a roof over our heads. As a fighter, I hadn't needed money either. It always seemed to be in my pocket, or if I was a little short, I'd hock myself to Mike Jacobs or Jim Norris for an advance.

But now that I was out of boxing, I not only had no money, I had no way of making any.

I had to borrow. I got a few thousand from Vincent Impellitteri, my mayor, who had become a judge. I got a few more thousand from some other friends. My ego had trapped me. Another man would have got a job, any job, for a hundred a week and lived on it. Not me, not Sugar Ray. I had established my style. I had to live that way, or no way. Our apartment was costing $365 a month. I could have rented a cheaper one, facing into the shadowy courtyard, but I had to have a balcony with a view of the sunset across the Hudson River. I had a card table, an old bed, and a view.

I had other expenses. Mom needed house money, so did Evelyn, who was separated from her husband. I had to meet alimony payments for Edna Mae and little Ray.

I thought about making an exhibition tour of South America, or the Orient, or Africa, anyplace where they hadn't seen me, but nobody would encourage me. Not even George.

"It would be good money," I said to him, "good paydays."

"You got to stop sometime, Robinson," he said, solemnly.

I contacted people who I thought might try to help me get a big job. They gave me the look I got to know well, the look that told me, "You were a great fighter, Ray, but . . ."

To make it worse for me, Millie had a job as a receptionist at the National Broadcasting Company.

In the morning, she would wait for the downtown bus across the street on Riverside Drive. I'd watch her from the window, and as she got on, she would wave up at me and I'd wave back. One morning she was shivering out there in the snow, and I was in a warm apartment, able to go back to a warm bed if I wanted to.

"Quit that job," I told her that night. "I don't care if we starve, you ain't working no more."

By that time, we had some furnishings. She had saved some money and bought a big mirror, the length of the living-room wall. Another time the doorman stalled me in the lobby for half an hour. He knew that Millie had purchased a surprise for me. When I got upstairs, a piano had been delivered. She knew how to shop, how to search for a bargain, something I had never bothered about. In my money years, if I liked something, I'd tell the salesman, "Ship it, man, and mail the bill." Half the time I never looked at the price tag.

I went through four million dollars, but I have no regrets. If I had a chance to do it over again, I'd do it the same way.

I did what I thought was the right thing at the time, and that's all anybody can do. I didn't gamble away my money. I used it to let people live. I took my family and my friends on trips with me. I loaned it to strangers to pay their bills, and sometimes I didn't get it back. I bought Mom a house, and a few years ago, when I didn't have much, I gave her a few thousand dollars to set up a Baptist church in a building not far from her house. I'd do that the same way any time.

Not long ago I drove along Seventh Avenue in Harlem and parked where my row of businesses had been.

My café had a new name, the Gold Lounge. Next door, where my office had been, was a place called Mister Benbow, a women's dress shop. Perry's Cleaners and the Playboy's Barber Shop were where my cleaners and my barber shop had been. On the corner at 124th Street, where the lingerie store had been, there was a beauty parlor, the House of Beauty. The new store fronts were nice enough, but Harlem has deteriorated. Junkies bobbing along the sidewalks with their blank faces. Blankest faces I ever saw.

I've got a little money now, from writing and from my roles as an actor.

I got started in a "Run For Your Life" television drama with Ben Gazzara. After that, Danny Thomas used me in a prison drama on his TV show. I worked with Mickey Rooney, Tony Randall, and Gary Crosby in the "Odd Couple" at Caesars Palace in Las Vegas. When the movie *The Detective* was on location in New York, Frank Sinatra got me a bit part as a cop.

"Hold it!" Frank yelled after I spoke my lines, and I thought I was awful. "Write more dialogue for this man. Build up his part."

I went to Rome to make *Candy*, with Richard Burton and Marlon Brando. My roles were obscure, but my name made them significant, just as I had made my preliminary bouts significant early in my boxing career.

During my money years, George Gainford once said, "There are no small fights for Robinson, only big ones."

To be honest, I wish I were still having big fights. I see my name in the newspapers, "Sugar Ray Robinson, the former champion . . ." and I try to visualize it without *former*. Once you've had acclaim as a world champion, once you move into that sphere, you never want to move out. But maybe someday I'll earn as much acclaim as an actor.

With my belief in God's help, maybe someday there'll be no small roles, only big ones.

Throughout my life, each setback prepared me for a greater triumph. One career is gone, but another is coming. I've never had a negative thought. To me, it's merely a matter of time for that greater triumph to happen. I continue to believe that I'm a chosen man, and I often think of the night I put my big gold trophy as "The World's Greatest Fighter" on the bare floor near the card table in my empty apartment.

I know it isn't supposed to end that way for me.

Afterword
by Dave Anderson

It didn't end that way. Even before this book was published originally in 1970, Sugar Ray and Millie had moved to Los Angeles, California, to their neat apartment on the second floor of a lime green duplex on the grassy corner of West Adams Boulevard and 10th Ave. Millie's uncle, Wright Fillmore, owned the duplex and lived downstairs.

In 1969 the Sugar Ray Robinson Youth Foundation was established to help youngsters develop their skills not only in sports, but also in the fine arts and the performing arts. His foundation is now his legacy.

"By offering youth opportunities to express themselves through sports, artistic activities and cultural enrichment," Sugar Ray said, "we can get to the children who are not reached by other methods and help keep them out of trouble."

At last count, the foundation has helped more than 40,000 youngsters in Los Angeles and Orange counties, including Florence Griffith Joyner, who won three track-and-field gold medals at the 1988 Summer Olympics in Seoul.

"For me," the Olympic champion has said, "the Sugar Ray Robinson Youth Foundation was my solid foundation. It kept me focused on reaching the finish line in a positive way. It gave me hope and a positive belief in myself, my community and my future."

Millie Robinson is now the foundation's executive director. Sugar Ray had been its chairman. And its symbol.

For a decade after settling in their Los Angeles apartment, Sugar Ray and Millie occasionally would go to Las Vegas, Nevada, for a big fight at Caesars Palace. On the cuff, of course. He was still Sugar Ray, still worth it to the promoters to have him photographed with the boxers in the days before the fight, still worth it to have him introduced at ringside. As dapper as ever, he hopped up the steps, slid through the ropes, waved and flashed that smile.

"Sugar Ray Robinson," you would hear people saying. "Pound for pound, the best. He still looks great."

But when he traveled to New York in 1981 for a party arranged by his friend and benefactor, Phil Rosenthal of TV Fanfare Publications, he suddenly didn't look that great anymore. The idea of the party was to bring together the boxers and other boxing people who had known Sugar Ray through the years: Jake LaMotta, Billy Graham, Willie Pep, trainer Ray Arcel and several others. Rocky Graziano was supposed to be there, but he never arrived.

"Rocky," joked Jake LaMotta, remembering Sugar Ray's third-round knockout of Graziano in 1952, "was afraid Robinson was going to hit him again."

By then Sugar Ray himself had been hit by Alzheimer's disease. Hit harder than any punch had ever hit him. No interviews at the party, Millie had requested. Nothing that might be embarrassing. As others came up to Sugar Ray, Millie would whisper the person's name and his face would brighten.

"My man," he would say.

Year by year after that, Alzheimer's kept outpointing him. The last time I saw him, I was in the Los Angeles area in January 1987 for pro football's Super Bowl XXI that the New York Giants won from the Denver Broncos, 35–19. Millie invited me to a party at their apartment. When I arrived, Sugar Ray, was sitting in a chair in the living room, staring straight ahead with Millie standing next to him.

"Ray, honey, Dave Anderson's here," she said. "Say hello to Dave, honey."

"Dave Anderson," he said, his face brightening momentarily. "My man."

It was that way with all the other guests. No matter how recently he had seen any of them, he didn't know them until Millie prompted him. When she did, his face would brighten, then he would return to his mental cocoon. Unless prompted, he never said a word. But at dinner, he ate heartily, as his waistline attested. He was no longer sleek.

I talked to Millie on the phone a few times after that, but never to Ray.

"He's resting," she would say. "My baby's tired. My baby needs his rest."

He died on April 12, 1989. Seven days later 2,000 mourners gathered at the West Angeles Church of God in Christ for his funeral. Boxing blended with show business. Mike Tyson, Henry Armstrong, Archie Moore, Ken Norton, Bobo Olson and Ruben Olivares were there. The actress Elizabeth Taylor, the singer Lou Rawls and the comedian Red Buttons were there.

"Sugar Ray Robinson," Reverend Jesse Jackson said in his eulogy, "was an original art form."

An original, a one and only. No matter how many other boxers dare to call themselves Sugar Ray.

DAVE ANDERSON

APPENDIX

Sugar Ray's Record

Born, May 3, 1920, Detroit, Mich. Height 5 ft. 11 in. Managed by George Gainford.
Won Golden Gloves featherweight title in 1939 and lightweight title in 1940 in New York and in intercity competition.
Engaged in 85 amateur bouts. Had 69 KO's (40 first round).

1940		
October 4—Joe Echeverria, N.Y.C.	KO	2
October 8—Silent Stefford, Savannah	KO	2
October 22—Mistos Grispos, N.Y.C.	W	6
November 11—Bobby Woods, Philadelphia	KO	1
December 9—Norment Quarles, Philadelphia	KO	4
December 12—Oliver White, N.Y.C.	KO	3

1941		
January 4—Henry La Barba, Brooklyn	KO	1
January 13—Frankie Wallace, Philadelphia	KO	1
January 31—George Zengaras, N.Y.C.	W	6
February 8—Benny Cartegena, Brooklyn	KO	1
February 21—Bobby McIntire, N.Y.C.	W	6
February 27—Gene Spencer, Detroit	KO	5
March 3—Jimmy Tygh, Philadelphia	KO	6
April 14—Jimmy Tygh, Philadelphia	KO	1
April 24—Charley Burns, Atlantic City	KO	1
April 30—Joe Ghnouly, Washington	KO	3
May 10—Vic Troise, Brooklyn, N. Y.	KO	1
May 19—Nick Castiglione, Philadelphia	KO	1
June 16—Mike Evans, Philadelphia	KO	2
July 2—Pete Lello, N.Y.C.	KO	4
July 21—Sammy Angott, Philadelphia	W	10
August 27—Carl Red Guggino, L.I.C.	KO	3
August 29—Maurice Arnault, Atlantic City	KO	1
September 19—Maxie Shapiro, N.Y.C.	KO	3
September 25—Marty Servo, Philadelphia	W	10
October 31—Fritzie Zivic, N.Y.C.	W	10

Reprinted by permission of *The Ring* magazine.

1942	January 16—Fritzie Zivic, N.Y.C.	KO 10
	February 20—Maxie Berger, N.Y.C.	KO 2
	March 20—Norman Rubio, N.Y.C.	KO 7
	April 17—Harvey Dubs, Detroit	KO 6
	April 30—Dick Banner, Minneapolis	KO 2
	May 28—Marty Servo, N.Y.C.	W 10
	July 31—Sammy Angott, N.Y.C.	W 10
	August 21—Ruben Shank, N.Y.C.	KO 2
	August 27—Tony Motisi, Chicago	KO 1
	October 2—Jake La Motta, N.Y.C.	W 10
	October 19—Izzy Jannazzo, Philadelphia	W 10
	November 6—Vic Dellicurti, N.Y.C.	W 10
	December 1—Izzy Jannazzo, Cleveland	KO 8
	December 14—Al Nettlow, Philadelphia	KO 3
1943	February 5—Jake LaMotta, Detroit	L 10
	February 19—Jackie Wilson, N.Y.C.	W 10
	February 26—Jake LaMotta, Detroit	W 10
	April 30—Freddie Cabral, Boston	KO 1
	July 1—Ralph Zannelli, Boston	W 10
	August 27—Henry Armstrong, N.Y.C.	W 10
1944	October 13—Izzy Jannazzo, Boston	KO 2
	October 27—Sgt. Lou Woods, Chicago	KO 9
	November 17—Vic Dellicurti, Detroit	W 10
	December 12—Sheik Rangel, Philadelphia	KO 2
	December 22—Georgie Martin, Boston	KO 7
	In U. S. Army	
1945	January 10—Billy Furrone, Washington	KO 2
	January 16—Tommy Bell, Cleveland	W 10
	February 14—George Costner, Chicago	KO 1
	February 23—Jake LaMotta, New York	W 10
	May 14—Jose Basora, Philadelphia	D 10
	June 15—Jimmy McDaniels, New York	KO 2
	September 18—Jimmy Mandell, Buffalo	KO 5
	September 26—Jake LaMotta, Chicago	W 12
	December 4—Vic Dellicurti, Boston	W 10
1946	January 14—Dave Clark, Pittsburgh	KO 2
	February 5—Tony Riccio, Elizabeth	KO 4
	February 15—O'Neill Bell, Detroit	KO 2
	February 26—Cliff Beckett, St. Louis	KO 4
	March 4—Sammy Angott, Pittsburgh	W 10
	March 14—Izzy Jannazzo, Baltimore	W 10
	March 21—Freddy Flores, N.Y.C.	KO 5
	June 12—Freddy Wilson, Worcester	KO 2
	June 25—Norman Rubio, Union City	W 10
	July 12—Joe Curcio, N.Y.C.	KO 2
	August 15—Vinnie Vines, Albany	KO 6
	September 25—Sidney Miller, Elizabeth	KO 3

	October 7—Ossie Harris, Pittsburgh	W	10
	November 1—Cecil Hudson, Detroit	KO	6
	November 6—Artie Levine, Cleveland	KO	10
	December 20—Tommy Bell, N.Y.C.	W	15
	(Won Vacant World Welterweight Championship)		
1947	March 27—Bernie Miller, Miami	KO	3
	April 3—Fred Wilson, Akron	KO	3
	April 8—Eddie Finazzo, Kansas City	KO	4
	May 16—George Abrams, N.Y.C.	W	10
	June 24—Jimmy Doyle, Cleveland	KO	8
	(Title bout)		
	Doyle died of injuries.		
	August 21—Sammy Secreet, Akron	KO	1
	August 29—Flashy Sebastian, N.Y.C.	KO	1
	October 28—Jackie Wilson, Los Angeles	KO	7
	December 10—Billy Nixon, Elizabeth	KO	6
	December 19—Chuck Taylor, Detroit	KO	6
	(Title bout)		
1948	March 4—Ossie Harris, Toledo	W	10
	March 16—Henry Brimm, Buffalo	W	10
	June 28—Bernard Docusen, Chicago	W	15
	(Title bout)		
	September 23—Kid Gavilan, New York	W	10
	November 15—Bobby Lee, Philadelphia	W	10
1949	February 10—Gene Buffalo, Wilkes-Barre	KO	1
	February 15—Henry Brimm, Buffalo	D	10
	March 25—Bobby Lee, Chicago	W	10
	April 11—Don Lee, Omaha	W	10
	April 20—Earl Turner, Oakland	KO	8
	May 16—Al Tribuani, Wilmington	Exh.	4
	June 7—Freddie Flores, New Bedford	KO	3
	June 20—Cecil Hudson, Providence	KO	5
	July 11—Kid Gavilan, Philadelphia	W	15
	(Title bout)		
	August 24—Steve Belloise, N.Y.C.	KO	7
	September 2—Al Mobley, Chicago	Exh.	4
	September 9—Benny Evans, Omaha	KO	5
	September 12—Charley Dotson, Houston	KO	5
	November 9—Don Lee, Denver	W	10
	November 13—Vern Lester, New Orleans	KO	5
	November 15—Gene Burton, Shreveport	Exh.	6
	November 16—Gene Burton, Dallas	Exh.	6
1950	January 30—George LaRover, New Haven	KO	4
	February 13—Al Mobley, Miami	KO	6
	February 22—Aaron Wade, Savannah	KO	3
	February 27—Jean Walzack, St. Louis	W	10
	March 22—George Costner, Philadelphia	KO	1

April 21—Cliff Beckett, Columbus, O.	KO	3
April 28—Ray Barnes, Detroit	W	10
June 5—Robert Villemain, Philadelphia	W	15
(Won Pennsylvania middleweight title)		
August 9—Charley Fusari, Jersey City	W	15
(Welterweight title bout)		
August 25—Jose Basora, Scranton	KO	1
(Pennsylvania middleweight title bout)		
September 4—Billy Brown, N.Y.C.	W	10
October 16—Joe Rindone, Boston	KO	6
October 26—Carl Olson, Philadelphia	KO	12
(Pennsylvania middleweight title bout)		
November 8—Bobby Dykes, Chicago	W	10
November 27—Jean Stock, Paris	KO	2
December 9—Luc Van Dam, Brussels	KO	4
December 16—Jean Walzack, Geneva	W	10
December 22—Robert Villemain, Paris	KO	9
December 25—Hans Stretz, Frankfort	KO	5

1951

February 14—Jake LaMotta, Chicago	KO	13
(Won world middleweight title)		
April 5—Holly Mims, Miami	W	10
April 9—Don Ellis, Oklahoma City	KO	1
May 21—Kid Marcel, Paris	KO	5
May 26—Jean Wanes, Zurich	W	10
June 10—Jan deBruin, Antwerp	KO	8
June 16—Jean Walzack, Liege	KO	6
June 24—Gerhard Hecht, Berlin	ND	2
(Robinson disqualified by Referee for kidney punch. Commission later reversed it to a no-decision bout.)		
July 1—Cyrille Delannoit, Turin	KO	3
July 10—Randy Turpin, London	L	15
(Lost world middleweight title)		
September 12—Randy Turpin, N.Y.C.	KO	10
(Regained world middleweight title)		

1952

March 13—Carl (Bobo) Olson, San Francisco	W	15
(Middleweight title bout)		
April 16—Rocky Graziano, Chicago	KO	3
(Middleweight title bout)		
June 25—Joey Maxim, New York	KOby	14
(For light heavyweight title)		
Announced retirement December 18, 1952.		

1954

October 20—Announced return to ring.		
November 29—Gene Burton, Hamilton, Ont.	Exh.	6

1955

January 5—Joe Rindone, Detroit	KO	6
January 19—Ralph Jones, Chicago	L	10
March 29—Johnny Lombardo, Cincinnati	W	10
April 14—Ted Olla, Milwaukee	KO	3

	May 4—Garth Panter, Detroit	W	10
	July 22—Rocky Castellani, San Francisco	W	10
	December 9—Carl (Bobo) Olson, Chicago	KO	2
	(Won world middleweight title)		
1956	May 18—Carl (Bobo) Olson, Los Angeles	KO	4
	(Middleweight title bout)		
	November 10—Bob Provizzi, New Haven	W	10
1957	January 2—Gene Fullmer, New York	L	15
	(Lost world middleweight title)		
	May 1—Gene Fullmer, Chicago	KO	5
	(Re-won world middleweight title)		
	September 10—Otis Woodward, Philadelphia	Exh.	2
	September 10—Lee Williams, Philadelphia	Exh.	2
	September 23—Carmen Basilio, New York	L	15
	(Lost world middleweight title)		
1958	March 25—Carmen Basilio, Chicago	W	15
	(Regained world middleweight title)		
1959	December 14—Bob Young, Boston	KO	2
1960	January 22—Paul Pender, Boston	L	15
	(Lost world middleweight title)		
	April 2—Tony Baldoni, Baltimore	KO	1
	June 10—Paul Pender, Boston	L	15
	(For world middleweight title)		
	December 3—Gene Fullmer, Los Angeles	D	15
	(For N.B.A. middleweight title)		
1961	March 4—Gene Fullmer, Las Vegas	L	15
	(For N.B.A. middleweight title)		
	September 25—Wilf Greaves, Detroit	W	10
	October 21—Denny Moyer, New York	W	10
	November 20—Al Hauser, Providence	KO	6
	December 8—Wilf Greaves, Pittsburgh	KO	8
1962	February 17—Denny Moyer, New York	L	10
	April 27—Bobby Lee, Port of Spain, Trinidad	KO	2
	July 9—Phil Moyer, Los Angeles	L	10
	September 25—Terry Downes, London	L	10
	October 17—Diego Infantes, Vienna	KO	2
	November 10—Georges Estatoff, Lyons	KO	6
1963	January 30—Ralph Dupas, Miami Beach	W	10
	February 25—Bernie Reynolds, Santo Domingo	KO	4
	March 11—Billy Thornton, Lewiston	KO	3
	May 5—Maurice Rolbnet, Sherbrooke	KO	3
	June 24—Joey Giardello, Philadelphia	L	10
	October 14—Armand Vanucci, Paris	W	10
	November 9—Fabio Bettini, Lyon	D	10

	November 16—Emile Sarens, Brussels	KO	8
	November 29—Andre Davier, Grenoble	W	10
	December 9—Armand Vanucci, Paris	W	10
1964	May 19—Gaylord Barnes, Portland	W	10
	July 8—Clarence Riley, Pittsfield	KO	6
	July 27—Art Hernandez, Omaha	D	10
	September 3—Mick Leahy, Paisley	L	10
	September 28—Yolande Leveque, Paris	W	10
	October 12—Johnny Angel, London	KO	6
	October :.4—Jackie Caillau, Nice	W	10
	November 7—Baptiste Rolland, Caen	W	10
	November 14—Jean Beltritti, Marseilles	W	10
	November 27—Fabio Beltini, Rome	D	10
1965	March 6—Jimmy Beecham, Kingston, Jamaica	KO	2
	April 4—East Basting, Savannah	KO	1
	April 28—Rocky Randall, Norfolk	KO	3
	May 5—Rocky Randall, Jacksonville	W	8
	May 24—Memo Ayon, Tijuana	L	10
	June 1—Stan Harrington, Honolulu	L	10
	June 24—Young Joe Walcott, Richmond	W	10
	July 12—Ferd Hernandez, Las Vegas	L	10
	July 27—Young Joe Walcott, Richmond	W	10
	August 10—Stan Harrington, Honolulu	L	10
	September 15—Neil Morrison, Norfolk	NC	2
	(Bout was ended in second round)		
	September 23—Young Joe Walcott, Philadelphia	W	10
	October 1—Peter Schmidt, Johnston	W	10
	October 20—Rudolf Bent, Steubenville	KO	3
	November 10—Joey Archer, Pittsburgh	L	10

TB	KO	WD	WF	D	LD	LF	KOby	ND	NC
202	109	66	0	6	18	0	1	1	1

Announced retirement December 10, 1965.

Key to abbreviations:

D—Draw
Exh.—Exhibition
KO—Knocked out opponent
KOby—Knocked out by opponent
L—Lost
LD—Lost decision
LF—Lost on foul

NC—No contest
ND—No decision
TB—Total bouts
W—Won
WD—Won decision
WF—Won on foul